Human-Computer Interaction Series

T0134634

Human-Computer Interaction is a multidisciplinary field focused on human aspects of the development of computer technology. As computer-based technology becomes increasingly pervasive - not just in developed countries, but worldwide - the need to take a human-centered approach in the design and development of this technology becomes ever more important. For roughly 30 years now, researchers and practitioners in computational and behavioral sciences have worked to identify theory and practice that influences the direction of these technologies, and this diverse work makes up the field of human–computer interaction. Broadly speaking it includes the study of what technology might be able to do for people and how people might interact with the technology. In this series we present work which advances the science and technology of developing systems which are both effective and satisfying for people in a wide variety of contexts. The human–computer interaction series will focus on theoretical perspectives (such as formal approaches drawn from a variety of behavioral sciences), practical approaches (such as the techniques for effectively integrating user needs in system development), and social issues (such as the determinants of utility, usability and acceptability).

For other titles published in this series, go to
www.springer.com/series/6033

Erik Champion

Playing with the Past

 Springer

Dr. Erik Champion
College of Creative Arts
Auckland School of Design
Massey University
0745, Auckland
New Zealand
e.champion@massey.ac.nz

ISBN 978-1-4471-2595-2   ISBN 978-1-84996-501-9 (eBook)
DOI 10.1007/978-1-84996-501-9
Springer London Dordrecht Heidelberg New York

British Library Cataloguing in Publication Data
A catalogue record for this book is available from the British Library

Printed on acid-free paper

Springer is part of Springer Science+Business Media (www.springer.com)

This book is dedicated to Wendy and Coco.

Acknowledgements

Images

I would like to thank the following for giving me permission to use these images.

Fig. 1.1: Virtual Calakmul, Dr. Rocio Ruiz Rodarte of Mexico, archaeologist Ramon Carrasco and architect Fernando Garcia Cuspineira. Dr. Rodarte was also very helpful to me when I visited Mexico during the author's doctoral research.

Fig. 1.2: Global Conflict: Palestine (as well as Figs. 5.8–5.10 which also features Playing History), Assistant Professor Simon Egenfeldt-Nielsen, Serious Games Interactive, Copenhagen. Simon was also instrumental in arranging support from a European Union project "Serious Games on a Global Market Place", which allowed me to visit both his company and DPU, Aarhus University in Copenhagen, in 2009.

Fig. 1.3: Virtual Parthenon interior, Chris Blundell, Brisbane.

Figs. 2.2–2.3: The SGI VRML model of Tenochtitlan ported to Bryce3D, placed on water, was originally created by SGI, thanks to them for releasing the project and the models via the Internet, and for promoting VRML.

Fig. 2.4: Qumulus, and Fig. 5.2 Dordrecht Monastery images are courtesy of Dylan Nagel, Paladin Studios, The Netherlands. I'd also like to thank Dylan for a model of the Temple of Inscriptions for my original Palenque environment.

Fig. 2.5: ActiveWorlds screenshot was in the public domain but thanks to ActiveWorlds for their continual evolvement of the project and for their ongoing help with academic research.

Fig. 2.6: The Renaissance Community screenshot was taken by the author, but the virtual environment was a cooperative European Union research project with the technical assistance of Blaxxun.

Fig. 4.1: Virtual Queenscliff, courtesy of Professor William Cartwright, RMIT University, and Tim Germanchis.

Figs. 4.2–4.5: Palenque in Unreal Tournament screenshots were from a student project involving Andrew Dekker and Mark Hurst.

Figs. 4.6–4.7: Car racing inside a tent image was from a University of Queensland student project that the author supervised, the team was Bonnii Weeks and Jonathan Barrett.

Figs. 4.13–4.14: Journey to the West was from a University of Queensland student project that the author supervised, comprised of Bonnii Weeks, Peter Claire and Wen Ling Pu.

Fig. 4.15: An Unreal bot (NPC) in the Unreal Palenque game level. Thanks to Mark Hurst and Andrew Dekker for the image.

Figs. 4.16–4.17: Elder Scrolls III: Morrowind and the Egyptian Temple of the Gods image was from a University of Queensland student project that the author supervised, the team was Alex Peters, Ryan Fairhurst, William Gordon and Benn Chisholm.

Fig. 4.18: Drawing Game (Chinese Writing Language) using Torque 2D image was from a University of Queensland student project that I supervised: AI Team Studios (Isaac Gibson and Amy Ng).

Fig. 5.1: The Blink3D image is courtesy of Dr. Glenn Gunhouse, Art History, Georgia State University.

Fig. 5.2: The Virtual Forbidden City image is courtesy of IBM.

Figs. 5.4–5.6: The Virtual Sambor images are courtesy of Professor Yehuda Kalay, University of California at Berkeley.

Fig. 5.7: Palace Kalhu, Assyria is courtesy of Dr. Melanie Stegman, Federation of American Scientists.

Figs.5.11–5.12: Virtual Egyptian Temple images are courtesy of Dr. Jeffrey Jacobson, PublicVR, USA.

Figs. 5.13, 7.5–7.6: The Mawson's Hut Reconstruction, Exterior and interior images are courtesy of Associate Professor Paul Bourke, WASP, University of Western Australia, and Dr. Peter Morse.

Fig. 5.14: Macquarie Light House in Oblivion is courtesy of Dr. Eric Fassbender.

Figs. 5.15–5.16: PLACE-Hampi and PLACE-Hampi, Opera House, Lille images are courtesy of Sarah Kenderine and Professor Jeffrey Shaw, iCinema.

Figs. 5.17–5.18: Spaces of Mjalnar from above and from in front were courtesy of Bernadette Flynn, the photographer was Heidrun Lohr.

Figs. 7.1–7.2: ARQuake and the HMD shot was courtesy of Professor Bruce Thomas, Director of the Wearable Computer Lab, School of Computer and Information Science The University of South Australia.

Figs. 7.3–7.4: The images of an early AR system and the asylum are courtesy of Professor Steven Feiner. The early AR system image is © 1997, Steven Feiner, Blair MacIntyre, Tobias Hoellerer, and Anthony Webster, Computer Graphics and User Interfaces Lab, Columbia University.

The asylum image is © 1999 Tobias Hoellerer, Steven Feiner, and John Pavlik, Computer Graphics and User Interfaces Lab, Columbia University.

Fig. 7.7: Layar Augmented Reality on a Phone image is courtesy of Layar Technologies.

Figs.7.8–7.9: The Virtual World with Real World Information image is courtesy of Philippe Kerremans, (www.Platini.com).

Fig. 7.9: The 34 North by 118 West image is courtesy of James Hight.

Fig. 7.10: The Biofed Single-Player game play image was from Andrew Dekker's University of Queensland student project that the author supervised in 2006.

Fig. 7.11: The Biosensor image was from a University of Queensland student project (Renee King, Matt Rhodes, Liam Miller and Aaron Fletcher) that the author supervised in 2006.

Fig. 7.12: The Gameplay augmented by audience image was from a University of Queensland student project that the author supervised. The students were Bonnii Weeks and Jonathan Barrett.

I was given permission to publish several other images. To Microsoft India, to Mellanium, Wolfire, Katalabs and so on, my apologies, time and space was against me.

Funding for the Palenque Project

An Australian Research Council SPIRT grant in collaboration with the industry partner Lonely Planet Publications and the University of Melbourne supported this research.

Academic Advice

Thanks to Lonely Planet Publications (especially to Dr. Ron Gallagher). I would also like to thank the University of Melbourne, to Dr. Graham Hepworth for statistics consulting, and to my supervisors Professor Ian Bishop and Associate Professor Bharat Dave.

Advice Scripting and Materials from

Martin Judd, Michael J. Hall, Ben Jordan, Stuart Forbes, Jim Coe, Tweex, Adobe Atmosphere Development Team, Agnes Davey, Paul from UTS, Americo Damasco, and Phil C. Initial 3D Studio Max/Viz modelling of the Temple of Inscriptions was modelled by Dylan Nagel. The Palenque temple models used in the evaluation were modelled in Adobe Atmosphere by Erik Champion and so were the other 3D Studio Viz models. Thanks to Planeta Vivo Society for use of the small Pyramid of the Sun at Teotihuacán Viewpoint model (used in the warm-up environment). Music used in the evaluations is by Xavier Quijas Yxayotl (http://www.yxayotl.com/).

General

Thanks to the Centre for Classics and Archaeology at the University of Melbourne, and to all the people who participated in the user evaluations. Thanks for ongoing advice and encouragement from Paul Bourke, Bernard Meade, Peter Murphy, and Sarah Kenderine.

Thanks also to KAIST for the offer of a conference grant to Korea, and to VSMM (and especially to Associate Professor Susan Tennant), for their ongoing interest in the project and for the recognition. In addition, thank you to Swinburne University of Technology for allowing me to test some of my ideas through supervision of postgraduate students, and for knowledge developed in co-ordinating the User Experience Design course. Thanks to Interaction Design, University of Queensland for initial funding and for give me so much leeway in organizing and supervising student projects. I am also greatly appreciated of the efforts of staff and students during my time there.

Archaeological Advice

Professor Peter Mathews for early archaeological and epigraphical advice, the FAMSI website for allowing me to use their amazing drawings as surface textures, and Justin Kerr for permission to use his photographs as surface textures. In addition, thanks to the musician Xavier Quijas Yxayotl for the breathtaking traditional music used in the evaluations. Thanks also to Associate Professor Phillip Hofstetter for permission to use his QuickTime panoramas (even though they were not used), Gilbert Griffin for advice on wall stucco texture, Doctor Ed Barnhart for sending me his terrain data, and Professor Dennis Tedlock for permission to quote from his translation of the Popol Vuh in the information used in the Palenque project.

"The Big Print Giveth and the Small Print Taketh Away" – *Step Right Up* by Tom Waits. I apologise in advance for any omissions, mistakes, dogmatic assertions, or other small print issues.

Contents

1 Introducing Virtual Travel 1
   1.1 Virtual Environments 1
   1.2 Moving Past the Picture Frame 3
   1.3 Being Not-There May Be More Achievable 4
   1.4 Being Not-There May Safeguard the Place 5
   1.5 Share by Being Not-There 7
   1.6 The Implications for Virtual Travel 8
   1.7 Learning via Virtual Travel 9
   1.8 The Thorny Issue of Engagement 10
   1.9 Four Major Problems 11
   1.10 Virtual Reality and Cultural Significance 13
   References 14

2 Virtual Environments 17
   2.1 Technological Limitations 17
   2.2 Lack of Widely Distributed Technology 17
   2.3 Size, Speed and Rendering Issues 18
   2.4 Lack of Meaningful Content 18
   2.5 We Experience More than Tangible Objects 19
   2.6 The World Is More than Visual Stimuli 19
   2.7 Different People See Different Things 20
   2.8 Personalization Is Missing 21
   2.9 Lack of Contextual Evaluation 21
   2.10 Summary of Implications for Virtual Environments 23
   References 24

3 Virtual Places 27
   3.1 Place in a Virtual Space.. 27
   3.2 Experiential Types of Place... 29
      3.2.1 Place as Unique Experience.. 29
      3.2.2 Sublime Places of Terror and Awe.............................. 30
      3.2.3 Evocative and Atmospheric Place 30

   3.2.4 Place as Stage and Playground.. 31
   3.2.5 Place as Trace and Palimpsest... 33
  3.3 Requirements for Creating a Sense of Place..................................... 34
   3.3.1 Place Requires Embodiment... 34
   3.3.2 Place Requires Paths and Centers.. 36
   3.3.3 Response to Place Requires Ongoing Feedback................. 36
   3.3.4 Place Requires Social 'Embeddedness'.............................. 37
   3.3.5 Place Is Mark-Able.. 38
  3.4 Evoking Place via Arts and Sciences.. 39
   3.4.1 Architecture.. 39
   3.4.2 Art and Artifacts.. 41
   3.4.3 Literature... 42
   3.4.4 Film... 43
   3.4.5 Cultural Geography in Place and Culture........................... 43
  3.5 Cyberspace Critics and Criteria... 44
   3.5.1 Cyberspaces Lack Limits.. 46
   3.5.2 Cyberspaces Lack 'Play' Through Objects......................... 48
   3.5.3 Cyberspaces Lack Life History.. 48
  3.6 Cyberspace Concepts and Terminology... 49
   3.6.1 Suggestions for Creating Cyberplace.................................. 50
  3.7 Three Types of Virtual Environments... 50
   3.7.1 Inert 'Explorative' Environments.. 51
   3.7.2 Activity-Based Environments... 53
   3.7.3 Cultural or 'Hermeneutic' Environments............................. 53
  3.8 Matching Virtual Environments and Technologies.......................... 55
  3.9 Terms.. 56
  3.10 Summary of Place Theory.. 58
  References.. 60

4 Cultural and Social Presence.. 63
  4.1 Why Photorealism Does Not Convey Cultural Significance........... 63
   4.1.1 Virtual Heritage Is Not Realism... 63
   4.1.2 Phobic Triggers and Experiential Realism.......................... 65
   4.1.3 Archaeology and History Is Not Set in Concrete................. 67
  4.2 Confusion over Cultural Presence... 69
  4.3 What Is Culture?.. 69
   4.3.1 What Is a Culturally Significant Place?.............................. 70
   4.3.2 How Culture Is Learnt... 71
   4.3.3 Social and Cultural Presence... 72
  4.4 Hermeneutic Richness, Cultural Agency... 75
  4.5 Culture in Virtual Worlds... 76
  4.6 Useful Cultural Presence... 76
  4.7 Summary of Cultural Presence Theory... 78
  References.. 80

5   Game–Style Interaction...   83
      5.1   Defining Games   83
      5.2   Defining Game–Style Interaction   84
             5.2.1   Useful Features of Games...   85
             5.2.2   Engaging Features of Games   87
      5.3   Case Study: Heretic II   89
      5.4   Dynamic Places...   90
             5.4.1   Dynamic Place Design: Unreal
                      Palenque and Xibalba   91
             5.4.2   Racing in a Tent: Spatial and Haptic Immersion   94
      5.5   Constrained Tasks and Goals   94
             5.5.1   Interaction Modes in Palenque Using
                      Adobe Atmosphere   95
             5.5.2   Constrained Tasks in Journey to the West   100
      5.6   Social Agency: Avatars Agents and Actors   101
             5.6.1   Agency in a Marco Polo Game.....................................   102
      5.7   Artifacts..   104
             5.7.1   Mapping to Aid Navigation
                      for Egyptian Mythology   108
             5.7.2   Mapping Through Drawing   110
      5.8   Game-Based Learning...   111
             5.8.1   Procedural Versus Prescriptive Learning   111
      5.9   Game Genres and Cultural Learning.......................................   116
             5.9.1   Snakes and Ladders   116
             5.9.2   Different Perspectives per Player...................................   117
             5.9.3   Role Playing...   117
             5.9.4   The Spy Game   118
      5.10   Issues of Time: Interaction Versus Historical Authenticity   118
             5.10.1   Ancillary Non-celebrity Characters   119
             5.10.2   Autonomous Action, Immutable Results..........................   119
             5.10.3   Groundhog Day   119
             5.10.4   Possible Worlds..   119
             5.10.5   Diary of Emotional Development...................................   120
             5.10.6   Surfing Memetic Drift   120
             5.10.7   Augment History with Real World   120
             5.10.8   Augmented Cultural Exchange......................................   121
             5.10.9   Dynamic Places   121
      5.11   Game-Based Evaluation...   121
      5.12   Summary of Games–Style Interaction   124
      References   126

6   Playing with the Past   129
      6.1   What Is Virtual Heritage?..   129
      6.2   The Problem of Culture...   131
      6.3   Virtual Heritage Case Studies   132

6.3.1   Art History in Online Worlds: Santa Maria, Italy............. 132
6.3.2   Virtual Forbidden City, China.. 133
6.3.3   Dordrecht Monastery, The Netherlands........................... 134
6.3.4   Urban Design and Virtual Sambor, Cambodia 135
6.3.5   FAS Palace, Mesopotamia 137
6.3.6   Culture and History Inside a Game: Palestine
         and Italy 139
6.3.7   Virtual Egyptian Temple.. 142
6.3.8   Dome Visualization: Mawson's Hut, Antarctica 144
6.3.9   Heritage Tour: Macquarie Lighthouse, Australia 145
6.3.10   Panoramic Explorations: PLACE-Hampi, India.............. 147
6.3.11   Performance and Archaeology:
         Spaces of Mjalnar, Malta 148
6.4   Summary 151
References.. 152

7   Augmenting the Present With the Past 157
7.1   What Is Augmented Reality? 157
7.2   Blends of Augmented Reality and Augmented Virtuality 160
       7.2.1   Inserted Walk-About Reality, University
                of South Australia.. 160
       7.2.2   Overlaid Walk-About Reality, Columbia University 160
       7.2.3   Bubbled Reality Example 3: Mawson's Huts,
                Antarctica.. 163
7.3   Other Types of Mixed Reality 164
       7.3.1   Data-Streamed Virtual Reality.. 164
       7.3.2   Augmented Virtuality 165
       7.3.3   Audio Augmented Reality 167
       7.3.4   Participant and Audience-Augmented Virtuality.............. 168
7.4   Augmented Reality and Virtual Heritage 171
7.5   Summary 172
References.. 174

8   Evaluating Virtual Heritage.. 177
8.1   Testing That Which Is Not Yet Fully Tested................................. 177
8.2   Evaluating Cultural Learning.. 178
8.3   Virtual Heritage Evaluation.. 179
8.4   What Types of Evaluation Are There?... 179
       8.4.1   Expert Testing 179
       8.4.2   Content and Media Comparison Studies 180
       8.4.3   Physiological Testing.. 180
       8.4.4   Task Performance 180
       8.4.5   Surveys/Questionnaires 181
       8.4.6   Ethnographic Evaluation.. 182
8.5   Evaluating Virtual Heritage Environments 182

        8.5.1   Task Performance and Game Evaluation 184
        8.5.2   Statistical Methods Suitable for Virtual
                 Heritage Projects 185
  8.6   Evaluation Case Study: Palenque 190
        8.6.1   Pilot Study 191
        8.6.2   Evaluation 191
        8.6.3   Evaluation Questions 192
        8.6.4   Schedule of Evaluation 193
        8.6.5   Observations 193
  8.7   Summary of Evaluation for Virtual Heritage 194
  References 196

9   Conclusion 201
  9.1   Cultural Understanding Through Digital Interactivity 201
  9.2   Future Research 207
  References 209

Index 211

List of Figures

Fig. 1.1 Virtual Calakmul (Courtesy of Rodarte,
Carrasco and Cuspineira) 4
Fig. 1.2 Global Conflict: Palestine
(Courtesy of Serious Games Interactive)........................ 5
Fig. 1.3 Virtual Parthenon interior (Courtesy of Chris Blundell) 9

Fig. 3.1 The Roman Coliseum at night...................................... 31
Fig. 3.2 The SGI VRML model of Tenochtitlan
ported to Bryce3D, placed on water........................... 32
Fig. 3.3 The same model from a more human perspective 33
Fig. 3.4 Qumulus: real-time weather system using Quest 3D
(Courtesy of Paladin Studios)...................................... 35
Fig. 3.5 ActiveWorlds screenshot 47
Fig. 3.6 Renaissance Community screenshot by author 47

Fig. 5.1 Virtual Queenscliff (Courtesy of William
Cartwright and Tim Germanchis)..................................... 87
Fig. 5.2 Palenque in Unreal Tournament 92
Fig. 5.3 Unreal Tournament and Sensor Pads:
artistic version of Xibalba 92
Fig. 5.4 Room projection using a curved mirror
(Courtesy of Paul Bourke).. 93
Fig. 5.5 Palenque prototype in Unreal Tournament
projected via curved mirror 93
Fig. 5.6 Car racing inside a tent.. 94
Fig. 5.7 Massage chair 95
Fig. 5.8 Initial warm-up environment 97
Fig. 5.9 A screenshot of the guide greeting
the visitor at the palace.. 97
Fig. 5.10 Fictional world setting using caiman and World-Tree 98
Fig. 5.11 Mayan Village 99
Fig. 5.12 Mayan Ballcourt world.. 99

Fig. 5.13   Journey to the West-Monkey encounters Raksasi
(Iron Fan Immortal) 100
Fig. 5.14   Journey to the West Loading Screen 101
Fig. 5.15   An Unreal bot (NPC) in Unreal Palenque game level 103
Fig. 5.16   Elder Scrolls III: Morrowind and the Egyptian
Temple of the Gods 109
Fig. 5.17   Egyptian game glyphic inventory 109
Fig. 5.18   Drawing game (Chinese writing language)
using Torque 2D. 110
Fig. 5.19   Shared avatars with personal worlds 117

Fig. 6.1   Blink3D (Courtesy of Glenn Gunhouse) 132
Fig. 6.2   Virtual Forbidden City, China (Courtesy of IBM) 134
Fig. 6.3   Dordrecht Monastery, The Netherlands
(Courtesy of Dylan Nagel, Paladin Studios) 135
Fig. 6.4   Virtual Sambor – the market (Courtesy of Yehuda Kalay) 136
Fig. 6.5   Virtual Sambor – tower (Courtesy of Yehuda Kalay) 137
Fig. 6.6   Virtual Sambor – ritual (Courtesy of Yehuda Kalay) 137
Fig. 6.7   Palace Kalhu, Assyria (Courtesy of Federation
of American Scientists) 138
Fig. 6.8   Global Conflicts: Palestine – dialogue with Imam
(Courtesy of Serious Games Interactive) 139
Fig. 6.9   Playing with history dialogue
(Courtesy of Serious Games Interactive) 141
Fig. 6.10   Playing history interface screen
(Courtesy of Serious Games Interactive) 141
Fig. 6.11   Virtual Egyptian Temple, Courtyard, Egypt
(Courtesy of Jeffrey Jacobson) 142
Fig. 6.12   Virtual Egyptian Temple, Earth Theatre,
(Courtesy of Jeffrey Jacobson) 143
Fig. 6.13   Mawson's hut reconstruction in an iDome
(Courtesy of Paul Bourke and Peter Morse) 144
Fig. 6.14   Macquarie Lighthouse in Oblivion
(Courtesy of Eric Fassbender) 146
Fig. 6.15   PLACE-Hampi (Courtesy of Sarah
Kenderdine and Jeffrey Shaw) 147
Fig. 6.16   PLACE-Hampi, Opera House, Lille (Courtesy
of Sarah Kenderdine and Jeffrey Shaw) 148
Fig. 6.17   Spaces of Mjalnar from above
(Courtesy of Bernadette Flynn) 149
Fig. 6.18   Spaces of Mjalnar from the user's perspective
(Courtesy of Bernadette Flynn) 150

Fig. 7.1   ARQuake (Courtesy of Bruce Thomas) 161
Fig. 7.2   HMD screenshot of monsters on campus
(Courtesy of Bruce Thomas) 161

Fig. 7.3   Early AR system (Courtesy of Steven Feiner) 162

Fig. 7.4   Asylum (Courtesy of Steve Feiner) 162

Fig. 7.5   Mawson's Hut Exterior (Courtesy of Paul Bourke
and Peter Morse) 163

Fig. 7.6   Mawson's Hut Interior (Courtesy of Paul
Bourke and Peter Morse) 164

Fig. 7.7   Layar Augmented Reality on a Phone (Courtesy of Layar) 165

Fig. 7.8   Virtual World with Real World Information
(Courtesy of Philippe Kerremans) 166

Fig. 7.9   34 North by 118 West (Courtesy of James Hight) 167

Fig. 7.10 Biofeedback in gameplay changes the shaders and NPCs 168

Fig. 7.11 Biosensor for Past Player Biofeedback For Minotaur Game 169

Fig. 7.12 Gameplay Augmented By Audience 170

Fig. 8.1   Dr. Jeffrey Jacobson of PublicVR.org,
testing his CAVEUT screens. 178

Fig. 8.2   A tourist attempts to explore a Virtual
Heritage Exhibit at Sydney Custom House 183

Fig. 8.3   Diagram of travel and tourism in a virtual environment 183

List of Tables

Table 1.1   Real world and virtual environment user requirements   10

Table 3.1   Features of real and virtual places   51
Table 3.2   Place-based typology of virtual environments   54
Table 3.3   Virtual place interaction and place features   55

Table 4.1   Ways in which we learn about a cultural context   72
Table 4.2   Social presence as it affects 'being there'   74
Table 4.3   Types of virtual presence   79

Table 5.1   Engaging features of games   88
Table 5.2   Schematic of cultural learning   96
Table 5.3   Interaction learning modes in games   112
Table 5.4   Procedural learning via social roles   113
Table 5.5   Prescriptive learning via social roles   114

Table 6.1   Comparison of case studies   152

Table 8.1   Evaluation measures and questions   192
Table 8.2   Table sequencing of environments in evaluation   193

Chapter 1
Introducing Virtual Travel

The central question of this book is: how can we increase awareness and understanding of other cultures using interactive digital visualizations of past civilizations?

In order to answer the above question, this book first questions the success of current virtual environments, and asks whether they are capable of producing a platform that supports the experience and understanding of place-inscribed culture and I outline a typology that defines different types of successful virtual environments. I suggest virtual environments are impeded by technological constraints, lack of evaluation techniques and results, and content-specific applications that contextually respond to user needs.

1.1 Virtual Environments

Why develop virtual environments?

Researchers of presence in virtual environments and websites advocating virtual medicine suggest that digitally mediated environments mentally, emotionally, and physically affect us (ISPR 2003). Hospitals have adopted virtual reality techniques for pain management (Lockridge 1999), and according to Heard (2003), virtual reality is used to help people enter calm meditative states while sitting together in large public spaces. An increasing amount of literature suggests that virtual environments have been successfully developed for simulation, entertainment, medicine and education. There are distance learning and virtual training environments for sports as well (Booth 2003).

> Soon a batsman will be able to play a virtual reality innings before he leaves the dressing room, reports Jenny Booth in London…The makers of the electronic umpire Hawk-Eye are developing virtual reality equipment that will allow batsmen to practice against the fastest or trickiest bowlers in the changing room before they face them on the pitch.
>
> Through a set of virtual reality goggles, batsmen will see opposition bowlers – Shaun Pollock of South Africa, for instance, or Muttiah Muralitharan of Sri Lanka – running in to deliver overs that are exact replicas of those bowled earlier in the match.
>
> The batsman will play at the balls with a bat wired to the Hawk-Eye computer, which will then let him know whether he has struck a boundary, nicked an edge or been clean bowled.

E. Champion, *Playing with the Past*, Human-Computer Interaction Series,
DOI 10.1007/978-1-84996-501-9_1, © Springer-Verlag London Limited 2011

Difficult deliveries can be played repeatedly until the batsman has perfected his stroke. "In the future I see no reason why it will not be realistic enough that international batsmen, particularly in 1-day cricket, will wear the headset while waiting to come in to bat, so when they get to the wicket they will already have their eye in," said Paul Hawkins, the scientist who invented Hawk-Eye…Michael Atherton, former England captain and opening batsman approves of this latest technological innovation.

"You try to construct your innings in your head before you play, and if virtual reality goggles could help you to do that, then all well and good."

Military training is taking similar strides (Malik 2003), and virtual environment technology (or virtual reality or VR as it is popularly known), is being developed for traumatic brain injury and phobia treatment (Haifa 2008; Robillard et al. 2003).

Marsh et al. (2001) defined four general types of virtual reality environments (VR): work-related; informative; entertainment; education and training. Extrapolating from their classification system, we could argue that virtual environments may be useful for the following seven reasons, if not more.

Virtual environments can help promote technology for the sake of technology (product showcases). You can see such various examples on the websites of commercial products such as Unity 3D, Blender 3D, Flash and Papervision 3D (which can be considered Adobe Flash with a 3D rendering engine).

Virtual environments might also enhance motor-coordination and related physical skill, especially in games. Recent research has suggested that games can help improve motor coordination for patients with brain injury (Huang et al. 2006) and even increase areas of the brain (Boyle 2010; Erickson et al. 2010).

We could utilize the multimodal potential of virtual environments to create more powerful synergized learning material that adapts to different learning styles. For example, 3D software has been used to create augmented reality models of the human heart (Grover 2009), as well as show how to service a car's engine.

The technology could also extend the perceptual experience or perceptual boundaries of observers. Various environmental art 'happenings' have been around for decades. Multimedia cinema was proposed as early as the 1950s (Tannenbaum 2000). Collaboration between sound composers and virtual reality designers is burgeoning; one of the fundamental criterions for acoustics is spatial presence, while audio in virtual environments appears to increase the sense of immersion and augments the learning experience (Richards et al. 2008).

Virtual environments can also present ideas, objects, or techniques difficult to perceive or conceive of in real-world form, or in conventional media. This can range from complex Japanese timber construction details (which I have been told are hard to visualize even in isometric drawings) to electric waves transmitted through the human brain or even to the formation of stars.

We can also develop the technology to preserve cultural artifacts through a three or even four-dimensional record of history. For example, the Virtual Heritage Society's website could incorporate 3D models, but their database is of academic papers *about* virtual heritage sites. So far the most accessible and well-known 3D models seem to be available via commercial software such as Google Earth. As recently as 2009 UNESCO has announced an alliance with Google on all their listed heritage sites, with

19 also being placed on Google's panoramic Street View (UNESCO 2009), but I am still waiting to hear of academic societies that share and collaborate *inside* these virtual sites, rather than present slides and movies *about* them.

Virtual environments (especially virtual worlds), can engender social discussion. Multi-user chat worlds include Second Life, HiPiHi ("China's Pioneer of The 3D Virtual World Platform"), IMVU, and There. Of course much of this technology and social community can disappear. Virtual environment platforms and technology arrive accompanied with much fanfare but disappear quickly and quietly.

Over the last 6 years I have lost trace of what happened to Outerworlds, Vnet, Cybertown, Blaxxun communities, Shout 3D, iCity, Galaxy Worlds et al. In fact, you can also take Metaplace off the list of active virtual worlds; it closed in January 2010. Even Google could not keep its interesting technology Lively open more than a few months. Blender 3D disappeared as a commercial product only to reappear as an open source cross-platform animation, modeling and real-time rendering solution. However, Second Life and World of Warcraft (often known as WoW) still seem to be wildly popular.

So if successful examples exist, why continue to research at a conceptual level rather than gradually improve on successful existing case studies? One potentially profitable and useful purpose of virtual environments that is often overlooked is also the one that *appears* to be catered for as a rudimentary requirement of virtual environments. That is, virtual travel. Yet the reason why we travel in the real world is not necessarily addressed by current design strategies for virtual environments. If my supposition is correct, then some of the fundamental concepts that virtual environments are founded on require critical inspection.

1.2 Moving Past the Picture Frame

Photo-realism may allow us to picture what a place currently looks like or looked like, but it does not give us the 'full picture' on the process of living in that place, and the perceptions that inhabitants of that place have developed. For example, Gillings (2002, p. 17) has decried the archaeological use of virtual environments, and their fixation on the creation of images rather than paying attention to a meaningful use for these models.

There are also many websites purporting to offer virtual travel or virtual tourism. However, what they offer are generally static or moving pictures of foreign places, set music clips, information on timetables and prices, or at most, 360 degree panoramic images that are interactive insofar as you can spin the camera around, and zoom in and out of the panorama. Two-dimensional images and three-dimensional panoramic images available through the Internet may allow us to identify objects, but they are not likely to help us experience inhabiting that place, moving through that place, or understanding the dynamic and ever-changing relationship of people and place.

Digital technology can integrate the real and the conjectural, as well as synchronous and asynchronous data, into conceptual user-specific information. This capability suggests that virtual environments may augment real-world travel and tourism experiences, rather than merely emulate them.

1.3   Being Not-There May Be More Achievable

Virtual travel may not be like 'being there'; it may offer more, 'being Not-there'. That is, it provides us with a portal into what could have been, not what still is. In this interpretative sense, it may in fact be even more educational, as it can rely on asynchronous multimodal data. And as noted by Aldrich (2004, p. 37) who cites Jane Boston (the general manager of Lucas Learning Ltd.), simulations can transport us to a time or place that we are unable or unlikely to experience directly.

Many ruins are bereft of their artifacts, which sit forlornly in the museums of past colonial powers. One example is Calakmul, this overgrown Classical Mayan site is impossible to fully visualize because it is so absorbed into the forest (Fig. 1.1). The website by the Virtual Calakmul project team (Rodarte et al. n.d.) warns of major challenges to those who plan to visit the real site:

> Calakmul, declared a protected World Heritage Site by UNESCO June 27, 2002, is an important ancient Mayan metropolis that played a key role in the history of this region for more than twelve centuries.
>
> Partially covered by a tropical forest, the buildings stand almost hidden from each other. The protected biosphere in which Calakmul is located prohibits the cutting of trees and the installation of towns.

The amount of vegetation prevents people from being able to visualize the entire site! So researchers in Mexico along with other researchers in the United States and the United Kingdom have used the game engine Unreal 2, to help visitors visualize the overall site before it was encroached on by vegetation and ravaged by warfare and the passing of time.

So at least in this respect, Internet media may prove more immersive, useful and educational than actually standing at site where history once took place. Sometimes

Fig. 1.1   Virtual Calakmul (Courtesy of Rodarte, Carrasco and Cuspineira)

Fig. 1.2 Global Conflict: Palestine (Courtesy of Serious Games Interactive)

we wish to understand people who live far away or in distant times that are not easily accessible to us. Multimedia and virtual environments as subsets of digitally mediated learning are great for conceptual understanding, "dealing with time and scale", or harmful or serious situations (Aldrich 2004, p. 37).

An example of a situation that is harmful and difficult to experience directly, yet educational for the very reason that so few settled people in Western countries experience it, would be border crossings in the Middle East. Serious Gaming Interactive in Denmark have created a series of educational games called Global Conflict, that are learning simulations designed for this very purpose (Fig. 1.2).

The ethical issue of the 'digital divide' may obscure another social phenomenon, that of the housebound who rely on their computers for news of the outside world. Virtual travel is not just useful for promoting future travel; it may negate the cost and fear of traveling. Virtual travel can help reach and educate the growing potential market of people who for whatever reason cannot leave the house.

1.4   Being Not-There May Safeguard the Place

Some tourist sites are so popular that the sheer number of the tourists themselves ironically threatens the travel experience. Freemantle (2000) wrote:

> No wonder the city attracts visitors by the millions each year...Venice both thrives on and suffocates from tourism....The city attracts numerous tourists, but it is becoming less attractive as a place to live for the local population or as a place for businesses to set up offices.

Tourism can destroy the local industry, and erode local culture. Businesses that have served the local populace for generations may have to move out of town because they are not believably 'authentic' or suitably 'historic' enough to be included in packaged tours. Tourism can even transform the urban fabric: the inner city may become crowded in summer and desolate in winter. 'Experiences' and 'artifacts' can be introduced that are actually not local at all; they just appear to be, and are easily placed in shopping bags and placed on mantelpieces. For example, Grabmeier (2003) decried the effect of mass tourism on Venice.

> It's no wonder that tourism may be killing Venice. "Every year Venice becomes more like an amusement park and less livable for Venetians," Davis said. "Of course it still exists as a city. But as a distinct culture, as a society, I can't say that Venice still functions anymore."... Most of the original Venetian culture has been swept aside, replaced by a tourist "monoculture," dedicated almost entirely to serving the 13 to 14 million outsiders who descend each year on this city of only about 65,000 permanent residents....Now, Davis said, gondolas are strictly for tourists, and they aren't even a means of transportation – they run pre-set routes that give a gondola "experience" without going anywhere...."Yet the tourists mostly don't seem to mind the crowds," Davis noted. "They largely accept the city as a giant strip mall and are happy to find all the tourist trinkets available to buy on every side, even though most of this 'touristware' was actually made elsewhere.

Real travel also creates a market for mass consumption, non-degradable consumer products, and resource-intensive transport that damages the environment. Holzman (1997) wrote that during summer in the United States up to 20% of all East Coast hospital admissions for respiratory problems may be ozone-related. And airports are huge emitters of volatile organic compounds (VOCs); John F. Kennedy International Airport is the second largest source of VOCs in New York City. Holzman concludes that pollution will further increase, with at least 32 of the 50 busiest US airports are planning to expand operations.

However, tourists can also travel without leaving home, through digital simulations of cultures and heritage sites. The flash of a camera will not damage a priceless artifact when simulated on a computer screen. Virtual travel can potentially help lessen the impact of tourist erosion. Many heritage sites are now being overrun; the Peruvian Government has proposed drastic measures to save Macchu Picchu from the ravages of one million tourists a year (Tuckman 2005), and urban design is threatening the traditional architecture of Kyoto (Milmo 2002; Smith 2009). In the future, we may need digital media to help save our cultural heritage from ourselves.

Tourists don't have to visit a site to destroy it. They can hasten its destruction or threaten its heritage status by demanding it is made 'prettier'. In another example from South America, tourists complained that the Akapana pyramid in the remote and windswept Bolivian Andes was not "pretty" enough (Adams 2009; Leonard 2009). It is true that the pyramid is 1,700 years old, the masonry was chipped with bricks missing, and Lonely Planet wrote that the pyramid was in a "sorry state" (Pringle 2009). And apparently the Peruvian government has the noble goal of reducing the pressure on Macchu Picchu by encouraging tourists to other heritage sites in the country. However the brown clay that the local authorities used to cover the pyramid in order to beautify its appearance has no historical reason to be there. As far as experts can tell, the original structure was entirely of stone.

UNESCO is visiting the site to decide if they should de-list the monument from its place on the World Heritage Site list. This would be a pity, because the Akapana pyramid is one of the largest of its type in all of South America, and an important part of Peruvian history. To add injury to insult, archaeologist Jose Luiz Paz believes the adobe coat could damage the structure, leading to the collapse of the pyramid.

This is a forceful reminder of the interconnection of tourism and heritage status and the role of politics in the safeguarding of what is not just nationally but also internationally important. Here is just one example of the (unwitting) power of travel publications to influence not just the tourist but also governments who will change their heritage landmarks because tourism is such income for them. Yet their solution could see their market being taken away from them through the heritage delisting of the site. Of course, the real horror is in tourists wanting ancient heritage sites to be "pretty".

On the other hand, sometimes the issue for heritage sites is that they are so picturesque, they can't escape punishment. In yet another tragic-comic incident from Peru, in the year 2000 a New York advertising company (allegedly) decided to sneak in a crane at dawn to film a beer commercial at Macchu Picchu. In the commercial, Intihuatana, the "Hitching Post For The Sun" (which may have been designed to be a stone sundial) was to be used as a beer bar. While the advertisement had been officially approved, the use of heavy equipment had not. And in a classic case of Murphy's Law, the crane fell on the edge of the irreplaceable Intihuatana, demolishing an 8 by 5 by 3 cm³ block of stone. The film company faced criminal charges for the incident (McGirk 2000).

There are also natural hazards that may prevent real-world travelers, for example, badgers. We are not allowed to step on Stonehenge boulders even though they are in danger of being uprooted by badgers! According to Jones (2004), badger burrowing are threatening remains and artifacts amongst the 5,000 year old stones of Stonehenge. The Ministry of Defence has stepped in (so to speak), to try to persuade the industrious badgers away from approximately ten of these archaeological sites.

You may now wonder how these stories could be of relevance to virtual environments. My point is that in contrast to vandals, pests and disasters, or destruction and endangerment by local authorities, digital media allows one to try out ideas and test hypotheses in order to learn, without destroying the actual thing that one is trying to understand.

1.5   Share by Being Not-There

Virtual environments can also act as collaborative virtual environments (CVEs). They may not just be experienced with others, they may also act as travel-diaries, the environment itself may be able to record our journeys, favorite views or spots, and either remind us of them later, allow us to transfer the 'highlights' to more portable appliances, or communicate our 'travels' to friends and family on the other side of the planet.

1.6   The Implications for Virtual Travel

We might argue that virtual environments and real-world travel share some very interesting issues. In augmenting real-world travel, successful virtual travel and heritage environments should attempt to provide some or all of the following capabilities. According to many writers (Gillings 2002; Mosaker 2001; Pletinckx 2003; Roussou and Drettakis 2005), it should provide the ability to travel across time and space in a way not possible in current reality in order to view what used to be there as opposed to what remains.

Virtual travel has the potential to provide an 'immersive' place-experience, the full and dramatic range of climate and topography (that is, experiences not usually accessible to short-term visitors). There are also opportunities to experience at first-hand important historical events; which requires the meaningful integration of artifacts, people and place.

Orientation and wayfinding are important functional elements of travel information, but they are not the only important components of travel experience. Some academics have already suggested that navigation is more important than wayfinding. Beynon (1998) wrote:

> In direct opposition to 'The Image of the City', 'The City and the Sign' (Gottdiener and Lagopoulos 1986) presents a number of views from urban semioticians that highlight the limitations of the Lynchian and cognitive perspective. The crucial thing missing from the traditional geographies is the failure to appreciate how environments are *conceived* by people as opposed to simply *perceived* by people.

To enrich and encourage our understanding of a certain place, we need to gain a conceptual understanding of what makes it significant and unique, and which elements (people, activities, events, and objects), make it a distinctive place. Only if the tourist market is intrigued by the prospect of traveling through, in, and to a place (as part of the 'travel experience'), is it then likely to be interested in 'travel information'. In other words, if we contextualize the travel experience via digital media, people may better understand the unique and significant aspects of that place as perceived by the inhabitants.

However, people do not want virtual environments to bombard them with too much information. There needs to be filtered relevance, ways that users can customize and filter the information. With travel there is also the problem of portability. Users want to be able to have the means of recording a travel experience and carrying it (as well as travel information) for future use.

Finally, the experience needs to have some potential aspect of social interaction; people usually find it more meaningful to be able to share their experiences with others. Many travelers want to have a pre-visit experience of a destination, as in knowing something about the place before they spend money and time visiting a place that they do not enjoy. If they do enjoy that destination, they want to be able to record or have a memento of that experience. We might even surmise that if on reaching the destination, the traveler achieved a goal contextually relevant to the local culture, this adventure would add to their sense of engagement.

1.7   Learning via Virtual Travel

There will always be questions of cost, time and resources, when creating virtual simulations. Franklin (2000) wrote:

> A question frequently asked is "Does the learning experience in a virtual environment offer any advantages over and above conventional learning experiences"? Even since the early days of VR people have made suggestions that a virtual environment will facilitate the learning process by allowing people to experience environments that are otherwise unavailable to them. This could include situations that are precluded because of safety, time or distance factors.
>
> As well as being able to represent environments that are based in conventional physics it is possible for the user to experience abstract environments. Therefore, it seems sensible to assume that virtual environments will be able to facilitate a range of different experiential learning inquiry. Of course, other learning technologies are able to support these different experiences. However, the flexibility of the VR system should make it easier to host different learning experiences on the one platform.

From the above quote, we can see that virtual environments may prove useful to travel in several ways. One in particular is through providing travel experience rather than just travel information. Virtual environment technology is potentially additive, multimodal, interactive, and open to real time augmentation. It lends itself to both social and cultural learning as vicariously explored through doing rather than imaginatively reconstructed (as in book reading) or experientially followed (as in linear media like films).

The real world has many constraints that prevent us from learning about objects in situ. For example, important elements of a virtual heritage site can be scattered around the world (for example, the scattered artifacts of the Parthenon, here reintegrated in a visualization by Blundell (2006), see Fig. 1.3) and only experts may know their cultural significance. Digital media can bring the landscape, the buildings, the

Fig. 1.3 Virtual Parthenon interior (Courtesy of Chris Blundell)

Table 1.1 Real world and virtual environment user requirements

Travel information/experience requirements	Related issues in virtual environments
People have trouble finding places on 2D maps and are often not sure which way is north	Orientation and moving from large-scale to small-scale examination of objects is a largely unexplored topic
People want to 'experience' place before they go there. They also want to get from A to B to C so they can enjoy their trip	VEs typically focus on objects, not objects in use; form should be separable from content so it is easily updateable; users can normally only explore, there is a lack of meaningful interaction
People want to travel light with downloadable and portable information	Again an issue of form and content; a lack of profiling; information is not divisible; user choice of interaction or 'realism' level could help reduce bandwidth problems etc
People want to personalize and filter their information to make it more accessible and relevant to them. They might even want to add personal mementos	User-based goals are inseparable from the overall model; VEs typically have no annotation ability; there is no record kept of user-environment interaction history
People want to interact with other travelers. On the other hand, they might want some control over the quantity or even quality of social interaction	Most VEs are single-user; sharing of information is usually restricted to chat, sending files or hyperlinks; control of social interaction is limited

artifacts, reasonably accurate reconstructions of the native music, representative animated avatars of the people, and past historical and environmental conditions all together in one multimodal interactive gestalt. In addition, it is deliverable over the Internet. The Internet does not just allow people to download 3D models and games, it allows them to share their own personal experiences, and discover and explore virtual worlds with others. Further, it can help update virtual worlds with real data, translate the explorations of real travelers into these virtual worlds, and modify and filter the data to help different audiences with different needs (Table 1.1).

The inherent capability of interactive digital media to afford learning was the starting motivation for this book. Basically, I wish to outline the issues and potential of cultural learning experiences available via virtual travel environments in general, and virtual heritage environments in particular. Which are the more effective and preferable types of interactivity and interactive elements available to three-dimensional virtual heritage environments? What are the philosophical issues that arise? Could interactivity actually obscure, help or hinder meaningful learning?

1.8   The Thorny Issue of Engagement

In 1997, Janet Murray published Hamlet on the holodeck: the future of narrative in cyberspace, which forecast the computer as a future platform for interactive drama (Murray 1997). Yet a great deal of recent literature has focused on the failure rather than on the success of virtual environments (particularly three-dimensional ones), as an engaging medium of entertainment and education.

Many critics have argued that virtual environments have yet to overcome a large number of impediments to their widespread dissemination, distribution, and use. Two fundamental restrictions are a lack of engagement and a lack of presence (as in, a feeling of "being there," of being transported to an actual place).

Virtual environments are often criticized for evoking 'cyberspace' but not 'place'. In other words, they lack the richness of the associations and encounters that occur in real space (Benedikt 1991; Coyne 1999; Johnson 1997). Even though place seems to be a central issue, how it can be clearly defined and demarcated, and its relation to presence and specifically to Cultural Presence is seldom discussed (Champion 2003). We have seen that there is scope for developing suitable context for virtual travel environments but the critical literature is so far descriptive rather than prescriptive. That is, it describes what is wrong or missing with virtual environments, but not how to test possible design solutions. More research is required to clarify and evaluate the key factors that improve the usability and user satisfaction of virtual travel environments for both education and for engagement, without one affecting the other.

I agree that issues with currently available virtual environment technology affect a sense of engagement in virtual heritage projects. While virtual environments can be used to simulate historically situated cultural perspectives, the above criticisms first need to be solved. That said, certain criticisms of the technology and use of virtual environments have been indirectly addressed by entertainment software design. A potential solution is to apply the interactive mechanisms used in games to virtual heritage environments. Modifying game–style interaction to suit the virtual reconstruction of a cultural site will allow for a more culturally immersive learning environment.

Interactive mechanisms commonly found in games can also be used for evaluation of user engagement without simultaneously interrupting the user's feeling of engagement. The more sophisticated computer games of today can evaluate user performance and change the difficulty of the tasks to suit. Some software and web browser additions also track user viewing patterns and preferences in order to improve the product. Via such devices, we may be able to gain useful feedback on the user travel experience without interrupting it, and without resource-intensive questionnaires or intrusive market surveys.

1.9 Four Major Problems

Even though interactive digital media has great potential, there are serious problems in designing virtual environments that in some way depict the values of past cultures. I wish to summarize these issues in the form of four major questions.

- Place Versus Cyberspace: What creates a sensation of place (as a cultural site) in a virtual environment in contradistinction to a sensation of a virtual environment as a collection of objects and spaces?

- Cultural Presence versus Social Presence and Presence: Which factors help immerse people spatially and thematically into a cultural learning experience?
- Realism Versus Interpretation: Does an attempt to perfect fidelity to sources and to realism improve or hinder the cultural learning experience?
- Education Versus Entertainment: Does an attempt to make the experience engaging improve or hinder the cultural learning experience?

The first problem is determining which elements of a cultural place are missing from virtual environments. Merely creating a reconstruction of a cultural site does not mean that one is creating a platform for understanding and transmitting locally specific cultural knowledge. We need to understand what distinguishes a cultural site from another site; we need to understand the features of place as a site of cultural learning.

The second problem is how to create an appropriate feeling of immersion or of presence in a virtual environment; how we make the past come alive for people so that they feel they are transported 'there'. This has often been seen as a technical constraint to the rendering of realistic virtual scenes (due to the speed of the Internet or network connection, limited processing power or the computer's capacity to render a large number of objects on the screen in real-time). I would however suggest designers should strive to foster engagement not only through realism, but also through contextually appropriate interaction.

Culture understood from the distance of a hotel or guidebook is obviously not the same as the dominant culture that guides, constrains, and nourishes a local inhabitant. In addition, a virtual traveler is not the same as a virtual tourist. Despite or perhaps because they have a goal to solve, and have more constraints and more direct immersion in the local way of doing things, people who travel rather than tour arguably have richer and more interesting experiences. Cipolla (2004) wrote:

> The tourist leaves home and brings in their luggage images and concepts about what and who they will meet; in this way the tourist 'has already lived' the contact with the inhabitants and their local culture…tourism creates [a sense of] **invulnerability**.

Tourists may want to share cultural perceptions and learn through doing, being told, observing, and asking. Yet in a real world environment, the industry may act as a cocoon. Real world tourism can lead to non-interaction, to being hermetically sealed in a sterile 'they lived like this' environment. Contextual engagement in the activity is missing, there is no locally related pressure, or necessity to understand the 'embedded' meaning of local cultural activity based on artifact. In order to be framed as an *experience*, local culture becomes high culture, non-invasive, and thus not so immersive.

In a virtual travel environment, you may want to be able to travel through time and space, to explore, and to interact with people, objects, and local goals, to explore thematically as well as spatially. Cipolla would see this as travel as opposed to tourism:

> The relation can begin when a traveler, without preconceptions or prefigured images, encounters a community, a monument, a natural environment or a cultural expression…

In a virtual environment, the setting should also be an interactive artifact. You should be able to interact with the environment as much as a local, to leave a trace, but also to communicate with the local inhabitants, and be able to understand or at least recognize their locally situated perspective.

Thirdly, our idea of what reality is may be at odds with understanding the past or a distant place from a local perspective. What does reality mean when we are trying to recreate and understand cultural perspectives? To what extent should we try to adhere to our normal concepts of reality?

In a virtual heritage environment, the more one can master local cultural behavior, the more one can understand significant events from the local cultural perspective. Mastery of dialogue and the contextually appropriate use of artifacts (as viewed from a local cultural perspective), may lead to enhanced cultural immersion. It may consequently lead to a heightened sense of engagement.

Yet it is possible that attempting to create contextual affordances and constraints will create too heavy a cognitive load on the virtual traveler, or require a high degree of skill and a large amount of time immersed in a virtual environment. Is it useful, desirable, or even possible to interact with digital reconstructions of different cultures in a meaningful way? Could interaction actually interfere with the learning process?

Fourthly, if we do manage to create an engaging and believable virtual environment, will the novelty or entertainment value actually interfere with the cultural understanding gained by the users? In virtual heritage environments, this is particularly evident in the conflict between individual freedom to explore and the more pragmatic need to convey historical information. For example, we may create an entertaining game. However entertaining that game may be, will it allow us to convey varying levels of historical accuracy in reconstructing the past?

1.10 Virtual Reality and Cultural Significance

One may well argue that such virtual representations cannot compete with actually visiting the site, but the point is whether such projects have a valid purpose and fit an important need; not whether they mirror reality. In fact, if we wish to understand how ancient people of long ago societies thought, believed, and acted, we need a non-realistic world to understand them and their beliefs. They saw, imagined, and related to things in a way a Westerner will not understand by merely traveling to the current remains of their past abode.

When I started my doctoral research, I looked for an exemplar, an archaeological site where the knowledge is hidden from the casual tourist, but discoverable through virtual interaction. I settled on a site, the Classical Mayan city of Lakam-Ha in Palenque Mexico. Although set in a spectacular location, the great majority of the artifacts of that city of inscriptions are simply no longer there. The people who live there now may not necessarily be the people who built the city, and even if they were the same people, they have lost the ability to read their own writing system.

A sense of being engaged with different local cultural perspectives is not always possible as a real-time tourist. Digitally mediated technology can attempt to reproduce existing data (archaeological impressions, extant ruins, the original condition of found artifacts, even typical weather patterns), but they can also make the user-experience more or less accessible and more or less contextual (i.e., augment, filter, constrain or optimize it).

In this book I will argue that there is a shortage of research integrating theory and practice on how best to augment or invoke the user-experience of place via digital media. By concentrating on achieving photo-realism rather than on under-standing the unique capabilities for digital media to enrich the user-experience, there are significant questions still to be answered. For example, we currently have little evidence as to whether virtual travel environments can afford useful and unique ways for augmenting and evoking awareness and understanding of distant places and foreign cultures. Critical research needs to be undertaken on the specific abilities of digital media to aid engagement, understanding, and awareness of other cultures.

One possible solution is to study why computer games are so popular, and whether their interactive elements can be applied successfully to interactive learning environments. Games have the ability to synthesize narrative, conjecture, computer-generated objects, contextually constrained goals, real-time dynamic data, and user-based feedback (Mateas and Stern 2001). It is possible that through this inter-active richness, rather than through a high-tech ability to reproduce elements of the real world, that people can both learn and enjoy alterity (experience of the 'other').

The intended audience that could most benefit from the theoretical part of this research are those who either communicate historical perceptions via digital media, or those who wish for more prescriptive (rather than descriptive) notions of 'place' and 'Cultural Presence'. The case study of Palenque that I will mention may also interest those designers interested in improving engagement via interactive elements. Finally, I hope to go some way in developing methods for addressing the user needs of potential virtual travelers and virtual tourists, especially when they wish to gain an atmosphere of a place before traveling there or are interested in a culture not easily accessed by conventional means.

References

Adams, G. (2009, 21 October). Botched facelift puts Bolivian pyramid at risk. *The Independent*. Retrieved 29 April 2010, from http://www.independent.co.uk/news/world/americas/botched-facelift-puts-bolivian-pyramid-at-risk-1806291.html

Aldrich, C. (2004). *Simulations and the future of learning: an innovative (and perhaps revolutionary) approach to e-learning*. San Francisco, CA: Jossey-Bass.

Benedikt, M. (1991). *Cyberspace: first steps*. Cambridge, MA: MIT Press.

Beynon, D. (1998, September 21–23). *Beyond Navigation as Metaphor*. Paper presented at the Research and Advanced Technology for Digital Libraries, Second European Conference, ECDL '98, Heraklion, Crete, Greece.

Blundell, C. (2006). *Investigation of the effectiveness of computer game-based virtual learning environments to facilitate students understanding of the features and history of ancient archi-tectural wonders*. Griffith University, Brisbane.

Booth, J. (2003). Hawk-Eye ushers in a brave new world [Electronic Version]. *The Telegraph*. Retrieved 30 April 2010, from http://www.smh.com.au/articles/2003/09/12/1063341777358.html

Boyle, A. (2010). Big brains for video games [Electronic Version]. *Cosmic log*. Retrieved 29 April 2010, from http://cosmiclog.msnbc.msn.com/archive/2010/01/20/2179437.aspx

Champion, E. (2003, 15–17 October). *Online Exploration of Mayan Culture*. Paper presented at the VSMM2003 - Ninth International Conference on Virtual Systems and Multimedia, Hybrid Reality: Art, Technology and the Human Factor, Montreal, Canada.

Cipolla, C.M. (2004). Tourist or guest: designing tourism experiences or hospitality relations? [Electronic Version]. *Design Philosophy Papers, 2*, n.p. Retrieved 25 April 2010, from http://www.desphilosophy.com/dpp/home.html

Coyne, R. (1999). *Technoromanticism: digital narrative, holism, and the romance of the real*. Cambridge, MA and London: MIT Press

Erickson, K.I., Boot, W.R., Basak, C., Neider, M.B., Prakash, R.S., Voss, M.W., et al. (2010). Striatal Volume Predicts Level of Video Game Skill Acquisition. *Cereb. Cortex*, 1–9.

Franklin, T. (2000). JTAP Project 305 Human Factors Aspects of Virtual Design Environments in Education: Project Report [Electronic Version], *48*, 1–151. Retrieved 25 April 2010, from http://www.jisc.ac.uk/uploaded_documents/jtap-048.pdf

Freemantle, M. (2000). Safeguarding Venice [Electronic Version]. *Chemical & Engineering News-C&EN (CENEAR), 78*, 23–31. Retrieved 25 April 2010, from http://pubs.acs.org/cen/coverstory/7835/7835sci1.html

Gillings, M. (2002). Virtual archaeologies and the hyper-real. In P. Fisher & D. Unwin (Eds.), *Virtual reality in geography* (Vol. 17–32). London and New York: Taylor & Francis.

Grabmeier, J. (2003, July 23). Life In The 'Bermuda Shorts Triangle:' Book Explores How Tourism Is Killing Venice. *Research News*. Retrieved 25 April 2010, from http://researchnews.osu.edu/archive/venice.htm

Grover, T. (2009, 17 March 2009). Basic Augmented Reality Heart in Flash. Retrieved 29 April, 2010, from http://www.imedstudios.com/labs/node/18

Haifa, U.O. (2008). Virtual Reality And Computer Technology Improve Stroke Rehabilitation [Electronic Version]. *ScienceDaily*. Retrieved 30 April 2010, from http://www.sciencedaily.com /releases/2008/03/080310110859.htm

Heard, C. (2003). Meditating on a cinema first [Electronic Version]. *BBC News Online,* heath. Retrieved 6 September 2010, from http://news.bbc.co.uk/2/hi/health/3151167.stm

Holzman, D. (1997). Plane Pollution [Electronic Version]. *Environmental Health Perspectives, 105*, 1300–1305. Retrieved 25 April 2010, from http://ehp.niehs.nih.gov/qa/105-12focus/focus.html

Huang, H., Wolf, S., & He, J. (2006). Recent developments in biofeedback for neuromotor rehabilitation. *Journal of NeuroEngineering and Rehabilitation, 3*(1), 11.

ISPR. (2003, May 2008). Tools to Measure Presence. Retrieved 12 March, 2010, from http://www.temple.edu/ispr/frame_measure.htm

Johnson, S. (1997). *Interface culture: how new technology transforms the way we think and communicate*. San Francisco, CA: HarperEdge.

Jones, M. (2004). Burrowing badgers mess with Stonehenge [Electronic Version]. *News in Science*. Retrieved 25 April 2010, from http://www.abc.net.au/science/news/stories/s1172316.htm

Leonard, T. (2009, 21 October). Ancient Bolivian pyramid 'could lose heritage status' after repairs. *The Telegraph*. Retrieved 30 April, 2010, from http://www.telegraph.co.uk/news/worldnews/southamerica/bolivia/6388640/Ancient-Bolivian-pyramid-could-lose-heritage-status-after-repairs.html

Lockridge, R. (1999). Hospitals try VR techniques for pain management [Electronic Version]. *CNN*. Retrieved 30 April 2010, from http://edition.cnn.com/TECH/computing/9905/21/t_t/pain.managment/index.html

Malik, T. (2003). Virtual Reality: Preparing for Terrorism in the Digital Age [Electronic Version]. Retrieved 6 September 2010, from http://www.space.com/businesstechnology/technology/vr_training_030319.html

Marsh, T., Wright, P., & Smith, S. (2001). Evaluation for the design of experience in virtual environments: Modeling breakdown of interaction and illusion. *CyberPsychology and Behavior, 4*(2), 225–238.

Mateas, M., & Stern, A. (2001). *Towards Building a Fully-Realized Interactive Drama*. Paper presented at the Digital Arts and Culture (DAC). Retrieved 24 April 2010, from www.stg. brown.edu/conferences/DAC/abstracts/mateas_stern.html

McGirk, J. (2000). Fury at sacred site damage [Electronic Version]. *BBC News Online*. Retrieved 30 April 2010, from http://www.independent.co.uk/news/world/americas/beer-ad-shoot-wrecks-inca-treasure-699395.html

Milmo, C. (2002, 8 November). List of world's most desirable destinations reveals canyon that lies between tourist dreams and reality. *The Independent*. Retrieved 29 April 2010, from http://www.independent.co.uk/travel/news-and-advice/list-of-worlds-most-desirable-destinations-reveals-canyon-that-lies-between-tourist-dreams-and-reality-746343.html

Mosaker, L. (2001). Visualising historical knowledge using virtual reality technology. *Digital Creativity, 12*(1), 15–25.

Murray, J.H. (1997). *Hamlet on the holodeck: the future of narrative in cyberspace*. New York: Free Press.

Pletinckx, D. (2003). Mapping the future: Intelligent Heritage – The user perspective. *Information Society Technologies, Cultural Heritage section*. Retrieved 30 April, 2010, from ftp://ftp. cordis.europa.eu/pub/ist/docs/digicult/pletinckx28012003.ppt

Pringle, H. (2009). Blame it on Lonely Planet? [Electronic Version]. *Archaeology Magazine Blog*. Retrieved 30 April 2010, from http://archaeology.org/blog/

Richards, D., Fassbender, E., Bilgin, A., & Thompson, W.F. (2008). An investigation of the role of background music in IVWs for learning. *ALT-J: Research in Learning Technology, 16*(3), 231–244.

Robillard, G., Bouchard, S., Fournier, T., & Renaud, P. (2003). Anxiety and presence during VR immersion: a comparative study of the reactions of phobic and non-phobic participants in therapeutic virtual environments derived from computer games. *CyberPsychology and Behavior, 65*(5), 467–476.

Rodarte, R.R., Carrasco, R., & Cuspineira, F.G. (n.d.). Calakmul (Virtual Calakmul). Retrieved 29 April 2010, from http://mezcal.fi-p.unam.mx/biorobotics/calakmul/index.htm

Roussou, M., & Drettakis, G. (2005). *Can VR be Useful and Usable in Real-World Contexts? Observations from the Application and Evaluation of VR in Realistic Usage Conditions*. Paper presented at the HCI International 2005 Conference, 1st International Conference on Virtual Reality, Las Vegas, Nevada USA

Smith, S. (2009, 6 October). From Kyoto to Machu Picchu: world's heritage at risk. *Google News*. Retrieved 29 April 2010, from http://www.google.com/hostednews/afp/article/ALeqM5iNHr-h8AEiYqkr92zlTSVwHrUJYQ

Tannenbaum, R.S. (2000). Multimedia developers can learn from the history of human communication. *Ubiquity, 2000* (October), 1.

Tuckman, J. (2005). £70m plan to save lost Inca city [Electronic Version]. *guardian.co.uk*. Retrieved 14 April 2005, from http://www.guardian.co.uk/travel/2005/apr/14/travelnews. artsnews.internationalnews

UNESCO. (2009, 3 December). Google and UNESCO announce alliance to provide virtual visits of several World Heritage sites. *News and Events*. Retrieved 30 April, 2010, from http://whc. unesco.org/en/news/570

Chapter 2
Virtual Environments

2.1 Technological Limitations

Virtual environments are generally assessed in terms of technological development (the amount or sophistication of data geometry or interaction that they can generate or deliver), or in approximation to reality (how realistic they appear to be).

Technological advances (technology for technology's sake), all too often drive the development and deployment of virtual environments. In the design of digital three-dimensional environments, the pursuit for exact duplication of visual form is all-important, as technological advances rather than content seem to be the main motivating factor of many web-enabled environments.

Technical issues include slowness, and a lack of realism. Other criticisms of virtual environments have pointed to a lack of meaningful content, confusing interface design, orientation and navigation difficulties, and a paucity of useful feedback mechanisms (Campbell 1997; Costalli et al. 2001).

To some extent, this may have been encouraged by limitations of early software, but even though both hardware and software are increasing in power and flexibility, new and more effective means of interaction are yet to appear. We could further argue that interaction is either limited or not appropriate to its context (Mosaker 2001; Turner et al. 2005). For example, Schroeder (1996, pp. 114–117) wrote:

> Interaction with virtual worlds mainly consists of changing the appearance of objects... there is little difference in terms of content between VR games and existing computer-based games.

2.2 Lack of Widely Distributed Technology

Part of the problem may be to do with the cost of dedicated virtual environment technology; such as the building and maintaining of CAVEs, which stands for Cave Automatic Virtual Environment (Cruz-Neira et al. 1993). In recent times, creating virtual environments typically required an army of programmers, a large space for

E. Champion, *Playing with the Past*, Human-Computer Interaction Series,
DOI 10.1007/978-1-84996-501-9_2, © Springer-Verlag London Limited 2011

front or rear projection, and computers far beyond the purchasing power of the typical home hobbyist.

Although online environments and 3D chat rooms have appeared in the last decade, the user is typically restricted to certain types of online browsers, operating systems, platforms, and graphic cards. On the other hand, where suitable applications exist or have existed (such as MetaStream, Metaplace, Adobe Atmosphere, Blaxxun, Google Lively, Pulse 3D, Shout 3D and Blink 3D), we cannot rely on them being around. Web-based 3D technology companies in particular seem to appear and disappear at a rapid pace.

2.3   Size, Speed and Rendering Issues

Virtual environments (VEs), and Collaborative Virtual Environments (CVEs), are too large in terms of file size or finding areas of interest when inside the environment. They contain too much data for many people to download, and walk through, especially on home computers, or on the computers that schools can afford to both buy and maintain. For example, Moshell and Hughes (2002) argued the following:

> For VR to have a significant role in school-based education, several things must occur. These include at least the following:
>
> - Reliable high speed, low cost multimedia systems must become available in schools. The next generation of video games, to appear in late 1999, seems likely to fulfil the performance and reliability requirements that are so clearly unfulfilled in schools by personal computers. However, their acquisition by schools depends on political and economic issues.
> - An adequate theory and body of practice of instructional design for virtual worlds must be developed.
>
> ...Environment that incorporates live instruction, tangible artifacts, and careful guidance for generalization. Virtual reality is like a field trip – fun, motivating but potentially hard to relate to the curriculum.

2.4   Lack of Meaningful Content

Where content is concerned, there are further varying aims and methods. Some virtual environments are assessed in terms of ergonomics, and their effective usability (Bowman 1997; Bowman et al. 1999). Unfortunately, few environments are directly assessed in terms of useful content (Champion 2002). Some virtual environments are assessed through how well they inspire a sense of spatial presence, negative feelings (phobic reactions), realism or naturalism, and subjective involvement/ engagement. These are generally considered factors of 'presence' or 'telepresence' ('the sense of being there' without noticing the experience is mediated by technology).

This field is still in its infancy – there is still confusion and debate as to the meanings of 'immersion' and 'presence' (Lombard 2000; Schuemie et al. 2001; Slater 1999).

2.5 We Experience More than Tangible Objects

Writers often criticize virtual environments for evoking 'cyberspace' but not 'place' (Benedikt 1991; Coyne 1995, 1999a, b; Heim 1998; Johnson 1997; Kitchin 1998). In other words, they are attacked for lacking the richness of associations and encounters of meetings that are found in real space. Yet compelling examples and prescriptive writings on exactly which elements help create a virtual sense of place are rare indeed. For instance, Weckström (2004, p. 9) decried the "hollowness" of virtual worlds:

> This thesis began from the fact that, when a group of students were exploring and researching other 'virtual worlds' in order to begin developing Marinetta, they reported that all the worlds seemed empty and hollow, like stage sets. There were neat buildings in these spaces but no sense that these buildings had been built for any real purpose. The students noted that these so called virtual worlds did not seem to be worlds at all, but just architectural spaces that did not give them any feeling of worldliness.

A class of Media students at Arcada in Helsinki also complained to Weckström that virtual worlds were sterile. Weckström's thesis surveyed simulators, chat-worlds and games, including *Microsoft flight simulator 2004*, *TRANSIMS Visualizer*, *Habbo Hotel*, *The Sims Online* and *EverQuest*. He then declared (2004, p. 38):

> …a virtual world has to support the following factors: there has to be a feeling of presence, the environment has to be persistent, it has to support interaction, there has to be a representation of the user and it has to support a feeling of specific worldliness.

Another reason for the existence of sterile environments may stem from a belief that we experience reality as something objective, settled and constant. Solid and immutable objects are also easier to conceptualize and model than what fully constitutes reality. For the real world includes many intangibles, including social behaviors and mental states.

2.6 The World Is More than Visual Stimuli

This issue is evident even in the debate over using the terms 'virtual reality' or 'virtual environment'. For example, Bryson (1995, p. 9.2) offered the following definition:

> **Virtual reality** is the use of various computer graphics systems in combination with various display and interface devices to provide the effect of **immersion** in an interactive three-dimensional computer-generated environment in which the virtual objects have **spatial presence**. [Bold is from original text].

Researchers testing the effects of presence and immersion in digital environments, list the above spatial criterion as only one of four (Lessiter et al. 2001). The four criteria are physical space, engagement, naturalism or realism, and negative feelings (such as phobia, motion sickness etcetera).

There is still an overwhelming tendency of 3D virtual environment designers such as Bryson (1995) to privilege spatial relations of visual representations over the other criteria found useful by psychologists (such as Baños et al. 2004; Botella et al. 2003).

The above quote from Steve Bryson is part of his more specific argument that objects have to be related to head movement of an observer via head tracking in order to have virtual reality. He also argues that visual fidelity is not necessary to have 'spatial presence' but his definitions and examples only relate to the visual medium. According to Bryson's argument, it would be impossible for a non-sighted person to feel a sense of presence in any virtual environment by definition. Therefore, using a reductio ad absurdum, there is either nothing that is not visual in our perceptions of reality (that cannot be simulated by virtual *visual* technology), OR non-sighted people cannot develop a sense of environmental presence. I find either claim to be unconvincing.

An emphasis on visual representation and realism is also not always of primary interest to social scientists, such as (Anderson 2003; Gillings and Goodrick 1996) or to educationalists such as (Roussos and Drettakis 2005). Research indicates that multimodal display of information may be more effective than one medium (Kray et al. 2003). However, many virtual environments are purely visual as seen in the following definition by Czernuszenko et al. (1997):

> Virtual Reality (VR) can be defined as interactive computer graphics that provides viewer-centered perspective, large field of view and stereo. Head Mounted Displays (HMDs) and BOOMs (TM) achieve these features with small display screens, which move with the viewer, close to the viewer's eyes.

While they do mention audio once, the emphasis of Czernuszenko et al is on the visual, not other sensory fields. Nor is 'interactive' defined as anything more than that the screen display is regenerated according to where the viewer is looking.

2.7 Different People See Different Things

There is another problem related to the ocular-centric tendencies of virtual environment designers. They seem to have a focus not just with visual fidelity, but a loyalty to a belief that in perceiving the world everybody sees the same thing.

What we see is not necessarily physical reality, but our concept-orientated brain tells us that it is. As soon as reality gets to our brain it has already been filtered not just by our eyes but also by our previous experiences of reality. Virtually everything in our head is put into a conceptual schema, a framework. Without content relating directly to how we perceive the world, an emphasis on formal realism is not creating a virtual reality, but a storehouse of visually represented objects.

2.8   Personalization Is Missing

Virtual environments typically have no annotation ability; there is no record kept of user-environment interaction history. User-based goals are also inseparable from the overall model.

Most virtual environments are single-user. Where they allow several people to see each other, sharing of information is usually restricted to chat, sending files or hyperlinks; control of social interaction is limited. People being social creatures may want to interact with and be recognizable to other travelers. On the other hand, they might want some control over the quantity or even quality of social interaction.

Interaction is also crucial to learning. The approach suggested here is constructivist, as explained by Weckström (2004):

> What is meant by constructivism? The term refers to the idea that learners construct knowledge for themselves – each learner individually (and socially) constructs meaning – as he or she learns. Constructing meaning is learning; there is no other kind. The dramatic consequences of this view are twofold;
>
> We have to focus on the learner in thinking about learning (not on the subject/lesson to be taught).
>
> There is no knowledge independent of the meaning attributed to experience (constructed) by the learner, or community of learners.

Hein (1991) argued that interactivity in exhibits creates more engagement by allowing the user to apply the tool directly to their own life:

> ... I have watched adults look at a map of England at the dock where the Mayflower replica is berthed in Plymouth, Massachusetts. Repeatedly, adults will come to the map, look at it and then begin to discuss where their families come from. ...Here is an interactive exhibit (even if there is little to "do" except point and read), which allows each visitor to take something personal and meaningful from it and relate to the overall museum experience. For me, the Diaspora Museum in Tel Aviv came alive when I had the opportunity to call up family genealogies on the computer in the reference center. The opportunity to view and manipulate a library of family trees covering several generations and a wide geographical distribution, gave personal meaning to the idea of a Diaspora.

2.9   Lack of Contextual Evaluation

Since most virtual environments are built in laboratories, they seldom reach mass-circulation. Their complexity and unique nature may hinder full-scale evaluation, especially of target audiences. Moreover, when the environments are evaluated, due to the scale or nature of the project, the evaluation findings cannot always be used to help fine-tune further environments.

However, there is also the problem that the academic community is still feeling its way as to which terms and criteria are best used to evaluate virtual environments.

Part of the problem is no doubt compounded by the complexity of the subject, and by the vast range of disciplines interested in virtual environments.

There is also an ongoing debate about the scope and nature of presence itself at http://www.presence-connect.com. For example, Slater (2003) posted the following on the presence-connect.org discussion forum:

> There is no 'true meaning' to the term 'presence'…The study of how to create emotionally rich, engaging, fantastic, entertaining, meaningful….experiences is very important and fundamental to the field of virtual environments, and to many other fields. However, the study of this is not the same as the study of pretence.
>
> Pretence is concerned with how to achieve successful substitution of real sensory stimuli with artificially generated sensory stimuli. This also involves the requirement that people experiencing such stimuli (participants) have the power to change it, within constraints. … The quest for high pretence in a virtual environment is not the same as a demand for high realism, i.e., this is not an attempt to 'reproduce reality'. Rather the interest is on what fundamental properties must sensory stimuli have, and how must they be structured as a totality in order to produce the 'pretense response'? …
>
> Preference is not the same as pretence. One doesn't have to like a situation to be in it…. Our only real disagreement is over the use of a label. We have been using the same label 'presence' to talk about different concepts. While this conflict remains, the field cannot advance since there can be no unifying paradigm that is the object of study of the group of researchers involved. We will always be arguing about true meanings. The term presence has now become so overloaded with different interpretations and meanings, perhaps I should abandon the pretence of working in this field, and use this other term.

The above posting by Slater highlights an ongoing discussion on the nature of Presence Research. One aspect of the research shared by both those attempting realism and those attempting to create engaging (aesthetic) experiences is that they are both concerned with which key stimuli are necessary and sufficient to enable people to feel they are 'there' (in a digitally supported environmental visualization).

In fact, we could say there are three divergent schools of thought in presence studies. The first, like Slater, believe that presence is acting or reacting as if one was acting or reacting to real world stimuli (a phobic sense of presence relies on evocative or phobic triggers). The second school believes presence is gained when the virtual environment is to all intents and purposes indistinguishable from the real world. This school of thought seems more and more evident in developing notions of presence. For example, Meehan et al. (2002) wrote:

> We hypothesize that to the degree that a VE seems real, it will evoke physiological responses similar to those evoked by the corresponding real environment, and that greater presence will evoke a greater response. If so, these responses can serve as objective surrogate measures of subjective presence.

The third school believes that presence is best reached when the participant has an experience of great aesthetic or sensory interest, and they leave the cares and concerns of the real world behind them (Riva et al. 2004). The aim of the first school (and the most challenging aim) would be of interest to people attempting to prove the power of the technology to simulate reality. The aim of the second school may be useful for curing phobias or for selling products (advertising). The aim of the third school may be useful for artists and designers. However, these distinctions are not *yet* widely distributed in the academic presence literature.

2.10   Summary of Implications for Virtual Environments

I argue that VR (or, as I refer to it here, virtual environments), before it can go forward, needs to address several issues that have prevented widespread realization of its potential. Many virtual environments lack meaningful content due to a paucity of meaningful interaction, few have feedback and evaluation mechanisms, most are devoid of a sense of place, do not offer personalization (such as annotation), there is no filtering of data, and no ability to adjust the 'difficulty level' of the interface to suit a particular user or experience.

Undoubtedly there are many successful uses for virtual environments. Yet virtual environments that have the noblest of aims are too often only showcases. For example, a major portal for virtual heritage, http://www.virtualheritage.net, records the most popular articles, but not the popular virtual heritage models. Virtual heritage models are still not considered worthy intellectual content even by societies dedicated to their advancement.

Major conservation organizations do not know of the potential of virtual environments to preserve both the formal specifications of the objects, and their cultural associations. In 2001 (but since updated) the ICOMOS (1988) charter did not list digital media as one of the many listed media to record cultural heritage.

In order to satisfy users of a virtual environment, they need to know the goals and significance of an environment-the reasons why they should immerse themselves in virtual environments and what they should particularly look out for and attempt to learn.

Meaningful interaction seems to be a crucial issue here. Research surveys indicate that when presented with realistic visual fidelity users also expect highly realistic interaction in order to be engaged (Mosaker 2001). While others have indicated that meaningful interaction is preferable to photo-realism (Eiteljorg 1998).

Visual depiction of objects does not automatically lead to full understanding of the social and cultural properties of these objects. Social critics have written that in creating authentic-looking objects, even our understanding of tourism has become *fetishized* (Crang and Franklin 2001). Many virtual heritage sites have brilliantly detailed temples, but are missing the element that 'places' the temple in its context.

That missing element is people, and the driving forces that compelled them to inhabit and modify their 'world'. Every group of people has their own viewpoints, issues, and outlook on the world. Without understanding this specific cultural agency, there is a danger that we may see the virtual heritage site only in terms of our own cultural perspective. This limited ability to represent social processes and 'intangible' heritage can create a second danger. The typically static and apparently immutable features of digital simulations can imply a certainty of knowledge that we actually do not possess.

Too many scientifically accurate virtual heritage environments lack the ability to store interaction history. The actions and paths taken by its visitors affect a truly interactive environment. Yet many virtual environments do not record traces of what happened. Visitors may be able to change part of the environment but seldom does the environment 'remember' the visitors, their paths, actions, or discoveries.

For both these reasons, visualization-based environments are only rough approximations for the conserving and preserving of history. Given interaction is needed in order to experience and learn about other cultures, there is still little research on which types of interaction are required.

Which varying modes of interactivity add to the experienced significance of, and engagement in, a virtual tourist environment? Do inbuilt evaluation mechanisms compare favorably to more traditional and formal feedback mechanisms when gauging engagement in an interactive virtual environment?

The survey by Mosaker (2001) on the missing elements of the user-experience of high-tech virtual reality museums is both unique and timely. There are indeed many technical issues to be resolved, but until we also resolve appropriate content issues, virtual environments may become highly usable, but they are unlikely to be useful (Davis et al. 1996, p. 3). In the following chapters I hope to show (with the focus on virtual heritage environments), that there are four major content-related issues blocking the development of useful virtual environments: place, Cultural Presence, experiential realism, and meaningful interaction.

References

Anderson, M. (2003). *Computer Games and Archaeological Reconstruction: The Low Cost VR, Enter The Past*. Paper presented at the CAA 2003 – Enter the Past + Workshop 8 – Archäologie und Computer Conference, Vienna, Austria.

Baños, R.M., Botella, C., Alcañiz, M., Liaño, V., Guerrero, B., & Rey, B. (2004). Immersion and Emotion: Their Impact on the Sense of Presence. *CyberPsychology and Behavior, 7*(6), 734–741.

Benedikt, M. (1991). *Cyberspace: first steps*. Cambridge, MA: MIT Press.

Botella, C., Baños, R.M., & Alcañiz, M. (2003). *A Psychological Approach To Presence*. Paper presented at the Presence 2003 Conference: The Sixth Annual International Workshop on Presence, Denmark.

Bowman, D. (1997). Interaction Techniques for Immersive Virtual Environments: Design, Evaluation, and Application. Invited talk at the Human Interface Technology Laboratory, University of Washington. Retrieved 1 January, 2009, from http://people.cs.vt.edu/~bowman/pubs.html

Bowman, D., Johnson, D.B., & Hodges, L.F. (1999). *Testbed evaluation of virtual environment interaction techniques*. Paper presented at the ACM Symposium on Virtual Reality Software and Technology, London.

Bryson, S. (1995). Approaches to the successful design and implementation of VR applications. In R. A. Earnshaw, J. A. Vince & H. Jones (Eds.), *Virtual reality applications* (pp. 3–15). London: Academic.

Campbell, D.A. (1997). Explorations into Virtual Architecture: A HIT Lab Gallery. *IEEE Multimedia, 4*(1), 74–76.

Champion, E. (2002, October). *Cultural Engagement in Virtual Heritage Environments with Inbuilt Interactive Evaluation Mechanisms.* Paper presented at the PRESENCE 2002 Conference: The Fifth Annual International Workshop on Presence, Porto Portugal.

Costalli, F., Marucci, L., Mori, G., & Paternò, F. (2001, 3–7 September). *Design Criteria for Usable Web-Accessible Virtual Environments.* Paper presented at the ichim01: Cultural Heritage and Technologies in the Third Millennium Conference, Milan Italy.

Coyne, R. (1995). *Designing information technology in the postmodern age: from method to metaphor.* Cambridge, MA: MIT Press.

Coyne, R. (1999a). *Technoromanticism: digital narrative, holism, and the romance of the real.* Cambridge, MA, London: MIT Press.

Coyne, R. (1999b). The Embodied Architect in the Information Age. Richard Coyne Inaugural Lecture delivered 16 February 1999 at the University of Edinburgh. Retrieved 11 April, 2009, from http://www.caad.ed.ac.uk/Coyne/Inaugural/

Crang, M., & Franklin, A. (2001). The Trouble with Tourism and Travel Theory? *Tourist Studies, 1*(1), 5–22.

Cruz-Neira, C., Sandin, D.J., & DeFanti, T.A. (1993). Surround-screen projection-based virtual reality: the design and implementation of the CAVE, *Proceedings of the 20th Annual Conference on Computer Graphics and Interactive Techniques* (pp. 135–142): ACM.

Czernuszenko, M., Pape, D., Sandin, D., DeFanti, T., Dawe, G.L., & Brown, M., D. (1997). The ImmersaDesk and Infinity Wall projection-based virtual reality displays. *SIGGRAPH Computer Graphics, 31*(2), 46–49.

Davis, S.B., Huxor, A., & Lansdown, J. (1996). The DESIGN of Virtual Environments with particular reference to VRML [Electronic Version]. Retrieved 10 May 2010, from http://www.agocg.ac.uk/reports/virtual/vrmldes/title.htm

Eiteljorg, H. (1998, Fall). Photorealistic Visualizations May Be Too Good. *CSA Newsletter, XI (2).* Retrieved 12 February, 2010, from www.csanet.org/newsletter/fall98/nlf9804.html

Gillings, M., & Goodrick, G. (1996). Sensuous and Reflexive GIS Exploring Visualisation and VRML [Electronic Version]. *Internet Archaeology*, n.p. Retrieved 10 May 2010, from http://intarch.ac.uk/journal/issue1/

Heim, M. (1998). *Virtual realism.* New York: Oxford University Press.

Hein, G.E. (1991). *Constructivist Learning Theory.* Paper presented at the Museum and the Needs of People CECA (International Committee of Museum Educators) Conference. Retrieved 28 April 2010, from http://www.exploratorium.edu/IFI/resources/constructivistlearning.html

ICOMOS. (1988). Australia ICOMOS Guidelines to the Burra charter [Electronic Version]. *Section 2.1*, from http://www.icomos.org/australia/burrasig.html

Johnson, S. (1997). *Interface culture: how new technology transforms the way we think and communicate.* San Francisco, CA: HarperEdge.

Kitchin, R. (1998). *Cyberspace: the world in the wires.* New York: Wiley.

Kray, C., Laakso, K., Elting, C., & Coors, V. (2003). *Presenting Route Instructions on Mobile Devices.* Paper presented at the IUI 03 Conference, Miami Beach, FL.

Lessiter, J., Freeman, J., Keogh, E., & Davidoff, J. (2001). A Cross-Media Presence Questionnaire: The ITC-Sense of Presence Inventory. *Presence: Teleoper. Virtual Environment, 10*(3), 282–297.

Lombard, M. (2000). Resources for the study of presence: Presence explication. Retrieved 12 June, 2007, from http://nimbus.temple.edu/~mlombard/Presence/explicat.htm

Meehan, M., Insko, B., Whitton, M., & Brooks Jnr., F.P. (2002). *Physiological measures of presence in stressful virtual environments.* Paper presented at the 29th Annual Conference on Computer Graphics and Interactive Techniques, San Antonio, Texas.

Mosaker, L. (2001). Visualising Historical Knowledge Using Virtual Reality Technology. *Digital Creativity, 12*(1), 15–25.

Moshell, J.M., & Hughes, C.E. (2002). Virtual environments as a tool for academic learning [Electronic Version]. *Handbook of virtual environments*, 893–910. Retrieved April 30, 2010 from http://depts.washington.edu/edtech/moshellHughes.pdf

Riva, G., Waterworth, J.A., & Waterworth, E.L. (2004). The Layers of Presence: A Bio-Cultural Approach to Understanding Presence in Natural and Mediated Environments. *Cyberpsychology and Behavior, 7*(4), 402–416.

Roussos, M., & Drettakis, G. (2005). *Can VR be Useful and Usable in Real-World Contexts? Observations from the Application and Evaluation of VR in Realistic Usage Conditions.* Paper presented at the HCI International 2005, The First international conference on virtual reality, Las Vegas, NV.

Schroeder, R. (1996). *Possible worlds: the social dynamic of virtual reality technology.* Boulder, CO: Westview Press.

Schuemie, M.J., van der Straaten, P., Krijn, M., & van der Mast, C.A.P.G. (2001). Research on Presence in Virtual Reality: A Survey. *CyberPsychology and Behavior, 4*(2), 183–201.

Slater, M. (1999). Measuring Presence: A Response to the Witmer and Singer Presence Questionnaire. *Presence: Teleoperators and Virtual Environments, 8*(5), 560–565.

Slater, M. (2003, 18 August). I'm only pretending -- response to the core of presence by J & A Waterworth. Retrieved 12 February, 2010, from http://presence.cs.ucl.ac.uk/presenceconnect/forum/viewmessage.asp?forumid=14&messageid=104

Turner, P., Turner, S., & Carroll, F. (2005). The Tourist Gaze: Towards Contextualised Virtual Environments. In P. Turner & E. Davenport (Eds.), *Spaces, spatiality and technology* (pp. 281–287). Dordrecht, The Netherlands: Kluwer.

Weckström, N. (2004). *Finding 'reality' in virtual environments.* Unpublished Masters, Arcada Polytechnic, Helsingfors/Esbo.

Chapter 3
Virtual Places

3.1 Place in a Virtual Space

What creates a sensation of place (as a cultural site) in a virtual environment in contradistinction to a sensation of a virtual environment as a collection of objects and spaces? It may be argued that a sense of place in virtual environments is related to how much 'presence' we feel. Presence researchers have often cited and used, the sense of 'being in a place' as a test of virtual presence. While there has been long-term discussion and disagreement over the concept of virtual presence, it is a tricky and elusive subject to define. Yet there is little debate on the concept of virtual place.

For example, Biocca (1997) noted people might feel present in real, imaginary or virtual places. Slater defined one aspect of presence as feeling that one is in another place, and not just viewing a set of images (Slater 1999). Researchers often use the term 'place' in their presence questionnaires (Lessiter et al. 2001; Schuemie et al. 2001; Slater 1999). Yet presence can only be clearly defined by relating it to place, if place itself is clearly defined and understood.

Presence in virtual environments is often defined as the subjective belief that one is in a place even though the participant knows that the experience is mediated by digital media (Slater 1999). Presence has many definitions yet the word 'place' itself has had a long history of changing meaning and usage.

When we talk of place, or a sense of place, we may mean socially or geo-physically defined locations, the feeling that one is in or surrounded by a type or kind of location, or the intensity of that feeling (some researchers ask in their questionnaires if a virtual environment felt like a 'place'). One can point to where they are on a map, they may feel spatially surrounded, or be able to say an event happened in a certain position in a virtual environment, without feeling that they were experiencing a strong or unique experience of place. In order to understand how and why people can feel a sense of presence, we need to have a clear and appropriate sense of place.

If we do not have a strong sense of presence, then perhaps we do not have a strong sense of place or a strong sense of social agency. We may have a sense of social agency in a virtual environment without a sense of place, but the events that 'take place' will be hard if not impossible to recover, retrieve, or re-enact. A sense of place allows us to locate and uniquely define cultural rituals, socially meaningful transactions using artifacts. This distinction will prove to be very important to the argument as I intend to demonstrate that place may not be a necessary and sufficient condition for a sense of presence but it is for Cultural Presence.

Perhaps there are elements of real places that somehow have been left out of virtual environments. Many writers, frequently from architecture, have made the distinction between place and cyberspace (Benedikt 1991; Coyne 1995, 1999a; Heim 1998; Johnson 1997).

Some of these researchers have further attempted to propose features that are needed for place making (Kalay and Marx 2001, 2003; Nitsche et al. 2002). However, they have listed all the features that create a sense of place, not which features create a sense of place for specific audiences and conditions. It is obviously impractical to attempt to provide all place-making features when one designs a place for a specific purpose, especially considering that real world places do not typically use all these place-making elements.

Given the premise that place is a necessary if challenging part of creating a meaningful virtual environment, what is the best way of gaining a sense of place via virtual environments? In addition, which features are desirable for which occasions?

Research into place-making can be described as involving three stages, critiquing the absence of place, prescribing which elements of place are needed, and evaluating and extending place-making in virtual environments.

Centers researching virtual places, and especially contextual realism, include the Cultural VR Lab (University of California, Los Angeles) and the Center for Design Visualization (University of California, Berkeley). Digital Studios-CUMIS (Cambridge) focuses on the cinematic expression of space and social agency. Crida (University of Melbourne), are evaluating modes of cultural learning via interactive elements such as dynamic environments, cultural constraints, and social agents. The University of Sydney's Key Centre of Design Computing and Cognition conduct research on agency and on-line learning via virtual environments. The University of Berkeley, and the European CAHRISMA project (also known as the Charisma Project), investigate social agency in virtual places.

Changing Places Research Group (MIT) hope to create mediated narrative enriched places. The "interactive institute" in Sweden has experimented with game engines to create interactive virtual environments, and are working on an 'intelligent street' project that reflects the cultures of its inhabitants. The Center for Virtual Architecture, (CVA University at Buffalo, New York), has recently been formed to create multimedia projects for architectural education. Architecture HKU (Hong Kong), research digitalization of heritage projects, while CASA at UCL (University College of London) has written reports on the inhabitation of virtual online worlds.

The above only name a few of the most advanced and profound research into place-making that I know of but there are many more. So there seems to be a multitude of centers that have a focal research interest in virtual environments. Yet this does not seem to translate to the actual place-making, even if there seems to be a recent explosion of research centers that name 'virtual place' as a research topic. So although the first stage place-making (the critique of virtual places) was reached as recently as the mid 1990s, we are still somewhere in the second stage of theorizing which elements of place go where. As we will see in the chapter on evaluation, concrete evaluative studies on popular and durable virtual environments are few and far between. My initial suspicion was that at least part of the reason why there have been so few studies of virtual environments in use, is that place is a complex and nuanced subject.

3.2 Experiential Types of Place

Writers in architecture, urban planning, philosophy and geography have defined place in a myriad of ways. Casey (1993) focused on the experiential sensation of place as an extension of the body. On the other hand Relph (1976) viewed place as that which surrounds the viewer existentially, in terms of attitude and intention. Relph defined many different types of place, and he described how each offered a mix of experiences.

The usefulness of 'place' can be considered a key feature of virtual communities in at least five major ways. The notion of place can identify and describe elements of a virtual environment through having the following features.

- A place can have a distinct theme, atmosphere, and contextually related artifacts.
- Some places have the capacity to overawe.
- Place has the power to evoke memories and associations.
- Place has the capability to act as either stage or framework in which communal and individual activity can 'take place'.
- Place has the ability to transmit the cultural intentions of individual participants and social 'bodies'.

3.2.1 Place as Unique Experience

In her doctoral thesis, Ciolfi (2004, p. abstract) wrote the following notion of place:

Place is a notion of space inextricably linked with the wealth of human experience and use occurring within it, and invested by values, attitudes and cultural influences. In other words, place is *experienced space*.

Place as a field or centre of unique associations and memories is a defining feature suggested by many writers (Coyne 1995; Kalay and Marx 2001; Massey 1993; Relph 1976). Massey (1993) made the further interesting point that a place may be unique not just as a thematically unified container of individual elements, but also as a container of the eclectic combination or selection of those objects.

3.2.2 Sublime Places of Terror and Awe

An experience of a place can range right across the comfort–discomfort and protected–unprotected spectrum. The experience may be comforting (the Danish 'hyggelig' or the German 'gemütlich' refer to the special 'cozy' nature of home when outside is cold and inhospitable) or it may be uncanny, sublime, or terrifying. This spectrum can range from a secure sense of territorial possession and domestic safety, to a sense of being completely overwhelmed, vulnerable, mortal, or otherwise insignificant.

By linking to 'heavenly' architecture, Benedikt may have foreseen 'cyberspace' in the latter sense, as an environment that over-awes and inspires (Benedikt 1991). Casey (1993) also described sites that were non-inhabitable and therefore non-places, as well as defining place-scapes as places that surround and dwarf us. There seems to be several methods by which a place can create a feeling of awe, through infinite scale and size, through immutability, through materialization of perfection, demonstration of unstoppable vast force, or through complete indifference to human visitation.

These notions are variations on the sublime, a theory of aesthetics that can be traced back at least as far as the Greek philosopher Longinus. The eighteenth century foresaw unbounded space, both in the etchings of Piranesi and in the aesthetic writings of the philosopher Immanuel Kant (1987) on the nature of the Sublime. Kant (1987) suggested that an over abundance of sensory data either too large to imagine, or so large it overpowered the senses, was an aspect of the sublime.

Popular cyber-literature often uses this idea to conjure up infinite spaces of overwhelmingly precise or overwhelming detail. For example, the book *Neuromancer* by Gibson (2000) described cyberspace as space without limit and with unbounded possibility. For the essence of the sublime as used by popular media's portrayal of Virtual Reality is to dwarf us and make our achievements seem physically insignificant by comparison. The idea of 'Eternal Space' was also a favorite concept of architects (Tyng 1984; Wrede 1980).

However, to suggest presence is attained solely by an over abundance of realistic objects (Kant's mathematical sublime) or by overpowering physical phenomena alone (such as in floods, and giant waterfalls, the natural sublime) is to create an environment that is devoid of cultural inscription.

3.2.3 Evocative and Atmospheric Place

Some writers suggest geography indirectly highlights our schemas of place. Relph (1976) suggested that place may be telluric, a series of projected landforms. While Kant (1987) argued that place is evocative. For example ruins like the Coliseum (Fig. 3.1) can evoke remembered sensations of its previous incarnations, or remind the visitor of related activities or even of similar places.

Many virtual environments including computer games use the use of place as an evoker of previous or imagined places. Yet writers who have noted the atmospheric

Fig. 3.1 The Roman Coliseum at night

sense of place have not yet fully described how it may be created (Johnson 1997; Kalay and Marx 2001; Neumann et al. 1996). To understand what builds atmosphere, we may need to wrestle the attention of game designers and cinematic directors away from their consoles and cameras.

3.2.4 Place as Stage and Playground

A place can frame space, it can also suggest activity through the way it frames and positions objects. A playground is a place that suggests activity through affordances (objects that can swing, carry and move), and constraints (swings and slides compel us to move in certain ways).

Place can be considered as a matrix of constraints and affordances that act on the body and mind, and this is not revolutionary concept. For example, Casey (1997) seems to favor the definition of place as that which provides boundaries, rest, is unique as well as being related to the human body. For example, the Gothenburg law court steps by the Swedish architect Erik Gunnar Asplund are so proportioned that running up them is difficult – people are induced to reach the courtroom in a slow and unhurried manner (Wrede 1980).

Architects such as Coyne, and geographers such as Relph have described how place functions as a filter of action, rest and movement. Coyne (1999a) actually suggested deliberately constructing constraints to force people to act in certain ways, a clear change in direction from the suggestion of Novak (1991) that virtual environments be 'Liquid Architecture'.

The metaphor of place as stage can be extended from being defined as choreographing (restricting) ways in which we move while inside it (as above) to a record of individual behaviors and significant ceremonial actions. As an example, the next two images are of a quick and dirty port of the famous Silicon Graphics VRML model of Tenochtitlan, into Bryce 3D, a now defunct 3D landscape modeler.

The model was a showcase of VRML 2.0 in 1996, in fact it accompanied the official manual by Silicon Graphics (Hartman et al. 1996). Yet even though the title of the book was *The VRML 2.0 Handbook: Building Moving Worlds on the Web*, the original model sat in the middle of empty space. This was not historically accurate, for the historic Aztec city lay in the middle of a giant lake (even though now it lies under the stone and concrete buildings of Mexico City). Yet by merely placing a body of water underneath the original VRML model (Fig. 3.2), and by selecting a more human scale and perspective (Fig. 3.3), we are much closer to understanding the situatedness of the original Tenochtitlan.

The original model featured pre-scripted animations but offered no possibility of personalization. A more inscriptive and write-able design theory of a virtual place could be viewed either in terms of the unavoidable marks left by environmental change and user action (archaeologists call these 'traces'), or by deliberate attempts at communication (when these inscriptions can be layered over each other when place acts as a 'palimpsest').

Fig. 3.2 The SGI VRML model of Tenochtitlan ported to Bryce3D, placed on water

Fig. 3.3 The same model from a more human perspective

3.2.5 Place as Trace and Palimpsest

Place as an artifact that records traces of its owners is a concept shared by cultural geographers, anthropologists, and archaeologists. For them, place is the interpretable staged slate on which historical interactions are inscribed by intent, accident, ritual, and habit. Deductions of historical places have allowed them to extrapolate cultural perspectives from dust, bones, and half believed tribal myths. Some have described a place as a storehouse of users' meanings and identities, rather than as a design portfolio of architects' intentions.

Many writers have remarked that places when viewed as artifacts are 'trace' museums (Beckmann 1998; Cantor 1974; Crang 1998; Johnson 1997; Rapoport 1982; Schiffer and Miller 1999; Tuan 1998). For Massey (1993), a cultural geographer, place is not merely a static physical background to action, but also a dynamic matrix or series of social interactions. Place is a process not a product, and can consist of multiple interpretations, conflicts, and a unique combination of borrowed histories.

Massey argued that place might be a record of social processes, consist of fluid boundaries, and be formed by internal conflicts. A place is evocative, fluid, and full of mementos from other places. To view a place as a container of x, y and z dimensions is to deny it a cultural content. A place is more like a nexus, or a web. Moreover, the strands that conspire to create a sense of place are never set in stone. Place involves a setting for social transactions that are location based and task specific. For what people do will depend on where they are and what they believe, and how the place is or could be viewed by others as a component of their 'social web'.

In this sense, place is a cultural setting, it gives cultural interaction a time and a location, which means that place is time-based. In the words of Crang (1998, p. 103), "Spaces become places as they become 'time-thickened'." To extend Crang's argument, virtual environments need to remember what 'takes place'. The effect of place on humans has obviously had a variety of interpretations, but the next question is to ask which elements are needed to create a 'sense of place' in real environments.

3.3 Requirements for Creating a Sense of Place

3.3.1 Place Requires Embodiment

Places identify more and less bodily-desirable locations. Whenever we move, sit, or place ourselves in the real world, in fact wherever we are, we orientate ourselves into the best relationship of task activity, behavioral intention, and environmental features. We will sit x inches into the shade of a tree, and within a certain visual field range (close to the band, the exit, and friends), but far enough away so that the sound is not so loud.

Some parts of our walk will be windy, dry, hot, or cold, and we will subconsciously try to navigate through all these conflicting, attracting, and repelling environmental processes and fields in the best possible way. This navigation is in a sense place making. Territory is place making, in the sense that we try to find the best possible site for all conflicting and varying possibilities.

We place artifacts in relation to our perception of how we appreciate or dislike environmental features. A bed may be close to the window but turned away from intense morning light. This might indicate the occupant is a late-riser.

Therefore, our idea of place is identifiable as a relationship between environmental features and personal or physical preferences. For example, 'placed' (platial) artifacts can indicate social relations between people and even between artifacts, such as houses close or far to each other (Schiffer and Miller 1999).

Culturally you could measure this; find the right or appropriate spatial relationship by measuring, say, the spatial distances between people in relation to their social prestige and familiarity. So the location and placing of self is often cultural (the science is called Proxemics), as well as physiological.

However, in a virtual environment, apart from in games (where one hides behind walls and windows, and guns may have a certain range), how one places oneself does not often matter or impinge on a task. You might walk forward to examine something, but that is purely to enlarge the object under view.

The environment itself has no particular features you wish to avoid or take advantage of or manipulate. Your only consideration is if you are close enough to an object to comprehend its visual form. This is not an issue of proximity but of visual acuity, screen resolution, and rendering detail. Nothing here is culturally filtered, but physiologically defined.

The diffusion and intermingling of a range of dynamically interactive environmental forces are almost always absent from a virtual environment (to some extent, range of sight is a factor in game design). Virtual space does not affect participants with dynamic environmental forces, with an interactive three-dimensional matrix of attenuating environmental influences.

In future journeys we will not stand too close to the kerb on a rainy day (so we do not get wet), we will not approach prisoners behind bars because they might grab us, and we sit down on a clean dry patch of grass. Activities, intentions, and environmental factors such as climate, weather (Fig. 3.4), light, dark, smell, sight, and sound all have a range that in turn depends on the range of other factors.

The diffusion and intermingling of this range of interactive forces, is almost always absent from a virtual environment. Space is x–y–z. Space is not phenomenologically dependent on or intentionally related in strength to the distance of the force or influence from the user. Nor is digitally simulated space amplified or affected negatively by the presence of other forces or influences.

Digitally simulated space is far too rarely constrained and contextualized by the presence of other forces or influences to convey accurately the embodied experience of real places. There is thus a need for location-specific variations in perceived physiological comfort and discomfort; we pick our place depending on personal tastes in comfort, light, privacy, and view.

Fig. 3.4 Qumulus: real-time weather system using Quest 3D (Courtesy of Paladin Studios)

3.3.2   Place Requires Paths and Centers

Virtual environments lack the affordances and constraints of paths and centers. For the virtual environment is only space, it does not 'afford' placing ourselves. So we only position, we do not place (centre) ourselves. In addition, we do not traverse a sensory field. We simply walk closer to an object or we stop.

As embodied stationary objects, we place, site, and centre ourselves optimally inside a flux of forces that affect our task efficiency, our social standing, and our feelings of comfort. As moving objects, we automatically choose the 'path of least resistance'.

Perhaps not surprisingly, examples of these suggested solutions reside in architecture. Architecture modifies behavior through symbolic cues, offers paths and centers so that we can navigate and place ourselves, and suggests the passage of time as well as records the meetings of people.

Borrowing from Venetian and Byzantine design motifs, architectural theory of the 1920s, made a distinction between path and centre, to decorate spaces of rest and eschew decoration in paths (Champion 1993). For ornaments make us rest, and a lack of ornamentation makes us search without distraction until we find a place we can centre ourselves. Decoration indicates the goal. Moreover, formal symmetry implies a ceremonial space that is less likely to change. Asymmetry implies influence from outside forces; a less regular spatial configuration can cater better for functional tasks than for formal rituals and ceremony.

3.3.3   Response to Place Requires Ongoing Feedback

Which factors that help create a sense of place are in need of restoring? Can we recreate some of them digitally or metaphorically?

For example, we walk under an eave when it rains or when we hear thunder. How would we inspire this behavior in a virtual world without the ability to soak the user? Could we use related triggers such as the sound of thunder?

The simulation of such 'triggers' would only work if the user thought they were in reality or a world that obeyed laws of physics completely. Following the thunder example, a user needs to be motivated by the apparent realism of the stimulus (the sound of thunder), or convinced that the stimulus had consequences for them if they did not seek shelter. Therefore, we need to aim for realism or we need to create rewards and punishments. If we opt for visual realism, the user will eventually lose the automatic reflex, as there is no reinforcing stimulus (i.e. they learn they cannot get wet even if they are outside and even can hear the sound of thunder).

If we opt for metaphor, depending on the level of realism, the user will also see through the analogy. There has to be a feedback mechanism somewhere that simulates dynamic environmental affordances. How can we create a believable and appropriate feedback system?

3.3.4 Place Requires Social 'Embeddedness'

Ironically, a sense of place is most apparent through its absence, especially in virtual environments, whether for games, for tourism, or for heritage preservation. The environments may have some simulated social interactions, but these social interactions do not richly inhabit or modify their environment. In such virtual environments people are stranded, for place does not recognize their presence.

Moreover, in the real world we seldom wander around without any sense of purpose. Flaneurs and peeping toms still have a purpose, to observe human behavior without themselves being drawn into direct social involvement (Ffytche n.d):

> Ah, the golden days of flanerie are gone. Saunter, stroll: dally, dawdle; loiter, linger … arm in arm those magical words float by me, trailing their irretrievable aura. The ability to set the pace of one's own life is the elusive dream of the urban loafer.

In actuality, the flaneur remained part of society even as they rebelled against it. Places reflect this wandering aspect of human behavior, through promenades, malls, and esplanades. For although flaneurs may have thought they were wandering completely without volition or direction, they were in fact drawn to spectacle and areas of interest. Virtual environments need to offer more than only the ability to wander, in order to retain interest they must offer some degree of social agency. Coyne (1999b) writes:

> Architecture is not only about the artifacts we see built around us, but it is about the process of designing and building, about the way we are all embedded, and embodied, in the practice/ praxis that is architecture.

In a sense, people are not just physically embodied; they are also socially embedded. Their motives, intentions, and actions can be fully understood only when referenced to a social perspective that makes sense of a specific physical environment. Recreating the objects that make up our society is however not recreating the society itself, as some of our cultural knowledge is not ostensive and is not directly tangible.

Undoubtedly, there are also many cultural and ethical issues. In the following paragraph, Sardar (1996, p. 19) describes the purely physical (or, in this case, digital) recreation of traditional societies as a typically Western phenomenon.

> Cyberspace is particularly geared toward the erasure of all non-Western histories. Once a culture has been 'stored' and 'preserved' in digital forms, opened up to anybody who wants to explore it from the comfort of their armchair, then it becomes more real than the real thing. Who needs the arcane and esoteric real thing anyway?

Sardar (1996) and Suzuki (1997) have argued that modern notions of place in Western literature may be ignorant of other cultural perceptions of place as opposed to space. Yet the obliteration or assimilation of other cultural histories is a trademark of all dominant cultures, not just Western ones.

Sardar's commentary seems unaware that culture is maintained and transformed online in a myriad of ways. Some communities administer their own cyber-worlds. Some communities require distance learning or websites to keep their own culture alive. Virtual environments can be dynamic, interactive and multi-perspectival; there is no inherent necessity for meta-narratives or Western-biased viewpoints. Nor does digital technology have to make virtual environments safe and homogenized.

Virtual environments can be abstracted multi-modal, multi-perspectival, challenging, and culturally constrained. They can choose their own form of presentation, interface, navigation, narration, and goal. It may turn out that this infinite range of interpretative possibilities and contextually related interaction is both more socially constraining *and* more engaging to participants than some bland Westernized cyberspace. Virtual environments can contain more than objects, they can also force us to be constrained by the social roles and rituals residing in the environment that has been digitally simulated.

While place is created, modified and inscribed by many varying beliefs and activities, virtual environments that offer a notion of place may appear to be complete and accurate when in fact they have ignored or distorted historical cultural or physical aspects of the real world. Place is a particularly difficult concept for virtual community designers, as its power lies through dynamic interaction as much as it lies through formal uniqueness or realistic detail. However, it is an essential staging device for atmosphere, for social identification, for personal orientation, and through adding a sense of uniqueness to user driven and observed events. As an artifact, place is also a treasure trove, a map and a storehouse of human–environmental interaction. A space used as a place reflects the attitudes, behaviors and intentions of the community that owns it. Hence, a virtual place must do likewise for a virtual community.

Communities identify and are identified not just by the clothes they wear or the language they speak, or the way they greet each other. Communities are often identified by where they feel compelled to do these things, how they use spaces to construct meanings, and the traces left by their social interactions. These trigger regions are thus not just points in space; they are also landmarks, havens, homes, ruins, or hells. Communities are identified, and identify with or against, not just space, but also place. Places do not just organize space; they orient, identify, and animate the bodies, minds, and feelings of both inhabitants and visitors.

3.3.5 *Place Is Mark-Able*

A virtual environment has to be writable; a user must be able to leave their mark on it. We have seen how in the literature a specific place gains its unique character through time and use. Place is not just adaptable, but also mark-able and recordable. It records signs of its use (user modification is persistent); it also erodes and denudes. Place is an artifact, as past events can often be inferred from it.

Through the wear and tear of graffiti, vandalism, environmental forces and human induced erosion, place is also personalized. Yet where in virtual environments, and specifically in virtual communities, do we see people leaving marks? The virtual houses that we might build in say ActiveWorlds are too crude to reflect either our activities inside it or our changing social identity. While current attempts at virtual 'placeness' often defy inhabitation, the places that surround and structure our lives reflect it.

Having summarized some key features of real world places, the next step is study how different mediums evoke a sense of place.

3.4 Evoking Place via Arts and Sciences

Other fields of human endeavor, such as architecture, literature and film, reveal that place is often imaginatively reconstructed through suggestion, rather than through realistic attention to detail alone. Which key ideas can we adopt from architecture, literature, film and other disciplines to extend and further articulate the role of place in virtual environments?

3.4.1 Architecture

In the creation of architecture, place is often highly referential. For example, architects skew fenestration in relation to paths in order to create glints of faraway vistas. Thematic separation of internal volumes into a tapestry of paths and centers that emphasize discrete building functions can also suggest another realm. In the writings of Nietzsche and Spengler and, from ancient monuments to buildings of the 'Heroic Modern' era, architectural environments appear to confront gravity and time.

Norberg-Schulz (2000) saw place as a dynamic unity of architectural elements that interact with inhabitants. Yet architecture is not just a collection of physical objects, it is also metaphorical, allegoric, and thematic, reliant for effect on the interactions between the building, dynamic external environment, and people along with their beliefs and values. Alexander (1977) similarly captured the essence of interactions between humans and the environment in terms of patterns and how these patterns help form distinct places. Archaeologists decipher the meanings of past worlds by using conceptual patterns. Architecture has cultural as well as formal properties, it codifies and helps codify culturally shared responses to possible situations.

Architects have also seized on commercial games, game mods (user modifications of a game level), and game-editors, however interactivity and usability is seldom discussed in depth or convincingly. For example, in his chapter "Gamespace" for the anthology *Space Time Play*, the architectural theorist and critic Mark Wigley (2007) declared "The real key to the architecture of game space, like any other architecture is the entrance and exit."

Considering modern architecture has long dithered over how to design either, and games have moved on from strict level progression, I find this worrying. Surely one key aspect of architecture is the movement and perception of movement through and across space, it is not an either/or, exit or entry. And secondly, many games are hybrids, situated between real and virtual. Presence is not necessarily a binary phenomenon. Thirdly, I am not yet sure enough architects really understand immersion or the effect of games on many gamers before, during or after the actual game-experience.

Theorists in architectural and game space have not yet created a convincing overarching theory that both describes and prescribes the notion of space in games. For example, in Michael Nitsche's recent book on the subject (2008), his overarching diagram describes game-space as including rule-based space, mediated space, fictional space (what the player imagines they are seeing), play-space (the physical space the player is in), and social space (when other players are physically present). Where is the cognitive space? It is not exactly the fictional space the player imagines, but rather the past experiences and future projections the player is extracting, collating, interpreting, and predicting.

The diagram also does not feature somesthetic space. And yet designing buildings to trigger a somesthetic, proprioceptive or kinesthetic response is nothing new. There are cantilevers in Egyptian architecture, knee-deep windows in Arne Jacobsen buildings (no doubt to heighten a sense of vertigo), the path-centre theory of Byzantine architecture, and of course Baroque architecture was designed to be experienced by bodies in motion.

Ilinx (vertigo, dizziness, disorientation on director or movement), is one of the four categories of game play as proposed by Roger Caillois (1962). Vertigo is also a prominent trigger and factor used in testing immersion in virtual environments. In Nitsche's book none of these three related terms (involving bodily responses to space and to movement through space) are mentioned in the index. Ironically, Hitchcock's film *Vertigo* is twice referred to, and at least one of Nitsche's projects described in the book involves a deliberate use of ilinx. So why isn't ilinx an important component of any theory of game-space? Thanks to virtual cues players may be technically sedentary, but their engaged minds are navigating, orienting and balancing as if they were actually in motion. Real or virtual, architecture works not just on the eyes, but also on our minds, memories and bodies.

The philosopher Schelling suggested that architecture could be viewed as clothing, which implied that rather than merely acting as a clumsy mass, architecture covers, modifies, and directs our imagined and real movement. We are, after all, kinetic sculpture. Morrison (1988, p. 322) writes:

> Viewers perceived the immobility of paintings in one way by moving into and out of the focal point in front of the works. They perceived that of statues in a second way, by circling statues in the round or by passive reliefs. In both cases, the viewers moved outside of the work of art. But, in architectural settings and galleries, viewers moved inside, and through the work of art, and - as gallery paintings indicate - they became kinetic components of those aggregated works, participating in the whole.

Modern architecture as the embodiment of rationality and the machine is also debatable. Many architects of the nineteenth and twentieth century, including even the early modernists, used spatial illusion. For example, Mies van der Rohe was concerned with the art of illusion, however much his supporters might talk of structural honesty. In almost every famous building by Mies, the structure was expressed, but only partially. Hidden and unexpressed supports were necessary for the external form to appear perfectly flat and freely floating, such as in the Farnsworth house and the Barcelona Pavilion (Champion 2004).

The canonical architecture of Mies, Le Corbusier, and Frank Lloyd Wright can be viewed as Apollonian pavilions but they were contrasted with the Dionysian wildness of a national park (the Barcelona Pavilion), French fields (Villa Savoye), and a waterfall (Fallingwater). Nietzsche (1967) outlined such a theory of aesthetic contrast in his doctoral thesis on the importance of aesthetic illusion (Nietzsche 1967).

Architecture may also create the appearance of popularity through the illusion of erosion. In the famous Woodland Crematorium in Stockholm, Asplund sawed into the marble columns so that they would prematurely age. In his Lister courthouse he even created a buried typology; part of a hall appears to be a dugout classical colonnade, implying the modern courthouse building had been built over another building dating from antiquity. Yet computer models do not normally incorporate these perceptual illusions and aesthetic contrasts.

I am suggesting that they *do* incorporate perceptual illusions and aesthetic contrasts. For virtual environments, limitations may also be desirable rather than unavoidable. In his essay, 'Liquid Architectures in Cyberspace' Novak (1991, pp. 225–254) defined the essence of virtual reality as freedom. Physically embodying and socially embedding a visitor in a virtual world may seem at first more confining than the liquid freedom proposed over a decade ago by Novak, but it may actually improve the user experience rather than detract from it.

3.4.2   Art and Artifacts

For Heidegger the notion of art cannot be merely the response to sensations. Heidegger argues that we hear sounds not acoustic sensations, and thus by implication all aesthetic phenomena (i.e. those sensations that the brain responds to) are actually distillations of experiences codified and responded to as the outcomes of deliberate, intentional activity.

> Much closer to us than all sensations are the things themselves. We hear the door shut in the house and never hear acoustical sensations or even mere sounds. In order to hear a bare sound we have to listen away from things, divert our ear from them, i.e., listen abstractly. (Heidegger 1975, p. 26).

There is thus, Heidegger argued, something to the work of art, let us call it the 'thingly character', which is not encompassed or created by the perception of mere sensations. Heidegger's argument has recently been bolstered by experiments in virtual environments. Handy et al (2003, p. 4) have suggested that there is indeed a 'graspable' quality to certain objects in virtual environments.

> Our ERP findings converge on the conclusion that graspable objects have the capacity to draw visual spatial attention to their locations, even if those objects are irrelevant to current behavioral goals.

We may further extend the argument to suggest there is an aspect of 'thingness' to our perception of our world that should be considered in designing virtual environments. In the nineteenth century, empathy theorists viewed architecture as little more than sculptural objects that we can create associations for (Morgan 1996, p. 321). A few years ago, the philosopher Anthony Savile attacked Richard Foster's work for the same reason: treating the essence of architecture as sculptural form (Savile 1993). For a thing, be it a hammer or a building, is not merely a three-dimensional object floating in space. Architecture also involves interior spaces, the linking of spaces (e.g., from inner to outer and the converse), and the placing or locating, using and imagining of symbolic objects (as well as the self and other people) in space.

3.4.3   Literature

Various writers have expanded on how literature creates an imagined sense of place (Casey 1993, 1997; Crang 1998, pp. 43–58; Malpas 1999; Relph 1976). As with architectural symbolism, literature suggests life-worlds by the use of patterns and motifs. Unlike architecture, the power of literature to signify place rests on continual and sustained evocation enlivened by dramatic tension or by descriptive power through a fixed story line. It conjures up an emotively charged setting, it is an imaginatively reconstructive projection, and suggests place via atmosphere that is an integral part of the characters' intentions and tasks.

Constructed through textual representations and linear format, Hein (1991) has argued that literature retrieves time, space and experiences, to move a reader from being a mere spectator to a participant, by appealing to a reader's personal experiences and associations. By suggesting rather than completely describing, the book only circumscribes reality by adding in our real-time imaginings of a place. In reading a book, we are really experiencing an imaginative construction of a world based on the interaction of our personal experiences and our inferences of what is happening along with, sometimes, the authorial intention. Realistic description is only part of the act of reading.

Literature is also famous for its foretelling of the future and the drastic ramifications of technology applied without thought to social consequences. Debatably, the first great make or break criterion of digitally or chemically mediated immersion was not *Neuromancer*, but Philip K. Dick's (1964) science fiction classic, *The Three Stigmata of Palmer Eldritch*. Set in an climate changed feature world, the author invites us to consider virtuality as drugged escape from mortality and existence on a terra-formed but banal Mars. Virtual presence is conflated with an alien religious presence, and the detective anti-hero is never sure whether he left the virtual reality after chasing the villain (who is god or devil of the virtual realm), or whether he is actually still trapped inside, but convinced that he is free.

Not only did Philip K. Dick use the term *Presence* long before Mel Minsky's famous *Telepresence* essay in 1981, he has created a parallel to a Turing test: you can tell you have created a successful virtual reality when you are never sure if you have escaped from it. Believable immersion does not necessarily rely on an exit/entrance, nor is it a simple binary phenomenon.

3.4.4 Film

Via transitions and fades, film is intentionally unrealistic (Laurel et al. 1994). Neumann et al. (1996), p. 8) reminds us via his quote of the architect Hugo Hāring, that spatial construction for film is ephemeral:

> As Hugo Hāring noted in 1924, "Space in film only needs to be unique, singular, designed for one event only, one instance of joyful bliss, one moment of horror."

Cinematic and linear representations mould places from a single perspective. Compared to literature, films offer a multi-sensory narrative albeit within a similar linear format, while challenging that constraint through various mechanisms such as transitions, fades, split-screens, and so on. Further, films suggest off-camera space but never show you it. By using fragmented perspectives, they coerce the viewer into believing asynchronous events and out-of-shot actions are happening now, and happening in a world that encloses the viewer.

3.4.5 Cultural Geography in Place and Culture

For cultural geographers, culture has a setting and this setting is enabled through a perceived sense of place. Culture requires a setting. According to Crang (1998, pp. 1–2) culture must be "embedded in real-life situations, in temporally and spatially specific ways". Cantor (1974) notes that the interactions between these objects and their setting may be quite complex.

Culture is a feedback loop. A visitor perceives space as place, and inhabits (modifies a place), place 'perpetuates culture', and thus influences the inhabitants in turn. We might say that social behavior is behavior between two or more people. Cultural behavior is a subset of social behavior, where behavior is governed by or understood in terms of a cultural setting. As culture almost inevitably involves transactions, there must be objects of shared transactional value.

'Place' is an important concept for virtual environment design. As I have noted earlier, place may have any of the following features: a record of social processes; fluid boundaries; and internal conflicts. It may leave 'traces' of the people who saw and used it as a place, or it may 'signpost' features that communicate something to us about how we see our place in the world. Places are often full of mementos from other places. So rather than a fixed and set experience; a place can be more like a nexus, a web of associations, cultural affordances and memories.

Thus, the old communication model of culture requiring only a sender and receiver of data is inadequate; culture is a highly interactive dialogue of human ideas transmitted via social and individually constructed places.

In order to create culturally evocative environments, we need to understand which interactive elements disseminate cultural information. According to Schiffer and Miller (1999), we learn about a culture through dynamically participating in the interactions between cultural setting (a place that indicates certain types of social behavior), artifacts (and how they are used), and people teaching others how to observe and how to behave (act and react in a shared social situation), along with one's personal motives.

One way to approach this issue is to view (and design) virtual environments depicting human cultures as hermeneutic (that afford an actively engaged interpretation of the lives and intentions of past inhabitants). The hermeneutic features of place in these environments are almost certainly more difficult to create digitally, but that does not negate their importance. Luckily, for virtual environment designers, these hermeneutic features have been described by social scientists. They maintain that people develop shared cultural perspectives of place in many different ways.

If place as location is a nexus of environmental forces or attributes, we can learn about places in the real world in relation to culture through observing human behavior. We may even infer specific mental attitudes by the ways in which humans respond to these environmental forces.

We can learn about the significance of a place by how old or worn it appears. These cues can tell us if it is popular, venerable or abandoned. We can also tell cultural behaviors by observation, such as inference from the properties of related artifacts. For example, properties in Japan near burial grounds are significantly cheaper than other housing areas. We can learn about the significance of a place by social learning (by people telling you or instructing you). We can learn about a place through task-based activity there (for example, we learn a swimming pool is suitable for swimming).

We have now seen the role of place in the real world. Given the above, how do we gain such a sense of place via virtual environments?

3.5 Cyberspace Critics and Criteria

Many virtual environments marketed as 'worlds' have limited capacity for personalization or for customization. They also often lack clear and precise navigation and general environmental affordances (Campbell 1997; Gibson 1979, p. 127; Schroeder 1996). This field is still in its infancy, as some of the most comprehensive research has been focused on combat situations (military simulations, online gaming), and not on what interaction is most engaging and usable in online communities.

In the real world, our understanding of the current locality is often colored by the places that we have just traveled to, or that we recognize as having some relation to our current place. In much Presence research, there is talk of being transported to a virtual environment, yet participants are in fact often teleported. That is to say, virtual environments are often experienced instantly; they typically do not offer a ritual of passage or 'arrival' that allows a suitable atmosphere or expectations to build up.

Hodder and Hutson (2003, p. 23) argued that "ritual regulates the relationship between people and environment", and that meaning is related to function. Tilley (1999, p. 29) agreed, noting, "Rituals not only say something, they *do* something."

Childe (1956) also made the point that myths are actually important. He argued that myths are instructions to do rational things; only the instructions often carry some additional irrational steps.

Further, there is little research so far on enhancing realism or completeness by using out of world stimuli to suggest there is more in the virtual environment than what is actually experienced (Marsh and Wright 2000). Writers have suggested adopting game engines and game–style interaction for the development of virtual worlds yet activity may create a sense of panic and reduce the level of attention paid to the enjoyment and learning of the virtual environment (Waterworth 1999).

Coyne (1999a) has written that tasks and social agents need to be part of virtual environments, as they provide purpose, meaning, and social feedback. The danger may be that talking to people will be more interesting than the place, or the place is so intimidating or imposing that social interaction is severely curtailed.

Cultural or physical constraints may be needed to control or free the participant in naturalistic or novel ways. As environmental psychology is a difficult and complex field for concrete results, our knowledge of which significant elements control or help human behavior in virtual environments is likewise curtailed and limited. Yet this knowledge is vital. A greater understanding of behavioral and perceptual cues helps a designer to design just enough that affords 'placeness' (Campbell 1997). We need to decide which real-world cues and constraints are desirable, while acknowledging that realism may sometimes hinder engagement (Eiteljorg 1998; Laurel et al. 1994; Mosaker 2001).

In their paper 'Cyber-Placemaking', Kalay and Marx (2001) identified eight types of virtual places or cyberspace places extrapolated from architectural and urban design theory. For them, places are settings for events, places are engaging, afford relative location (i.e. orientation), are imbued with authenticity, are adaptable, afford a variety of experiences, provide choice and control over transitions, and are inherently memorable.

Granted, it is hard to argue with the appropriateness of the above attributes, for many writers have used similar criteria. Coyne (1999a) talked of association, authenticity, activity and task-based criteria. Laurel et al. (1990) spoke of the need for engagement and personalization. Inspired by both the Memex and the Memory Palaces of Simonides, Johnson (1997, pp. 120–122) argued that the most engaging three-dimensional environment would be socially associative, interactive, and task-oriented with a 'recall' or a 'trail' of the users.

Extrapolating from anthropological stages of 'going native', Relph (1976) suggested three dimensions of relating to feeling inside or outside place. These dimensions are behavioral (observing behavior modified by place cues), emphatic (participating in an understanding of place), and existential (feeling an integral part of a place).

Champion and Dave (2002) wrote that 'existential insideness' was one approach to place not fully covered by the Kalay and Marx paper. Our solution was to extend and apply Relph's classification of urban places to virtual places. In that paper we divided virtual environments into three major types, visualization-based, activity-based, and hermeneutic.

We argued that the intention of virtual environments is to afford visualization, to support activity-based tasks, or to offer an interpretative framework for different cultural beliefs, individual perspectives, and world-views. The hermeneutic environment, as we then defined it, allows people to gain an idea of the indigenous social and cultural beliefs, and further allows users to inscribe the environment with the results of their own interaction with it. We suggested unique and personalized user action that modifies the environment would deepen time-associations and hence increase a sense of place.

This leads me to propose that when we are creating a virtual heritage environment with a notion of a 'place' (a region recognizable to a user as a culturally coded setting); we need to have more than merely identifiable or evocative virtual environments. Instead, we need to create a virtual environment that evokes and identifies a place that carries cultural indications of inhabitation driven by a different cultural perspective to that of our own.

This virtual place should suggest ideas of thematically related events, evidence of social autonomy, notions of territorial possession and shelter, and focal points of artifactual possession. In other words, the virtual environment must provide a perspective of a past culture to a user. Such a perspective is normally only deduced by trained archaeologists and anthropologists from material remains (fossils, pottery shards, ruins, etcetera).

3.5.1   Cyberspaces Lack Limits

It may seem counter-intuitive to suggest that one issue with cyberspace is that it lacks limits, but it is actually meaningful constraints that help evoke a sense of place. For example, "ActiveWorlds" (at least of the 2004 era), allows one to build houses and thus it might seem to feature some kind of place-ness (Fig. 3.5: ActiveWorlds screenshot., image source: screenshot taken by author while visiting http://www.activeworlds.com, 16 December 2004). However, these virtual worlds have typically lacked meaningful constraints. They lack dynamic environmental or physiological features that would constrain and thus uniquely identify places.

Some users now talk of vandal police (as users could destroy other participants' houses) but apart from that interesting social development, one is confronted with an absence of tasks, limited social interaction and movement, and an absence of any historical context (for more information, refer the CASA diary online at http://www.casa.ucl.ac.uk/30days/news9.htm).

The Renaissance Project does not have an exterior, agents walk around a predefined place, and one cannot modify the environment (Fig. 3.6, image source: screenshot by author). However, agents do remember user profiles, and one is given tasks to complete in line with a Renaissance book of manners, in order to become rich or famous. Still, as the place itself does not retain footprints of users, it does not seem to have a great deal of place-ness, especially as the agents could exist in any of the rooms.

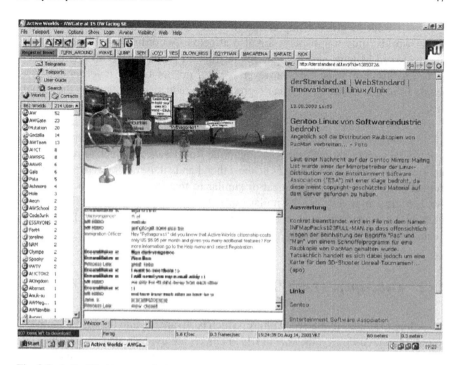

Fig. 3.5 ActiveWorlds screenshot

Fig. 3.6 Renaissance Community screenshot by author

I don't want to give an impression that the issue lies only with commercial virtual worlds; museum displays are also affected. According to Mosaker (2001) who reviewed Miletus and Bologna reconstruction projects, it is all architecture, no life forms. For stage sets, however perfect, do not tell us much about how people lived there. These historical reproductions reduce authenticity to the visual surface.

The above examples, on the one hand, demonstrate that place-making notions are becoming crucial in such projects, e.g., territorial demarcation in ActiveWorlds, scripted encounters through role-playing in the Renaissance Project, or reconstructions of past moments in time. On the other hand, it is not clear if 'place' in ActiveWorlds is somehow identical or similar to that in the Renaissance Project. Nor is it clear how they are dissimilar (apart from in appearance or delivery) that might allow us to distinguish one place (if there is any) from another. Evaluation mechanisms may help, but how?

3.5.2   Cyberspaces Lack 'Play' Through Objects

According to studies in material culture, which is advancing into the field of anthropology from archaeology, the way in which objects are used, created, and exchanged gives us not just new insight into past and long extinct cultures, but also into our own (Schiffer and Miller 1999). Material culture theory argues that human interaction is between humans, humans and the environment (and externs-objects that are not artifacts), between humans and artifacts, from humans to humans via artifacts and so on.

The range of interaction is also extremely broad, and in every facet of interaction, artifacts can play a major or even essential role. Hence, unlike verbal studies of culture that only account for audio research, material culture studies may offer a wide range of insights across all the domains of interactivity.

That is not to say 'Material Culture Studies' is fundamentally a visual-based research field. For example, Schiffer and Miller (1999, p. 5) argued that even though only 6–7.7% of major research journals in anthropology deal with artifacts or technology, "every realm of human behavior and communication involves people–artifact interactions."

3.5.3   Cyberspaces Lack Life History

Typically, the role of place in virtual environments has been as a locator of objects. Yet cultural geographers argue place is more a constrained and malleable container of localized activities, evoking associations of past events and stimulating future tasks. In fact, virtual environments are often criticized for evoking 'cyberspace' rather than a culturally shared notion of 'place'. In other words, they lack the richness of associations and encounters of human transactions in real space (Benedikt 1991; Coyne 1999a; Heim 1998; Johnson 1997).

Without content relating directly to how we perceive the world, an emphasis on formal realism is not creating a virtual reality, but a storehouse of visually represented objects. A possible reason why early environment builders aimed for realism rather than for content may have been a belief that we experience reality as something objective, settled and constant. Solid and immutable objects may be easier to conceptualize and model than what reality is really made up of, matter and energy interacting according to laws of physics continually interpreted by human perception fuelled by need and imagination.

However, our notions of reality are actually cultural notions of a constructed reality (Riegler 2001). Digital simulation of objects by itself will not enable meaningful content that contextually places a virtual environment in an engaging way. For if the purpose of virtual heritage models is to preserve the culturally significant articles of the past, they must demonstrate reasons for simulating that past material culture. Yet they are generally used as showcases for technology rather than to reveal the views and beliefs of the owners of that culture. In most current digital environments, objects are not digitally simulated as objects-in use, with life histories, with formal or associational traces. They are simply three-dimensional objects.

Even if the models did bear formal traces of a life history, of a series of interactivities (interactive activities), they fail to communicate effectively the knowledge required to infer why that particular artifact was contextually meaningful. This may be due to the difficulty of conveying the worth of objects from a different cultural background, and conveying its cultural significance, its imagined presence.

Yet an idea of Cultural Presence must mean that people with a similar or different cultural perspective to ours, can occupy a place, and be identified as like or unlike, by us. This sense of Cultural Presence should allow us to feel that we recall having, in the words of Slater (1999, p. 561) "visited a 'place' rather than just having seen images generated by a computer."

3.6 Cyberspace Concepts and Terminology

A paucity of clearly defined concepts prevents designers from developing appropriate place making elements for virtual environments. The challenge of selecting appropriate place making features is not helped by the slippery (and circular) nature of language in the literature and discussion of virtual environments. Additionally, until recently many designers considered the degree of visual correspondence between real and virtual worlds as a sufficient measure of successful virtual environments.

For example, Kalay and Marx (2001) used such a scale to classify 'cyber' environments into the following: hyper-reality; abstracted reality; hybrid cyberspace; hyper-virtuality. However, terminology based solely on appearances or delivery does not explain the aims of designers, the goals of users, or the interactive content that arises out of virtual interaction and interpretation between users in their attempts to solve tasks. Indeed, apart from the magnetic attraction of ever expanding vocabularies, such terms do not even help us understand why we would want to be in those virtual environments in the first place.

I should note here that since their paper, and after some interesting debate, they have changed their approach to place. Still, it is worth mentioning this paper because it was meant to introduce the topic in order to help educators bring social worlds into the classroom (the implications for virtual heritage environments was probably not the main aim of the paper).

3.6.1 Suggestions for Creating Cyberplace

Although the criteria proposed by Kalay and Marx (2001) are useful, they do not help us to determine which design features are most important, necessary, or even desired, for different types of virtual environments. Further, they do not address several important features of place. In *Place and Placelessness* Relph (1976, p. 61) noted:

> The identity of a place is comprised of three interrelated components, each irreducible to the other, physical features or appearance, observable activities and functions, and meanings or symbols.

So the place-making criteria of Kalay and Marx address only two major types of environments addressed by Relph, environments that afford 'physical features or appearances', and those that afford 'activities'. The Kalay–Marx criteria, based on modes of reality, do not address virtual environments that attempt to offer interpretations of past and present cultures. Partly this omission is due to the difficulties of simulating virtual culture. As Tuan (1998, p. 6) wrote, "Seeing what is not there lies at the foundation of all human culture", yet virtual environments typically only attempt to simulate what is there.

I have suggested five major types of place experiences. We could summarize how to evoke these experiences in virtual places as follows (Table 3.1). This table explains how five types of place-experiences may be conveyed via digital media by analyzing which real world experiences of place are left out of virtual environments. Yet this approach may compel the designer to overload their virtual environment with every possible place feature. The danger of such an approach appears to be already happening in some of the academic literature (Kalay and Marx 2001, 2003; Kalay 2004; Nitsche et al. 2002).

Real world places only have some place making features, and practical considerations suggest we only create those place features that most effectively trigger the required sensation of place. With this in mind, we can also approach place-experience through designing for different types of audiences and intentions.

3.7 Three Types of Virtual Environments

Instead of using the Kalay and Marx taxonomy, which relies on a degree of visual correspondence between real and virtual worlds to discuss place, I proposed a matrix derived from an observation of both real world place experiences and virtual

Table 3.1 Features of real and virtual places

Features of real-world places	Desired features of a virtual place
Places are dynamic and changeable. Their boundaries may be vague and amorphous	Attenuating environmental forces (for example, wind, fog, rain, directional and dynamic lighting, sound, perhaps even varying vision acuity)
Places can range from the comforting to the uncanny, the sublime, the terrifying.	Scale, detail, atmosphere replication or phobic triggers heighten the experiential realism
A place is full of references and evocations of related places via the movement of people and their artifacts. It may also evoke images of its previous self, related activities, or other places	Can trigger past associated environments or events that the virtual environment thinks a visitor has been to. This is one of the most challenging yet interesting of place-attributes, how to create place-associations
A place constrains, suggests and localizes activities. The constraints may be highly variable, and affect the physical, conceptual, or cultural sides of human experience. This in turn means that place frame communities – you can read a place from the way it frames individual ritual and communal activity	Tasks, events, artifacts and some degree of social agency (people), which is specifically place-associated. For example, participants may be able to move certain artifacts, but they will only be able to place or leave them in specific places, or, some interaction (e.g. skills), may or may not be transferable across places. The ability to piece together understanding of a community through viewing its artifacts and the way people relate to those artifacts in certain places

environments (Table 3.1). Such a graduated categorization, on the one hand, allows us to correlate place-making features to general aims of virtual environments. On the other hand, it also suggests that a hermeneutic virtual environment (one that has to be actively interpreted by a participant), is the most difficult to engender.

3.7.1 Inert 'Explorative' Environments

The first and most common type of three-dimensional virtual environment available on the Internet is the visual (sometimes with sound). An extension of the scripting language used to write web pages (HTML) was developed in the 1990s to create the sense of three-dimensional objects on a webpage. This language was called VRML (and confusingly either pronounced V.R.M.L or 'Virmil'). It was difficult for non-programmers to learn and required a great deal of effort to make interactive. Worse, it was very slow. One of the great hyped technologies of the Internet, even VRML's inventors have admitted that it never truly took off (Parisi 2001, p. xxxviii).

VRML environments were good examples of the limited interactivity of virtual environments that targeted visualization. One can walk around objects, magnify the view or pan the camera around objects (say buildings), occasionally move between preset viewpoints, and that was about it. Orientation and view were often manipulable, but the environment was not truly interactive, as it did not affect the participant's actions, nor could it be modified by the participants. However, visualization-based environments do have their uses. For example, they can be used to create a three-dimensional fly-through of a building for an architect's clients. The advantage and disadvantage is that the environment is only a finished product: it is not affected by inhabitants, and so manages to be definitive, immutable, and appear consistent in appearance.

Due to the success of these architectural computing-based models, it has been suggested that Virtual Environment design be informed by architectural and planning theory (Kalay and Marx 2001). It might be argued that Computer Aided Drafting (CAD) applications are directly synonymous with building three-dimensional digital environments and therefore the CAD programs used by architects are tailor-made for designing virtual environments.

The problem is that CAD was designed to get buildings built, to quantify rather than qualify the architectural experience. They show static additions to the environment, rather than environmental changes acting and interacting over time. There is no fog, no dirt, no wind, and often even no people. Yet the real world experiencing of architecture is always mediated through a dynamic and imperfect sensory interface: our minds and our bodies.

Computer reconstructions created from CAD programs typically do not allow for sensory cues, illusions, and limitations. The suggestion of dissolution of form, of mood (often through dramatic lighting), of multiple thematic interpretations, or personalization and the erosive effect of time are generally missing from virtual reconstructions. These factors, along with limited interactivity in general, may help explain why few virtual heritage environments are popular or engaging, especially when compared to chat-worlds or to computer games.

Lack of atmosphere is not the only issue. Virtual heritage environments are designed to preserve historically significant archaeological sites. Conserving and preserving a sense of history is an important and difficult task. Part of the problem is that history is not a static and immutable object, but a dynamic mass of interpretations, actions, intentions, and beliefs.

Every group of people has its own viewpoints, issues, and outlook on the world. Without understanding this specific cultural agency, there is a danger that we may see the virtual heritage site only in terms of our own cultural perspective. This limited ability to represent social processes and 'intangible' heritage can create a second danger: the static and apparently immutable aspect of digital reconstruction can imply a certainty of knowledge that we actually do not possess.

In addition, too many scientifically accurate virtual heritage environments lack the ability to store interaction history. The actions and paths taken by its visitors affect a truly interactive environment. Yet many virtual environments do not record traces of what happened. Visitors may be able to change part of the environment, but the virtual environment seldom 'remembers' the visitors, their paths, actions, and discoveries.

For these reasons, visualization-based environments are of limited use in designing virtual heritage environments that conserve, preserve, and communicate history.

3.7.2 Activity-Based Environments

Activity-based virtual environments allow activities to take place. Many are games or training programs. More than a straight visualization of objects, an activity based virtual environment allows one or more users to alter some character or element in pursuit of a defined goal. Video games such as Pacman are activity based, as are Tic-tac-toe and Microsoft's Flight Simulator game. Activity-based virtual environments are arguably the most commercially successful type of virtual environment.

The technological limitations of Internet-available visualization-based virtual environments (such as VRML 'worlds') do not seem to have hindered the popularity of complex games. The most popular form of virtual environments is arguably the computer game. Entertainment software is the fastest growing of all types of entertainment, outselling films. The computing power of current game consoles also rival supercomputers used a mere decade ago. Computer game engines are also used for research into artificial intelligence.

Games can have 'atmosphere'. There are tasks to complete, navigation reminders, inventories, records of interaction history (such as damage to surroundings), and social agency (such as real or computer directed opponents). Most popular games contain a personalized representation of the user (known as an avatar), and similar representations of allies and opponents. In creating effective virtual heritage environments, these features of games could be used. They could be designed around a task or goal, and include visual representations of the users and other significant characters.

3.7.3 Cultural or 'Hermeneutic' Environments

In order to create a virtual heritage environment with a notion of a 'place' (a region recognizable to a user as a culturally coded setting), we need to have more than merely identifiable or activity-based virtual environments. A place can also carry cultural indications of inhabitation driven by a similar or different cultural perspective to that of our own. A virtual heritage environment must allow us to see through the eyes of the original inhabitants, or at least make us believe that this place once belonged to someone else.

Hermeneutics argues that we must grasp the world of the interpreter as well as the world of the interpreted in order to gain the meaning of the text or an artwork. For example, the philosopher Hans-Georg Gadamer wrote that language is inter-subjective, exemplified by how children learn. Children learn by seeing how others respond to them: learning is an interactive process; a language itself constitutes our life-world. To quote Gadamer's translator David Linge (Gadamer 1976, p. xii), "the hermeneutical has to do with bridging the gap between the familiar world in which we stand and the strange meaning that resists assimilation into the horizons of our world."

According to Table 3.2 the simplest stage of visualization is capturing and manipulating and visualizing three-dimensional objects, a more advanced stage is the ability to navigate through landscapes. Technology now allows us to capture adequately realistic detail, and to mimic more accurately physical laws, so this type of digital environment, while achievable and useful for various scientific purposes, only represents spatial configurations and navigation through them. The second type of virtual environment, the one that affords activity-based interaction, allows a more interactive form of wayfinding. Tasks can be completed inside the environment through interaction.

Computer games and flight simulation perhaps best convey this type of digital environment. However, only if the environment evokes a notion of other people interacting with the environment in ways similar or dissimilar to us, does the digital world begin to form. A hermeneutic environment requires the ability to personalize and communicate individual perceptions through artifacts, and the more deeply this cultural communication can be unselfconsciously expressed through our modification of our surrounds, the more this environment becomes a dwelling, a home, a place.

Table 3.2 Place-based typology of virtual environments

Type of virtual environment	Relph's categories	Features	Personal/cultural attachment
Spatial visualization	Existential outsideness (objective)	Locational (links)	Locates setting
		Navigational (orients)	Locates paths, and centers
Activity-based	Vicarious-behavioral-empathetic insideness (activities and events)	Memorable (unique)	Has uniquely occurring events
		Territorial (protects)	Locates shelter; repose in regards to dynamic environment
		Modifiable	Artifacts and surrounds can be modified
Hermeneutic (symbolic)	Existential insideness (culturally coded)	Supports an idea of agency-directed symbols, reveals secrets of the environment	
		Abandoned inhabitation	Evokes an idea of social agency and past inhabitation
		Lived-in inhabitation	Supports interpersonal social behavior through human and or computer agents
		Home	Affords personal shelter, primary orientation, identification, possession and collection of artifacts

The degree of complexity of such a virtual environment may range from merely believing people with a different world-viewpoint existed in an environment, to feeling that we are being rejected or assimilated by another culture, to feeling that we are 'home'. At time of writing, I know of no virtual environment that can compare in emotional attachment to a real world home, and hence we argue that this is the most difficult type of virtual environment to create. However, we can test for 'mild' hermeneutic immersion in a virtual world, where a participant begins to use and develop the codes of other cultures in order to orient and solve tasks, and to communicate the value and significance of those tasks and goals to others. The particular type of virtual environment that might be required thus depends on the amount and intensity of cultural perspective that needs to be generated and conveyed.

3.8 Matching Virtual Environments and Technologies

In order to choose an appropriate technology, we need to determine the extent of place making features necessary to convey the required information, be it for visualization, activity-based, or for hermeneutic understanding (Table 3.3). As virtual environments typically involve spatial representations, it would help to consider the overall form. Is it to be a self-contained object, an object in the landscape (similar to theatre in the round), as a frame filtering you from the external view (as in a panorama), or as a complete world? Architecture as a self-contained but externally realized object can be embedded directly in a webpage, and it can allow for annotation (audio or visual) via mark-up technologies tied to an external database.

Objects in landscape offer the opportunity to bury markers (annotations) in culturally coded ways supported with spatial and temporal databases. They can be made more

Table 3.3 Virtual place interaction and place features

Virtual world	Goal	Interaction (over time)	Feature
Observational (audio visual worlds)	Navigate, and recognize	Physiologically inactive to reactive	Objects, background, navigation metaphors, time recording (sometimes)
Process-driven (activity worlds)	Enact, test skill level, and learn	Physiologically reactive To intentionally proactive	As above plus artifacts, performance recording
Hermeneutic (culturally/personally identifiable worlds)	Inhabit, identify otherness (alterity), and communicate	Personally and socially symbolic	As above plus it affords the perception that one can either personalize artifacts or that artifacts have been personalized by distinct individuals or societies

powerful with realistic recreations of weather patterns as well. The frame and panorama idea allows hyperlinked objects, the tracking of x, y, z co-ordinates, and the selection and hence annotation of three-dimensional objects.

This technology could be used for visualizations of plazas, open spaces, and interior spaces (but not so convincingly together). However, for the inside-outside evocation of architectural form game engines are more powerful. Breaking down the environment into cells, game engines support real-time interaction, particle physics, fully interactive artifacts, dynamic physical environments, multi-user participation and chat logs. They may also allow for annotation and personalization (if only via gun scorched walls and corpses), simulated weather conditions, as well as terrain modeling (see for example game engines such as Unreal, Quake, Max Payne, Crytek, PlaneShift, Torque, Black and White).

The first type of environment surrounds and orientates us (it has spatial presence). It allows us to visualize things. The second type creates a background in which activity is possible. It allows us to do things (it allows for interaction).

The third type of environment identifies both us and our personal form of physical embodiment through how we modify artifacts and the environment. Alternatively, it identifies and helps us understand the identity and intentions of other intelligent beings through how they appear to have modified artifacts and the environment. For either purpose, it caters for symbolic interaction. This third type of environment is thus like a symbolic stage or palimpsest. It either allows us to express our identity and intentions to other people, or it allows us to feel that we can interpret identity and intentions of others through how they appear to have modified and personalized the environment to better express themselves.

I now intend to expand on useful theoretical concepts, terms and techniques, as well as overall research areas and research questions that may help us critically evaluate the success and failure of virtual environments.

3.9 Terms

In order to apply and improve virtual environments designers need to share a clear design terminology. Sharing of research and language between disciplines, such as the field studies of cultural anthropologists, environmental psychologists testing criteria of presence, and virtual environment designers, would help create virtual environments that are more meaningful and engaging.

Presence: I have previously argued that Presence as in 'being there' and when tested as Social Presence, Engagement, Negative Feelings, Spatial Presence etcetera in a virtual environment does not fully evaluate Cultural Presence. Hence, it is not fully suitable as it stands for testing simulations of cultural environments. Yet travelers typically travel to cultural environments, hence a virtual travel environment should address the issue of presenting Cultural Presence.

Presence researchers have conflated Cultural Presence and Social Presence. On the other hand, I suggest that we should distinguish between the two as below:

- Social behavior is behavior between two or more people.
- Cultural behavior is a subset of social behavior, where behavior is governed by or understood in terms of a cultural setting involving the constrained use of artifacts.

As discussed above, I believe that appropriate context (and especially intangible content such as cultural heritage), is missing from a great deal of virtual environments (Champion 2003). With the view to analyzing cultural interactions in a virtual environment, I propose that terms used in both environmental psychology and in anthropology and archaeology would be suitable. These fields offer a scholarly framework for digital environments due to a focus on environment–people interaction, cultural behavior (people–people interaction), and the interaction of people with their culturally defining use and creation of artifacts (people–artifacts interaction).

The terminology between information design and archaeology is similar, adding weight to the use of a related terminology, as it appears to be in some currency across disciplines. Moreover, a terminology acceptable across disciplines must surely be a requirement in the discussion of virtual environments for cultural learning.

A major part of Schiffer and Miller's theory relies on a three-way means of communication (Schiffer and Miller 1999, p. 59); information is transmitted person to person via artifacts, not directly person-to-person ('receiver–sender') as in linguistic theories. A person modifies an artifact, which is decoded eventually by an archaeologist's 'relational knowledge'. There are thus three interactors (further described below).

The theory is also based on interactivity, allows for interaction independently of humans, and allows for quantifiable research insofar as there can be discrete (i.e., observable) interactions. Weaknesses may include an over generous definition of materiality (materiality seems to include everything), and an inability to discern mental states of participants in a virtual environment (due to its behavioral focus).

Interactors: An interactor is any object that can take part in interactions, which is in a way a circular definition (Schiffer and Miller 1999, pp. 12–13). An interaction must arise from one or more performances by interactors (each interactor has a range of performance characteristics). There are three types of interactors: people (actors), artifacts, and externs.

People (Users): In a virtual environment, people may be visitors (travelers or tourists), or inhabitants. They may wish to loiter, to be guided, or seek out certain views or tasks. They may differ in their purpose (goal), in their preference for mythology or history, ability to navigate or solve complex tasks, and desire to personalize the environment or socialize with other avatars.

It may be necessary to evaluate the effect of interactive components on engagement in virtual environments, assess the popularity of 'travel' versus 'tourist' levels of interactivity, and weigh up the needs of 'inhabitant' and 'visitor'.

One way of describing the overall elements of a digital environment might be to borrow from performance media. Terms that could be used include the actor (the visitor to a digital environment); the backdrop (the default environment); the audience (those observing but not taking part); props (artifacts and naturally occurring objects); dialogue (in multi-user chat rooms); cues; motives; and plot devices. There may also be improvisation (as metaphors for triggered events, agent behaviors, predefined scripts, and random or actor-directed actions and events).

Schiffer and Miller (1999, p. 16) give a long list of academics in the social and behavioral sciences using the actor metaphor. Schiffer and Miller further extend the actor/performer metaphor but in reference to what they call anthropological archaeology and its attempt to re-focus on people–artifact interactions. The terminology focuses on material culture interaction, using interactor, artifacts, and externs as the basic elements.

Artifacts: "are phenomena produced, replicated, or otherwise brought wholly or partly to their present form through human means" (Schiffer and Miller 1999, p. 12). Types of artifacts are platial ("reside in a place...include portable artifacts [artifacts] stored there"), personal artifacts (actual or temporarily associated with the human body), and situational artifacts "arrive with people or turn up at a place for the conduct of an activity" (Schiffer and Miller 1999, pp. 21–22).

Extern: An Extern "takes in phenomena that arise independently of people, like sunlight and clouds, wild plants and animals, rocks and minerals, and landforms" (Schiffer and Miller 1999, pp. 12–13). This is a useful term as interaction in a virtual environment seldom makes the distinction between that inherent in the environment and that triggered by a user.

Trace: Although not included in the above three-term interaction theory, another important Schiffer and Miller term is the formal trace, properties of material that have been modified. For example, by analyzing food residue left in a pot, archaeologists can infer that it was used for cooking rice.

Life history: A life history is "the specific sequence of interactions and activities that occurs during a given interactor's existence" (Schiffer and Miller 1999, p. 26). Sets of closely linked activities are called processes, which in turn are subsets of life histories.

The creation of a common terminology may be helped by Schiffer and Miller, but listing design goals, intended audiences, environment elements, and interactive methods used would also help focus attention on creating content-rich virtual places, rather than mere form.

3.10   Summary of Place Theory

This chapter argues that a sense of presence in virtual environments and real experiences is not just a consequence of being surrounded by a spatial setting, but of being engaged in another place. A place is particular, unique, dynamic, and memorably related to other places, peoples, and events, and it is hermeneutic.

In later chapters I will propose that the broad objectives of virtual heritage environments are to impart the significance of a place, and its importance to local cultural values and perspectives. Two major related issues would then be how we best convey both a sense of place and a sense of Cultural Presence in the experiencing of virtual environments. Yet surprisingly, they are often not discussed. The most accurate, realistic and powerful virtual heritage environments do not necessarily produce a corresponding increase in user enjoyment (Mosaker 2001). Such research indicates that lack of engagement with cultural perspectives of the past may have been due to a lack of meaningful content rather than to a lack of realism.

It has been suggested that virtual environment design be informed by architectural and planning theory. However, places are not just built environments; they are lived and inhabited by non-designers. The interaction of environment dwellers and visitors give place their final character. Design by a single mind will not cover the complexity and contradiction engendered by those that are affected by place. Moreover, the pristine nature of digitally simulated or abstracted environments often lacks the blur between clear form and infinite space that creates mood and character (Neumann et al. 1996). Real world built environments are often vague and amorphously designed, as well as incorporating deliberate illusions to tease evoke or trigger our perceptions and memories.

Place is particular, unique, elusive, dynamic, and memorably related to other places, peoples, and to events (tasks and happenings). Place may also have a cultural and personal significance as well as a social history shaped by how it helped, hindered, and was modified by humans. Place may also act as a decipherable record of human interaction (a 'history').

Some of the most effective constraints in both physical and virtual realms that offer and often dictate behavioral cues are derived from the dynamic nature of real-world environments. Modeling such dynamic environments can range from shelter and familiar territory, to a hostile world where survival is dependent on task completion, artifacts collected, and their impacts on users' abilities.

The dangers and opportunities of the environment could be contextually related to the local cultural perspective. Some parts of the environment may impede the progress of the user in order for the user to recognize trails and paths, and socially accepted ways of traveling through the environment. The other parts of the environment may be deleterious to the avatar's metaphorical health, in other words, they act as constraints.

To encompass all the above features of various places into cyber places is a huge and currently impossible undertaking. One possible solution is to adopt a more graduated approach for understanding features of different kinds of virtual places, and the cultural and social functions they facilitate, in order to guide selection of appropriate interaction, content, and technology.

In this regard, Kalay and Marx articulated eight specific notions of place that are missing in virtual environments (Kalay and Marx 2001). However, Champion and Dave (2002) have previously argued that these features were important but not comprehensive. The Kalay–Marx criteria, as they are based on modes of reality, do not address virtual environments that offer interpretations of past and present cultures.

I have instead offered a categorization of virtual environments (derived from Relph's tripartite notion of place). These categories were the observational (visual), the activity focused (such as games), and the hermeneutic (capable of transmitting cultural perspectives between users, and between past and present inhabitants).

There are still many issues and problems with the above theories. The first is how realistic places need to be. A key issue in the creation of place is whether the goal is to reproduce accurately aspects of the real world or to create virtual environments that defy, extend or inspire our concept of what is real. There is ongoing discussion in presence research, for example, over whether the term 'presence' measures subjective or objective sensation of being in a simulated or abstracted virtual environment (refer http://www.presence-connect.org).

To approximate reality requires settings for social transactions that are location specific and task specific (elements that help define a place). Although designers are hindered by a lack of haptic interfaces, there is also a need for transition zones of perceived physiological comfort and discomfort (navigated and defined by user-perceived paths and centers). Yet these elements, though they may help create a place, do not necessarily create a hermeneutic environment.

Finally, especially in light of a community, a virtual environment has to be writable; a user must be able to leave not just their footprint but also their 'mark' on it. For a comprehensively hermeneutic environment requires ciphers indicating cultural agency, and these ciphers, marks, glyphs or artifacts must appear to afford some form of interpretation. This notion of cultural agency and the related notion of Cultural Presence is the subject of the next chapter.

References

Alexander, C. (1977). *A Pattern Language*. New York: Oxford University Press.

Beckmann, J. (1998). The Virtual Dimension: Architecture, Representation, and Crash Culture. New York: Princeton Architectural Press.

Benedikt, M. (1991). Cyberspace: First Steps. Cambridge, MA: MIT Press.

Biocca, F. (1997). The Cyborg's Dilemma: Progressive Embodiment in Virtual Environments. Journal of Computer-Mediated Communication, 3(2), n.p.

Caillois, R. (1962). Man, Play and Games (M. Barash, Trans.). London: Thames & Hudson

Campbell, D.A. (1997). Explorations into Virtual Architecture: a HIT Lab Gallery. IEEE Multimedia, 4(1), 74–76.

Cantor, D. (1974). Psychology for Architects. London: Applied Science Publishers.

Casey, E.S. (1993). Getting Back into Place: Toward a Renewed Understanding of the Place-World. Bloomington, IN: Indiana University Press.

Casey, E.S. (1997). The Fate of Place: A Philosophical History. Berkeley, CA: University of California Press.

Champion, E. (1993). Scandinavian Architecture Redefined. Architecture New Zealand, 81–84.

Champion, E. (2003, 15–17 October). Online Exploration of Mayan Culture. Paper presented at the VSMM2003 – Ninth International Conference on Virtual Systems and Multimedia, Hybrid Reality: Art, Technology and the Human Factor, Montreal, Canada.

Champion, E. (2004). The Limits of Realism in Architectural Visualisation. Paper presented at the LIMITS, 21st annual conference of the Society of Architectural Historians Australia and New Zealand, (SAHANZ), Melbourne, Australia, 26–29 September 2004.

Champion, E., & Dave, B. (2002, 24–27 October 2002). Where is this place? Paper presented at the ACADIA2002, Association for Computer Aided Design in Architecture 2002 Annual Conference, Pomona USA.

Childe, V.G. (1956). *Piecing Together the past: The Interpretation of Archeological Data*. London: Routledge & Kegan Paul (http://catalogue.nla.gov.au/Record/866509).

Ciolfi, L. (2004). Situating "Place" in Interaction Design: Enhancing the User Experience in Interactive Environments. Limerick: University of Limerick.

Coyne, R. (1995). Designing Information Technology in the Postmodern Age: from Method to Metaphor. Cambridge, MA: MIT Press.

Coyne, R. (1999a). Technoromanticism: Digital Narrative, Holism, and the Romance of the Real. Cambridge, MA, London: MIT Press.

Coyne, R. (1999b). The Embodied Architect in the Information Age. Richard Coyne Inaugural Lecture delivered 16 February 1999 at the University of Edinburgh. Retrieved 11 April, 2009, from http://www.caad.ed.ac.uk/Coyne/Inaugural/

Crang, M. (1998). Cultural Geography. London; New York: Routledge.

Dick, P.K. (1964). The Three Stigmata of Palmer Eldritch (2007 ed.). Kent: Orion Publishing Group.

Eiteljorg, H. (1998, Fall 1998). Photorealistic Visualizations May Be Too Good. CSA Newsletter, XI (2) Retrieved 12 February, 2010, from www.csanet.org/newsletter/fall98/nlf9804.html

Ffytche, M. (n.d). Flaneurs [Electronic Version]. THE IDLER. Retrieved 28 April 2010, from http://idler.co.uk/practical-idling/flaneurs/

Gadamer, H.-G. (1976). Philosophical Hermeneutics. Berkeley, CA: University of California Press.

Gibson, J.J. (1979). The Ecological Approach to Visual Perception. Boston, MA: Houghton Mifflin.

Gibson, W. (2000). Neuromancer. London: Voyager.

Handy, T.C., Grafton, S.T., Shroff, N.M., Ketay, S., & Gazzaniga, M.S. (2003). Graspable objects grab attention when the potential for action is recognized. Nature Neuroscience (March 17 2003).

Hartman, J., Wernecke, J., & Silicon Graphics. (1996). The VRML 2.0 Handbook: Building Moving Worlds on the Web: Addison-Wesley Professional.

Heidegger, M. (1975). Poetry, Language, Thought (A. Hofstadter, Trans.). New York: Harper & Row.

Heim, M. (1998). Creating the Virtual Middle Ground [Electronic Version]. TECHNOS Quarterly For Education and Technology, 7. Retrieved 10 May 2010, from http://www.ait.net/technos/tq_07/3heim.php

Hein, G.E. (1991). Constructivist Learning Theory. Paper presented at the Museum and the Needs of People CECA (International Committee of Museum Educators) Conference. Retrieved 28 April 2010, from http://www.exploratorium.edu/IFI/resources/constructivistlearning.html

Hodder, I., & Hutson, S. (2003). Reading the Past: Current Approaches to Interpretation in Archaeology (3rd ed.). Cambridge; New York: Cambridge University Press.

Johnson, S. (1997). Interface Culture: How New Technology Transforms the Way We think and communicate. San Francisco, CA: HarperEdge.

Kalay, Y., & Marx, J. (2001). Architecture and the Internet: Designing Places in Cyberspace. Paper presented at the Proceedings of ACADIA 2001: Reinventing the Discourse, USA.

Kalay, Y., & Marx, J. (2003). Changing the Metaphor: Cyberspace as a Place. Paper presented at the Digital Design – Research and Practice, Proceedings of the 10th International Conference on Computer Aided Architectural Design Futures, Tainan, Taiwan.

Kalay, Y.E. (2004). Virtual learning environments. Journal of Information Technology in Construction (ITCon), 9 (Special Issue ICT Supported Learning in Architecture and Civil Engineering), 195–207.

Kant, I. (1987). The Critique of Judgement. Indianapolis, IN: Hackett Pub. Co.

Laurel, B., Strickland, R., Tow, R. (1994). Placeholder: Landscape and Narrative in Virtual Environments. ACM Computer Graphics Quarterly, 28(2).

Laurel, B., Strickland, R., Tow, R. (Ed.). (1990). The Art of Human–Computer Interface Design. New York: Addison-Wesley Pu. Co.

Lessiter, J., Freeman, J., Keogh, E., & Davidoff, J. (2001). A Cross-Media Presence Questionnaire: The ITC-Sense of Presence Inventory. Presence: Teleoper. Virtual Environments, 10(3), 282–297.

Malpas, J.E. (1999). Place and Experience: a Philosophical Topography. Cambridge; New York: Cambridge University Press.

Marsh, T., & Wright, P. (2000). Maintaining the Illusion of Interacting Within a 3D Virtual Space. Paper presented at the Third International Workshop on Presence. Retrieved 28 April 2010, from http://www.temple.edu/ispr/prev_conferences/proceedings/98-99-2000/2000/Marsh%20 and%20Wright.pdf

Massey, D. (1993). A Global Sense of Place. In A. Gray & J. McGuigan (Eds.), Studying Culture: An Introductory Reader. London: Arnold.

Morgan, D. (1996). The Enchantment of Art: Abstraction and Empathy from German Romanticism to Expressionism. Journal of the History of Ideas, 57(2), 321.

Morrison, K.F. (1988). I am You: the Hermeneutics of Empathy in Western Literature, Theology and Art. Princeton, NJ: Princeton University Press.

Mosaker, L. (2001). Visualising Historical Knowledge Using Virtual Reality Technology. Digital Creativity, 12(1), 15–25.

Neumann, D., Albrecht, D., David Winton Bell Gallery, Deutsches Architekturmuseum, Deutsches Filmmuseum (Frankfurt am Main, G., & Academy of Motion Picture Arts and Sciences: Academy Gallery. (1996). Film architecture: set designs from Metropolis to Blade Runner. Munich, New York: Prestel.

Nietzsche, F. (1967). The Birth of Tragedy. New York: Random House.

Nitsche, M. (2008). Video Game Spaces: Image, Play and Structure in 3D Game Worlds. Cambridge, MA: MIT Press.

Nitsche, M., Roudavski, S., Penz, F., & Thomas, M. (2002). Narrative Expressive Space. SIGGROUP Bulletin 23(2), 10–13.

Norberg-Schulz, C. (2000). Architecture: Presence, Language, Place. Milan, London: Skira Editore; Thames & Hudson.

Novak, M. (1991). Liquid Architectures in Cyberspace. In M. Benedikt (Ed.), Cyberspace: First Steps (pp. 225–254). Cambridge, MA: MIT Press.

Parisi, T. (2001). Foreword. In A. Walsh & M. Bourges-Sévenier (Eds.), Core Web3D. Upper Saddle River, NJ: Prentice Hall.

Rapoport, A. (1982). The Meaning of the Built Environment: a Nonverbal Communication Approach. Beverly Hills, CA: Sage Publications.

Relph, E.C. (1976). Place and Placelessness. London: Pion.

Riegler, A. (2001). Virtual Science: Virtuality and Knowledge Acquisition in Science and Cognition. In A. Riegler (Ed.), Virtual Reality: Cognitive Foundations, Technological Issues & Philosophical Implications. Frankfurt am Main: Peter Lang.

Sardar, Z. (1996). alt.civilizations.faq: Cyberspace as the Darker Side of the West. In Z. Sardar & J. Ravetz (Eds.), Cyberfutures: Culture and Politics on the Information Superhighway (Vol. 1, pp. 14–41). London: Pluto Press.

Savile, A. (1993). Kantian Aesthetics Pursued. Edinburgh: Edinburgh University Press.

Schiffer, M.B., & Miller, A.R. (1999). The Material Life of Human Beings: Artifacts, Behaviour and Communication. London: Routledge.

Schroeder, R. (1996). Possible Worlds: the Social Dynamic of Virtual Reality Technology. Boulder, CO: Westview Press.

Schuemie, M.J., van der Straaten, P., Krijn, M., & van der Mast, C.A.P.G. (2001). Research on Presence in Virtual Reality: A Survey. CyberPsychology and Behavior, 4(2), 183–201.

Slater, M. (1999). Measuring Presence: A Response to the Witmer and Singer Presence Questionnaire. Presence: Teleoperators and Virtual Environments, 8(5), 560–565.

Suzuki, H. (1997). Introduction. In K. Sakamura & H. h. Suzuki (Eds.), The Virtual Architecture – the Difference Between the Possible and the Impossible. Tokyo: Kenchiku Hakubutsukan, Yonsei University.

Tilley, C.Y. (1999). Metaphor and Material Culture. Oxford, UK; Malden, MA: Blackwell Publishers.

Tuan, Y.-F. (1998). Escapism. Baltimore, MD: Johns Hopkins University Press.

Tyng, A. (1984). Beginnings Louis I. Kahn's Philosophy of Architecture. New York: Wiley.

Waterworth, J.A. (1999). The Scope of Virtual Presence. Paper presented at the Second International Workshop on Presence. Retrieved 28 April 2010, from http://www8.informatik. umu.se/~jwworth/PresenceScope.html

Wigley, M. (2007). GAMESPACE. In F. von Borries, S. P. Watlz & M. Böttiger (Eds.), Space Time Play: Computer Games, Architecture and Urbanism: The Next Level (pp. 484–487). Basel: Birkhauser.

Wrede, S. (1980). The Architecture of Erik Gunnar Asplund. Cambridge, MA: MIT Press.

Chapter 4
Cultural and Social Presence

4.1 Why Photorealism Does Not Convey Cultural Significance

In the last three chapters I have cited various papers that declare a lack of engagement in a virtual environment due to technology or application issues, and this is to some degree the crude and limited ways in which realism can be reached by recent technology. On the other hand, even though more powerful and accurate technology may edge closer to photo-realistic rendering and enhance the speed of computation, that does not mean the resulting virtual environment will be more useful, usable, and insightful.

For virtual environments that aim to preserve explain and inform on culturally significant places need to do more than replicate objects; they need to replicate *and* communicate the processes that made those artifacts culturally significant. And virtual heritage environments are far too often examples of this lack of meaningful interaction (Mosaker 2001). Many writers have stated that virtual environments lack meaningful content, and virtual heritage environments are a case in point. "VR systems do not offer an alternative 'reality'; they do, however, provide simulated worlds that seem 'realistic,' " wrote Schroeder (1996, p. 115).

Photo-realism has been the goal of many virtual environments designers. Can photo-realism exist in tandem with physically embodied, socially embedded and culturally inscribed virtual environments? In the following section we will discuss specific issues that may result from attempting to develop photo-realistic virtual heritage environments.

4.1.1 Virtual Heritage Is Not Realism

A desire for realism often conflicts with a need for interpretability. Does an attempt to perfect fidelity to sources and to realism improve or hinder the cultural learning experience? Greeff and Lalioti (2001, p. 1) argued that virtual identities

E. Champion, *Playing with the Past*, Human-Computer Interaction Series,
DOI 10.1007/978-1-84996-501-9_4, © Springer-Verlag London Limited 2011

are needed to allow engagement in "interactive cultural experiences....People create meaning through narrative or stories....Culture influences our perspectives, values and behavior....Many applications, such as culture, are dynamic and therefore static representations are not efficient for portraying them." Yet personal creation through interaction would however threaten realism and authenticity.

There seems to be a conflation in popular usage between the word 'virtual' meaning to have the effect of the 'real' without actually having material or form and 'virtual' as a synonym for the word 'digital'. A similar problem appears with the common use of realism: 'appears to be real' could mean, 'an object looks like something that really exists', or 'I can believe that it exists'.

Virtuality can be defined as existing or resulting in essence or effect though not in actual fact, form, or name, for example, the virtual extinction of the buffalo. It may refer to that which exists in the mind, especially as a product of the imagination (used in literary criticism of a text). In computer science, an online dictionary also defines virtual as that which is "created, simulated, or carried on by means of a computer or computer network, such as virtual conversations in a chatroom"(Dictionary, n.d.).

Designers may use this conflation to persuade the viewer that high-resolution images imply a high degree of archaeological certainty, when this is not the case, "...the distinctions between real and hypothetical are not simple but subtle, complex, and far-reaching... As Mr. Emele pointed out in his article, a partially known site cannot be reconstructed satisfactorily... Our reconstructions are also too clean and neat" (Eiteljorg 1998, p. 2).

When we talk of limits applied to virtual environments we may mean that fidelity to the real world is conceptually rather than visually realistic. Realism has its uses, but so does the expanding of perception and cultural understanding. Information may be highly selective (more appropriate to the learning curve of the audience), interaction could be metaphorical and dramatic rather than god-like (omniscient and omnipotent), or we may have deliberately reduced the cognitive loading required to complete tasks.

The cultural significance of a world heritage site, say a Neolithic cave, may be intangible, alien, and hence unreal to the tourist. Yet to a Stone Age cave dweller the marks on the wall may be more than unrealistic drawings; they may be the culturally inviolable and hence 'real' ciphers that create and sustain a cultural setting.

The recent developments of highly accurate and large-scale virtual heritage scanning technology indicate that the impedance to capturing a sense of place in digital models is not a problem with capturing realism. Virtual environments exist with photo-realistic laser-scanned artifacts, augmented by textures scanned in from real-world materials. However the reason why such environments lack a sense of engagement and therefore lack a sense of place is too often because they lack thematic interactivity, the interactivity that has helped make computer games so popular (Eiteljorg 1998; Laurel et al. 1994; Mosaker 2001).

While visual correspondence to reality may be a great help for visualizing layout and orientation of a site, our knowledge of a place is deepened by our activities as shaped by that place, and our identification with or against that place. If a feeling of presence depends on a feeling of active participation in a place, I would argue that a hyper-realistic spatial setting by itself does not necessarily create presence.

Advances in digital media technology hold great promise for photo-realistic and historically authentic reconstructions of heritage monuments and culturally significant places. In order to attain a degree of 'reality', computer visualizations have focused on reducing technical limitations in order to approach visual fidelity and accurate reproduction of real and historical environments. Yet this love of technology as progress per se may blind us to the amorphous nature of history. A computer model can imply certitude when the data it is based on is not as reliable and authentic as the environment it was meant to portray. Further, exacting technology may not always capture culture, particularly the more intangible aspects of culture, accurately. UNESCO (2005) seems to agree, for it has recently developed a policy on the importance of intangible heritage.

> The Convention for the Safeguarding of the Intangible Cultural Heritage defines the intangible cultural heritage as the practices, representations, expressions, as well as the knowledge and skills, that communities, groups and, in some cases, individuals recognize as part of their cultural heritage....intangible cultural heritage is transmitted from generation to generation, and is constantly recreated by communities and groups, in response to their environment, their interaction with nature, and their historical conditions of existence. It provides people with a sense of identity and continuity, and its safeguarding promotes, sustains, and develops cultural diversity and human creativity.

If history is not a precise science, we may be presumptuous in attempting visual fidelity without considering what techniques and media best afford an engaging and fulfilling experience of the cultural significance of that site (Boskovic 1997).

4.1.2 Phobic Triggers and Experiential Realism

Realism is not necessarily the same as visual fidelity; it could also mean conceptual fidelity. A person might believe something exists and is 'real' even if it does not look 'realistically' like anything unknown; as long as he or she believes it may affect him or her, as we are discovering with VR used for medicine. For example, Hoffman (2004, p. 60) wrote:

> Researchers are finding that some of the best applications of the software focus on therapy rather than entertainment. In essence, virtual reality can ease pain, both physical and psychological....The results have been so promising that a few hospitals are now preparing to explore the use of virtual reality as a tool for pain control. In other projects, my colleagues and I are using virtual-reality applications to help phobic patients overcome their irrational fear of spiders and to treat post-traumatic stress disorder (PTSD) in survivors of terrorist attacks.

Problems can actually arise from the depiction of too-realistic human avatars. Thompson (2004) noted:

> In 1978, the Japanese roboticist Masahiro Mori noticed something interesting: The more humanlike his robots became, the more people were attracted to them, but only up to a point. If an android become *too* realistic and lifelike, suddenly people were repelled and disgusted.

Mori (1981) called this phenomenon 'The Uncanny Valley', and it is further described and illustrated in Bryant's (2000) online article, *The Uncanny Valley, Why are monster-movie zombies so horrifying and talking animals so fascinating?*

The latest development in game engines and interfaces is further blurring the distinction between physical and cognitive presence. Robillard et al.(2003, p. 473) built a virtual environment using to a game engine help people overcame phobias and noted in their discussion that:

> The first goal of this study is to determine if TVEDGs [therapeutic virtual environments derived from computer games] can induce anxiety in phobic participants. The results demonstrate that despite their low cost and flexibility, TVEDGs can be phobogenic. Moreover, virtual environments derived from games can produce the mid-range levels of anxiety that are most useful in therapy.

What is most interesting to me is that the VR equipment involved does not need to be high cost, inaccessible to the public, or capable of high resolution. The phobic 'triggers' are so strong that photo-realistic digital environments, according to Jacobson (2000) are not needed:

> Virtual reality (or VR) therapy already helps many patients overcome phobias, from fear of flying to fear of spiders. Similar systems are being tested to see if they can reduce bouts of anorexia and bulimia.

Philosophers of science have argued for many centuries that what we see is filtered reality, not actual reality (Ferko et al. 2003; Riegler 2001). So virtual environments can be used to engage, distract, or stimulate learning styles or particular phobias.

In dealing with extreme phobia cases, photo-realistic detail is not needed, significant detail is. We may extrapolate these findings to capturing the cultural perspectives of a certain society: capturing what they find evocative and important is arguably the most important aim. Photo-realism is a great aim if we wish to test the extent of technology, but it may not be the most suitable aim for content.

For example, game designers do not all vie for photo-realism. Just as with VR phobia studies, if a game correctly stimulates a user by such methods, the participant is too busy experiencing the sensation (horror, terror, etcetera) to worry about nitpicking the quality of detail. My term for this is experiential realism. On reflection, the participant feels that they experienced the same degree and nature of experience (of feeling) as if they had been in a similar situation in the real world. Experiential realism is afforded when the experience was visceral atmospheric and evocative, *rather* than photo-realistic capture of detail and rendering.

Realism may obscure specific information (more appropriate to the learning curve of the audience). It is not necessary for metaphorical and schematic interaction. Realism has potentially misleading connotations of 'god-like' knowledge (omniscient and omnipotent), and too much detail can increase the cognitive loading of participants to the point where they have difficulty completing or being inspired to complete tasks. In such a case, there may be occasions where virtual environment designers might actually wish to limit or restrict the degree of visual fidelity, as pointed out by Eiteljorg (1998):

> ...The distinctions between real and hypothetical are not simple but subtle, complex, and far-reaching... As Mr. Emele pointed out in his article, a partially known site cannot be reconstructed satisfactorily... Our reconstructions are also too clean and neat.

Designers may use the common confusion between visual fidelity and historical fidelity to persuade the viewer that high-resolution images imply a high degree of archaeological certainty, when this is not the case.

4.1.3 Archaeology and History Is Not Set in Concrete

Writers have noted that culture is improvised and transformative, for social rules are not set instructions like chess (Tilley 1999, pp. 29, 272). Experiencing a virtual environment may be enhanced if the social rules and cultural artifacts can be modified. However, there are two aspects to this; the social world as lived by people inside the 'world', and the perceived social world projected into the environment as seen by people outside that 'world'.

A classic example would be the archaeological dig. The reconstructed palace of Knossos on Crete is a dynamic blend of archaeological dogma and controversial projections as well as actual uncovered remains. How could we digitally recreate the many views and ideas of the palace?

Being part of society, archaeologists are as interested in controversy and the degree of agreed upon accuracy as they are in the historical reconstruction itself (Kensek et al. 2002). This is also a highly specific form of etic cultural transmittance. Current digital reconstructions do not in general show the process by which archaeologists reconstruct likely scenarios as to what has taken place.

When onsite, through deducing patterns of behavior from artifacts, knowledge of other comparative cultures, and by testing changes to the landscape, anthropologists and archaeologists may develop their own 'detective knowledge' of a past culture which is not accessible to the general public via either trips to the actual site or through tourist literature. Yet this could be incorporated into virtual heritage environments (Champion 2002).

Part of the problem with virtual heritage projects is thus semantic in nature. Historical reconstructions may be measured in terms of their fidelity, but history is not one story but a series of interpretations. Anderson (1997, p. 25) noted this self-deception:

> One convenient falsehood that we embrace is that scholarship is best undertaken in solitude...We will welcome the arrival of a multifaceted interpretive model, our artworks, offering numerous ways to enlighten our visitors about our artworks, rather than offer up a single point of view that has been traditionally held.

Fidelity can be seen as faithfulness to obligations, duties, or observances. It may mean exact correspondence with fact or with a given quality, condition, event, or accuracy. It may also refer to the degree to which an electronic system accurately reproduces the sound or image of its input signal (definitions from http://www. dictionary.com, accessed 28 April 2010).

Yet in virtual heritage projects, the fidelity is not conceptually or even physically faithful to the past. Fidelity of reproduction is often a high resolution capture of the static leftovers of the present; using scientific extrapolation of past circumstances through analysis of remaining data, or a monument based on a singular (historically situated) archaeological insight.

Virtual environments do not tend to show how the local past inhabitants modified, interacted with, and inhabited their environment through their own view of reality. Yet hermeneutics argues that we must grasp the world of the interpreter as well as the world of the interpreted in order to gain the meaning of the text or object of art. The philosopher Hans-Georg Gadamer (1976, p. xii) defined hermeneutics as follows:

> Hermeneutics has its origin in breaches in intersubjectivity. Its field of application is comprised of all those situations in which we encounter meanings that are not immediately understandable but require interpretative effort....

According to Gadamer's definition of hermeneutics, one could not negate the temporal (and spatial) difference that separates the reader from the author of the text they are reading. To be able to read the author of a past era or society as if nothing is lost in translation or from the passing of time implies that modern humans can separate any modern human being from their historical background. Reflection cannot hold at a distance and objectify the past, for the present is always a given. Gadamer (1976, p. xiv) asserted that "To be historical....means that one is not absorbed into self-knowledge."

On the other hand, that does not mean that virtual heritage environments cannot entertain. Recent research has also indicated that realistic but non-interactive installations of virtual heritage projects may bore the audience (Mosaker 2001). However, allowing participants to talk to each other in a virtual heritage world may improve the sense of engagement, but at a cost to Cultural Presence. A further issue with realism is whether computer simulations can convey archaeological disagreements and alternative viewpoints. How do we present scientific uncertainty? Can we convey historical interpretation, hunches or imagined reconstructions in virtual environments?

For example, archaeologists have already developed interactive games to train students to make educated guesses. ArcDig is a two-dimensional game that allows students to guess where things are buried, and then dig for them. It then provides answers as to where and why by professional archaeologists. Such a theme could be extended into a genuine three-dimensional game that explores the probable validity, the professional controversy and the eventual outcome of archaeologists' hunches.

> Recommendations for designing a VR-experience are at the outset that 'augmented reality' should better be 'augmented fiction,' not so much by increasing the number and quality of realistic features but by increasing the relevance of a situation, providing features that tune in to the goals and concerns of the user....(Hoorn et al. 2003, p. 25)

The cultural significance of a world heritage site, say a Neolithic cave, may be intangible, alien, and hence appear unreal to the tourist. We may well agree that computer generated worlds and images are (ironically) limited by their lack of limitations (by views that seem to last until infinity). Yet a focus on visual fidelity rather than on atmosphere is not always a necessary or desirable component of either virtual heritage or digital architecture.

4.2 Confusion over Cultural Presence

There is a great deal of research still to be done on what social and cultural cues are most significant to people, and which cues most aid education and engagement. These factors vary according to the audience, their background, beliefs, and intentions. Due to the gestalt-nature of cultural understanding, it may not be enough to experiment with restricted content, research on Cultural Presence may require significant and contextually appropriate content.

We still do not have agreed definitions of Cultural Presence or data to help determine which elements most aid a sense of Cultural Presence. We do not know, for example, which interactive features and type of cultural agency are most preferable, most informative, or most afford a sense of place as a cultural setting.

Even the evaluation of Cultural Presence, cultural understanding, and cultural learning is problematic. We do not have a clear mutual understanding of what exactly is cultural information and how to provide for it or communicate it digitally. The first step is almost certainly to aim for shared acceptance of terms and methods, such as of Cultural Presence, Social Presence, and Co-presence.

4.3 What Is Culture?

Kroeber and Kluckhohn (1952, p. 357) have attempted to encapsulate the many differing definitions of culture:

> Culture consists of patterns, explicit and implicit, of and for behavior acquired and transmitted by symbols, constituting the distinctive achievement of human groups, including their embodiment in artifacts; the essential core of culture consists of traditional (i.e. historically derived and selected) ideas and especially their attached values; culture systems may on the one hand, be considered as products of action, on the other as conditioning elements of further action.

Jenks (1993) wrote that most definitions of culture include the notion of organized knowledge and the use of symbolic representation. He noted one reason for the confusion is that culture is often used to separate, as between humanity and nature or between humanity and machine, and to unify, culture is that which humans have (and animals do not). Historically culture may be a level of perfection (a person of culture), a stage of social development (a society with a developed culture), the collective works of art and intellect (the cultural output of a society), or the way of life of a people (their cultural traditions and social perspectives).

In contrast to culture as an organization of knowledge via symbolic representation, culture is rules-based, according to Bourdieu (1984). For Crang (1998, p. 57) culture is best defined as "sets of beliefs or values that give meaning to ways of life and produce (and are reproduced through) material and symbolic forms." Crang extended Sauer's early writings and remarks that landscape is a 'palimpsest'. Crang argued that culture is spatially and temporally embedded. Anderson noted culture was seen to refer to non-western people and to elites as in 'high culture' (Anderson 1997, p. 47; Crang 1998). Tuan (1992, p. 44) wrote that place "helps us forget our separateness and the world's indifference. More generally, culture makes this amnesia possible. Culture integrates us into the world through shared language and custom, behavior and habits of thought."

These definitions do share similar features. Culture is in some way socially created, defined and managed. Culture is expressed via language and artifacts, and culture is both vaguely bounded and open to interpretation. To demarcate the boundaries of culture clearly and accurately is thus highly problematic. Culture is an intangible connection and rejection of threads over space and time. How cultures are spread over space and how cultures make sense of space is thus interdependent. A visitor perceives space as place, place 'perpetuates culture' (frames it, embeds it, erodes it) and thus influences the inhabitant.

4.3.1 What Is a Culturally Significant Place?

We could consider a virtual heritage environment to be a representation of a culturally significant place. Scientists can learn about a place from artifacts, environment, size, scale, form, location (placement in landscape), and relation to other built forms. These cultural cues may help the designers of virtual heritage environments to layer the environment with historically based beliefs, intentions, and interactions of past inhabitants. For culture and place are entwined. This is reflected in the ICOMOS (1988) charter:

> Cultural significance is a concept which helps in estimating the value of places. The places that are likely to be of significance are those which help an understanding of the past or enrich the present, and which will be of value to future generations.

If culture is or can be seen as a web of behavior or system of meaning, then the significance of a cultural place is how richly and powerfully and singularly it emphasizes, filters, and directs a certain culture's way of behaving. Moreover, by extension, Cultural Presence is the strength to which the uniqueness of that culture is perceived through the experiencing of that place.

Designers of virtual communities may also use the detective-style methods of archaeologists and film directors to provide their 'worlds' with the ability to leave traces and artifacts of its users, and to provide the setting with a mood, an atmosphere.

Can we provide understandable cultural cues in a virtual environment? The answer is yes if we could create cues that inspire people (travelers, tourists, or role players) to behave in similar ways to the way they behave when confronted by real-world cultural cues and settings. If people were now to engage in a virtual environment, one would expect a series of rich and clear cultural settings and or cues that would induce certain response behavior.

Would cultural cues add to engagement? If a sense of presence is enhanced by a sense of social realism (cultural learning being a subset of social behavior); then creating a cultural context with these cultural cues would add to the engagement of the 'actors' (actual people participating in the virtual environment).

Would these cues be an improvement to learning, say, over traditional media? A related question would be whether the participants would learn more from a culturally encoded virtual environment than from a typical virtual environment, or perhaps even from traditional media information.

Therefore, there were at least three major questions to be answered if we wish to evoke the sense of Cultural Presence. These questions are as follows: how is cultural coding possible? Secondly, how is it value adding (in terms of entertainment)? Thirdly, how is it educationally significant when delivered through digital media? In order to answer these three questions, we have to have a theoretical model of cultural learning.

4.3.2 How Culture Is Learnt

When we visit other cultures we often learn cultural perspectives through copying others' behavior, through listening (to their language, to their myths and music), or through reading text and viewing media (as tourists and students). When we visit cultural heritage sites as social scientists, we also develop pictures of the past inhabitants. This is done through deducing patterns of behavior from artifacts, knowledge of other comparative cultures, and changes to the landscape (studied by geologists, anthropologists and archaeologists).

We learn about a culture through dynamically participating interactions within its cultural setting (Place). That is, through artifacts (and how they are used), and through people teaching us social background and how to behave (through dialogue devices such as stories and commands), along with our own personal motives (Table 4.1). As we have seen from above, one can gain an idea of a culture indirectly, through artifacts (Schiffer and Miller 1999, pp. 12–16).

In the real world, we learn culture socially, through other people telling us how to behave, or advising us when what we have done is not in accordance with social beliefs. Therefore, there are two major ways of transmitting culture: through other social agents (through the language, actions, and reactions of other people), and through artifacts (the objects created and modified by people).

Table 4.1 Ways in which we learn about a cultural context

Real-world cultural learning	Suggested Methods for VE cultural cues
The ways in which humans collectively respond to environmental forces	Location-dependent filters or clues for allowing you to interactively solve a task
We can learn about the significance of a place by how old or worn it appears	Ability for attrition and user-role based erosion of place
Learning about a place through task-based activity there	A variety of tasks relevant to the progress and enjoyment of the user
The properties of ritual and habitual-related artifacts	Allow for audio or visual cues in artifacts event-driven and or location-driven
The significance of a place by social learning (by people telling you or instructing you)	Computer-scripted agents that answer certain questions, and remember who passed by and what they did, ability for potential users to leave messages for each other

4.3.3   Social and Cultural Presence

Presence has been defined as being in a place that has some present meaning to the viewer (Slater 1999). I would rather suggest a new definition of Cultural Presence, a feeling in a virtual environment that people with a different cultural perspective occupy or have occupied that virtual environment as a 'place'. Such a definition suggests Cultural Presence is not just a feeling of 'being there' but of being in a 'there and then', not the cultural rules of the 'here and now'.

A sense of a Cultural Presence, when one visits a real site, is inspired by the suggestion of social agency, the feeling that what one is visiting is an artifact, created and modified by conscious human intention. For example, when one visits a cultural heritage site of a long since lost people, signs and audiovisual tapes prompt us to look at specific items, and tell us the cultural significance of that site to its now deceased inhabitants.

Yet to social scientists on a dig, a site visit evokes images of the past, for them the place itself is a cultural artifact. They extrapolate a sense of the Cultural Presence that once inhabited and modified the site. If we were trying to create a virtual heritage environment that engaged and educated people, we would be aiming at eliciting this sense of Cultural Presence. Therefore, in this sense Cultural Presence is a perspective of a past culture to a user, a perspective normally only deduced by trained archaeologists and anthropologists from material remains (fossils, pottery shards, ruins, etc.). They recreate an idea of place from broken objects and expert deductive knowledge not immediately available to the public.

Rykwert (1996) wrote:

> Anthropologists can set out the condition of building: they can tell us what people expected from them in the past; how they interpreted what they saw and experienced, even about the most obvious pieces of a building – doors and windows, walls, roofs and floors; how the experience of each part related to the whole – as the building, the district, the city were walked through, penetrated, integrated by use, their fragments compacted into a body.

If a robot was created and abandoned without defined rules or human contact, it is unlikely to attempt to express itself through artifacts left from the wreckage of past civilizations. For adherence to cultural rules and mores are ultimately socially governed. It is the acceptance or condemnation of other people in a society that separates cultural behavior from individual habits. Even on a desert island, a human would endeavor to live according to his or her previous mores, in case people returned. Humans seek social affirmation.

For if a person were to be left on a desert island, the amount of information they garnered from the leftover artifacts of previous inhabitants would reflect their understanding of the local level of Cultural Presence. Cultural Presence may also be of currently existing cultures. A tourist who is lost in a market in an exotic town but manages without understanding the local laws, language, or custom, to suspect the sellers are from a separate tribe, may have some sense of Cultural Presence.

To improve our understanding of Cultural Presence, and why it is missing from many virtual environments, we need to distinguish it from Co-presence and Social Presence. Many research papers that have 'culture' in the title do not clearly distinguish Cultural Presence from Social Presence (Greeff and Lalioti 2001; Riva et al. 2002, 2004). It is also not clear that we can say Social Presence is a group of people in a virtual environment aware of each other, because the general and more specific meaning of a society is of one with shared values beliefs and/or identity. Further, people in a chat room may be experiencing Social Presence without feeling that they are experiencing a strong sense or level of Cultural Presence.

Schroeder (2002) distinguished between Co-presence ("the sense of being there together") and Social Presence, although he seems to think the latter is an individual's experience of being with another in a virtual environment, or, describes how well the medium helps generates this experience. He does note that this feeling does not describe what is done together or how well, which is important, as the range of interaction in shared virtual environments is actually very limited.

However, he does not draw the conclusion that Social Presence is limited as interaction is limited and that therefore more research is needed on what affords Social Presence. We could add that one significant aspect of social interaction is via culture. Culture is a way of transmitting social beliefs in a more permanent form than by random dialogue. Culture requires interaction and inscription into the virtual environment, it requires musical instruments, pens, brushes, and materials that can be sculpted, inscribed, and imprinted. Culture leaves marks; it requires an indirectly socially interactive communication medium.

Swinth and Blascovich (2002) reviewed definitions of Social Presence, from being together in a virtual environment, to having a sense of another intelligent being in a virtual environment, to feeling that one is communicating directly to another person without acknowledging that technology is creating this impression. They state that after nearly 30 years of research the boundaries between Co-presence and Social Presence are still ambiguous and unclear. Swinth and Blascovich (2002, p. 319) wrote:

> [Co-presence is]…a person's perception and feeling that others are co-situated within an interpersonal environment…Social Presence can be thought of as whether or not there are

social cues that signify the presence of others within some interactional content, copresence
might be better thought of as one's perception and awareness of those social cues and the
corresponding feeling, sense, or belief that others are "there".

An unwieldy definition, it does make the crucial point that the realization
others are 'in' the same virtual environment does not mean that one can socially
interact with them. However, their slightly changing definitions on the next page
confuse the issue again. Swinth and Blascovich (2002, p. 320) here defined
Social Presence as "the actual, imagined or implied presence of others". No,
this is still Co-presence; two people in a virtual environment from different
languages and cultures may not know how to understand each other. Only when
they manage to communicate or interact as intelligent beings in a meaningful
and understood manner can we agree they have a comprehensive sense of Social
Presence.

Alternatively, perhaps Social Presence also occurs when an observer can see
social interaction taking place between two intelligent beings (for surely an observer
can perceive social interactions of virtual ants). Hence, we have an emic and etic
spectrum of Social Presence.

The emic Social Presence is the degree to which someone feels part of potential
or actual social interaction with at least one other being also capable of social interaction. The etic degree of Social Presence is the degree to which they see social
interaction (mutually perceived and understood) between two or more intelligent
beings. In addition, the social interaction can range from full inclusion to full exclusion – the exiling of dangerous citizens from ancient Greek city-states was an act
of exclusion but it was still a social act.

Heeter (1992) argued for a personal presence, Social Presence, and
Environmental Presence. The former is how much you feel part of a virtual environment, social is how much others exist in virtual environment, and environmental
is how much the environment acknowledges and reacts to the person in the virtual
environment.

I suggest that we further need a distinction between active presence and
passive presence, and it has also added a different form of Social Presence, 'how
much I notice people affecting each other'. We can be aware of social interaction
without feeling part of the society itself. Heeter seems to be conflating awareness
of society with social awareness, and social belonging. They are all different
categories (Table 4.2).

Table 4.2 Social presence as it affects 'being there'

Factors in 'being there'	Awareness of self	Awareness of others
Self presence	The degree my presence affects others	The degree others presence affects me
Social awareness	How much I notice society affecting me	How much I notice people affecting each other
Social identity	How much I identify with society	How much others think I am part of society

4.4 Hermeneutic Richness, Cultural Agency

Being able to observe a distinct Cultural Presence does not necessarily indicate a great amount of cultural learning has taken place. In order to evaluate the effectiveness of cultural learning there needs to be a measure of the cultural 'immersivity' of a virtual heritage environment. For want of a better term, I advance the term *Hermeneutic Richness*: The depth and vividness of a medium that allows for interpretation of different cultural and social perspectives as judged from an emic or etic viewpoint.

Hermeneutic richness does not mean photo-realism, or Social Presence. If Cultural Presence is a measure of how deeply a cultural force is perceived to imprint or ingrain itself on its surroundings; hermeneutic richness may be the depth of affordance that a virtual environment gives to the interpretation of a natively residing culture in that virtual environment.

Hermeneutic richness may allow awareness of Cultural Presence, or awareness of one's own ability to express oneself symbolically to oneself or to others in the virtual environment. In other words, it is the range and intensity of overlaying inter- pretations afforded to a visitor through a virtual environment which either

1. Allowed a culture to express itself symbolically through its modification and augmentation of the local environment and artifacts, or
2. Allowed one or more individuals to express or reveal (to others or to themselves) their personal identity, values, and expectations.

Cultural presence can only happen with version (1), if we perceive a cultural framework when afforded a virtual environment with hermeneutic richness. Otherwise, we perceive social agency, as in an auteur, the sense of another person expressing themselves and their relation to their world through their symbolic inter- actions in the environment, but we do not perceive Cultural Presence.

For example, one could test the richness of Cultural Presence in a digital place by placing a highly sophisticated and fast-learning artificial intelli- gence (AI.1) in a digital environment. The length of time AI.1 can enjoy exploring the world gives an indication of the sensory richness of the place. More importantly, the length of time it can learn from interaction in the digital environment without being bored gives one an idea of the richness of the inter- active experience.

However, there is no social agency; at no time does the artificial intelligence develop an idea of an 'other' – of a foreign social agent. This lack of social agency may be resolved by creating a different type of artificial intelligence (AI.2) and placing it in the same virtual environment, which results in social encounters between AI.1 and AI.2.

Yet only if AI.1 and AI.2 develop a common understanding (hopes, dreams, and fears) of the world, and they manage to interpret and share that understanding via artifacts, can we say that there is an emergent cultural agency and Cultural Presence. Cultural Presence exists via artifact-mediated communication between social agents (the creator and the recipient), even when the creator is not there. The ability of an artifact to convey a sense of that creator's agency is a reflection of its hermeneutic richness (akin to the archaeological notion of the 'trace'). The perceived sense of that creator's agency through an artifact is itself cultural agency. For an artifact is itself a cipher, a mark of cultural agency.

This hermeneutic richness is passive if AI.1 can observe and understand it. It only becomes activated if AI.1's survival becomes directed by it. In an online community, active hermeneutic richness may be a possibility and some degree of perceived social agency is a necessity. However, in a historic situation we are dealing with what was communally shared, not with what is currently shared and participated in. Completely free user-based interaction contaminates historic authenticity. It may also damage the hermeneutic richness that suggests past cultural frameworks, which is necessary for a sense of Cultural Presence. In order to evoke cultural learning of a historic nature, this passive hermeneutic richness is the elusive and intangible quality one should aspire towards.

4.5   Culture in Virtual Worlds

Agnew (1999, p. 90) once declared that:

> ...All people live in cultural worlds that are made and re-made through their everyday activities.

A cultural place via cultural characteristics identifies its inhabitants. We can digitally recreate a built form, but how do we recreate a web or system of behavior? The only behavior system online is via forums and chat rooms, and apart from dialogue, interaction is very limited (Schroeder 2002). One might ask if 3D chat rooms add any significant filters or cues to a system of behavior (Johnson 1997).

There has been little online reconstruction of cultural heritage of traditions. We have data, multimedia applications and three-dimensional models, but no cultural 'place' in terms of identifiers as to how to behave in another culture. To gain a full sense of Cultural Presence and hermeneutic richness we need to experience culture itself as a process rather than as a product.

4.6   Useful Cultural Presence

Why do we need to worry about Cultural Presence? Addressing the issue of Cultural Presence is to determine what makes the experiencing of a virtual environment meaningful, and, by extension, more engaging. Virtual reality research has been concerned with the usability offered rather than usefulness. Yet games, arguably the most successful virtual environments, also add tasks, goals, user-personification and social status for successful task performance but they do not aim for usability, they aim for provocation, stimulation and challenge. This is exemplified in the following passage by Nielsen (1998):

> Finally, **entertainment applications** and some educational interfaces can benefit from the fun and engaging nature of 3D, as evidenced by countless shoot-them-up games. Note that 3D works for games because the user does not want to accomplish any goals beyond being entertained. It would be trivial to design a better interface than *DOOM* if the goal was to kill the bad guys as quickly as possible: give me a 2D map of the area with icons for enemy troops and let me drop bombs on them by clicking the icons. Presto: *game over* in a few seconds and the good guys win every time. That's the design you want if you are the Pentagon, but it makes for a boring game. (His emphasis).

In order for virtual technology to gain widespread acceptance, we also need to evaluate the usefulness of virtual environments. For cultural environments, that means replicating reproducing or evoking cultural responses. For example, Riva et al. (2002), suggested that reality is not the only component of experiencing the real world, and therefore non-real experiences should be included in virtual environments. They suggest Cultural Presence involves a "cultural framework" and "the possibility of negotiation" (Riva et al. 2002, p. 307). For them this must include recognition that the experience is mediated by digital technology, that it recognizes the social context, and that it allows for ambiguity.

Virtual communities thus require a stage for social events, social beings, and props that can be modified shared and created to express these social interactions and beliefs. This also appears to be the view of Kalay and Marx (2003). A virtual environment with socially active Cultural Presence is a stage for presenting ambiguous social roles and allusive cues (symbols) that allow participants to identify both themselves and each other via communication and cooperation. Hence, while a virtual environment can have a sense of Social Presence, to have a dynamic sense of Cultural Presence, we need to have a sharable way of expressing socially understandable beliefs and behavior (active Cultural Presence).

For Weckström (2004, p. 21), in order to achieve 'worldliness', a virtual environment must also allow for various ways of doing things:

> The worldliness of "the Roman world" is in the multitude of different characters involved in making it a world. For this Roman world to be rendered virtually, it should offer the user the possibility to choose from a multitude of things to do, and lives to lead.

Weckström seems to be arguing both that a world should be specific, and it should allow you to do different things in different ways. He may mean that 'worldliness' consists of three components:

- The virtual environment offers at least one thematic cultural way of looking at things (for example, being a Roman).
- There is more than one way of interacting with the world (you can invade countries, build roads, or deliver speeches to the senate).
- The way of interacting with the virtual environment depends on your selection of a certain social role (although you can select different actions this depends on whether you are a Roman centurion, engineer, or senator).

His idea of 'worldliness' may also mean that there should actually be at least two thematic cultural ways available in the world, i.e. a Roman way, and a Barbarian way. In other words, the social and cultural framework is defined not just by how it allows people to communicate, but also by the existence of a distinguishing framework.

However, while some writers on virtual place, such as Kalay and Marx (2003), argue that cultural immersion requires the perceived presence of other real social beings, we do not have contextually based evaluation data on how embedded and culturally constrained visitors to a virtual heritage site need to be. For example, if we use our own language to communicate we will not be fully embedded in the recreated culture. Other visitors will almost certainly distract from the contextually situated embedded and embodied cultural experience.

There is however, another level of Cultural Presence. If the virtual environment contains a collection of artifacts that can be observed, interpreted, or understood as a coherent materialization by intelligent beings of a shared social system, this may be considered passive Cultural Presence. We can see culture, but we either cannot participate in it or with it due to a lack of culturally constrained creative understanding, or because the originators have long since passed away. This view is reflected in the writing of Weckström (2004, p. 26):

> Culture arises over time because people put their perception of their culture into everything they say or make. This means that outsiders can sense the culture of a place even when there are only objects present, but no people. This is usually done in archaeology where researchers try to interpret the symbolic meaning of objects that are left behind from ancient cultures.

There may also be more than one group of originators. A virtual environment can be a palimpsest ("products of action"), where past social interactions are layered echoed and carved into the fabric of the environment. In other words, a virtual heritage environment that allows us to breathe in the past. The premise that visitors require other real people in the virtual environment in order to feel Cultural Presence is thus unsubstantiated and highly problematic. Cultural Presence, albeit in a weakened form, is possible in the absence of Social Presence.

In academic literature, one can find use of the term 'aura' in a way that suggests a definition of Cultural Presence. For example, MacIntyre et al(2004, p. 1) defined aura as a description of "...the cultural and personal significance that a place (or object) holds for an individual." However, Cultural Presence as it has been used here is a more specialized notion than that of 'aura'; Cultural Presence creates the feeling that a place or object also contains significance for a society.

4.7   Summary of Cultural Presence Theory

People intending to travel to a heritage site may have different requirements to people just exploring a virtual world. People may want to use virtual technology in different ways; to use the information as a travel guide, to imagine explore or understand the past, or to meet and socially participate with other people. Virtual environments that would be helped by a sense of Cultural Presence could be virtual communities, virtual travel and tourism sites, or virtual heritage sites.

Experiencing Cultural Presence is an important issue not just for virtual heritage environments, but also in varying ways for virtual travel and tourism sites, and for virtual communities. Merely experiencing Social Presence is ephemeral and fleeting, and does not layer the environment with a felt 'history'. Culture is more the deliberate material embodiment of social values; it has a sense of permanence that attempts to outlive its immediate originators. Either Cultural Presence requires the sense of layered interaction history of culturally constrained agents, or it requires full social interaction with other social agents via interactive media. Thus we need to distinguish between shared Social Presence and Cultural Presence (Table 4.3).

If we allowed participants to appear in avatar form as typical tourists, and to chat about whatever they liked in an online world, this Social Presence of like-minded others may destroy the cultural immersion necessary to understand the virtual environment from a historical and locally constrained perspective. If we instead give them contextually appropriate goals rather than let them wander around at will (i.e. as travelers or inhabitants rather than as tourists), and provide contextual constraints and affordances (just as some games do); this may actually increase their enjoyment, and increase their understanding.

Whether Cultural Presence is transmitted via reading a palimpsest or by participating on a social stage, one must keep in mind it can be perceived from the outside (etic Cultural Presence), or lived from the inside (emic Cultural Presence). Interaction is crucial in the creation of culture, and, by extension, in the understanding of culture. Where our environment refers to a long extinct civilization, such a bridging is perhaps impossible, unless we somehow can bring the ghosts of the culture back to life. In other words, a feeling of strong Cultural Presence requires being physically *embodied* (we have a body that affects and is affected by other objects and forces), socially *embedded* (there exists the presence of others to whom we feel socially bound) and culturally *inscribed* in the world (our actions leave a lasting and meaningful impression on the world).

Via advances in virtual simulation technology, we are now able to create online interactive worlds that also communicate a perceptual sense of light, space and time, the evanescent, diaphanous, inter-spatial and eroded features of architecture.

Table 4.3 Types of virtual presence

Shared Social Presence	Dominant and shared cultural perspective	Passive other: Cultural Presence	Active-other-Cultural Presence
We notice other people in the environment	We turn on the television, write a letter, say hello to the next-door neighbor, without really noticing what we are doing or that we are acting and behaving in a certain way	Passive: we develop a sense of a long ago and distinctly 'alien' culture once inhabiting the site that we are visiting. There are 'traces' of past inhabitation	Active – we feel surrounded by a people and their cultural perspective that is very different to our own. The place is 'alive' and inhabited

If they had appropriate interactive tools at their disposal, virtual travelers will not just feel far more 'embodied' but also culturally immersed and socially 'embedded'. Then they will be able to gain a far greater idea of the 'horizon' of the original inhabitants. The next chapter discusses how studying the features, genres and learning style of computer games may help a visitor to a virtual heritage environment perceive contextual embodiment and a feeling of Cultural Presence, as well as socially embed them into such a shared 'horizon' of cultural understanding.

References

Agnew, J. (1999). Place and politics in Post-War Italy. In K. Anderson & F. Gale (Eds.), *Cultural Geographies* (pp. 71–93). South Melbourne: Addison Wesley.

Anderson, M.L. (1997). Introduction. In K. Jones-Garmil (Ed.), *The Wired Museum* (pp. 11–34). Washington DC: American Association of Museums.

Boskovic, A. (1997). Virtual Places: Imagined Boundaries and Hyperreality in Southeastern Europe [Electronic Version]. *Ctheory.net*, article A054. Retrieved from http://www.ctheory.net/text_file.asp?pick=97

Bourdieu, P. (1984). *Distinction: a Social Critique of the Judgement of Taste* (R. Nice, Trans.). London: Routledge & Kegan Paul.

Bryant, D. (2000, 2006). The Uncanny Valley, Why are monster-movie zombies so horrifying and talking animals so fascinating? Retrieved 28 February 2010, from http://www.arclight.net/~pdb/glimpses/valley.html

Champion, E. (2002, October). *Cultural Engagement in Virtual Heritage Environments with Inbuilt Interactive Evaluation Mechanisms.* Paper presented at the Fifth Annual International Workshop PRESENCE 2002, Porto Portugal.

Crang, M. (1998). *Cultural Geography.* London; New York: Routledge.

Eiteljorg, H. (1998, Fall). Photorealistic Visualizations May Be Too Good. *CSA Newsletter, XI (2)* Retrieved 12 February, 2010, from www.csanet.org/newsletter/fall98/nlf9804.html

Ferko, A., Grabner, M., Schwann, G., Sormann, M., & Schindler, K. (2003, February 3–7, 2003). *Navigation Functionality for Virtual Archaeology.* Paper presented at the WSCG: POSTERS Plzen, Czech Republic.

Gadamer, H.-G. (1976). *Philosophical Hermeneutics.* Berkeley, CA: University of California Press.

Greeff, M., & Lalioti, V. (2001). *Interactive Cultural Experiences Using Virtual Identities.* Paper presented at iCHIM2001, Politecnico di Milano, Italy.

Heeter, C. (1992). Being there: the subjective experience of presence. *Presence: Teleoperators and Virtual Environments, Fall, 1*(2), 262–271.

Hoffman, H.G. (2004). Virtual Reality Therapy. *Scientific American, August,* 58–65.

Hoorn, J.F., Konijn, E.A., & Van der Veer, G.C. (2003). Virtual reality: Do not augment realism, augment relevance [Electronic Version]. *Upgrade - Human-Computer Interaction: Overcoming Barriers, The European Online Magazine for the IT Professional, 4,* 18–26. Retrieved 30 April 2010 from http://www.upgrade-cepis.org/issues/2003/1/upgrade-vIV-1-low-res.pdf

ICOMOS. (1988). Australia ICOMOS Guidelines to the Burra charter [Electronic Version]. *Section 2.1.* Retrieved 30 April 2010 from http://www.icomos.org/australia/burrasig.html

Jacobson, L. (2000, 14 August 2000). A Virtual Class Act Technology Aims to Help Hyperactive Students. *Special to the Washington Post.* Retrieved 28 February 2010, from http://www.washingtonpost.com/ac2/wp-dyn?pagename=article&node=&contentId=A21148-2000Aug13&notFound=true

Jenks, C. (1993). *Culture: Key Ideas.* London: Routledge.

Johnson, S. (1997). *Interface Culture: How New Technology Transforms the Way We think and communicate*. San Francisco, CA: HarperEdge.

Kalay, Y., & Marx, J. (2003). *Changing the Metaphor: Cyberspace as a Place*. Paper presented at the Digital Design – Research and Practice, 10th International Conference on Computer Aided Architectural Design Futures.

Kensek, K., Swartz, D.L., & Cipolla, N. (2002). *Fantastic Reconstructions or Reconstructions of the Fantastic? Tracking and Presenting Ambiguity, Alternatives, and Documentation in Virtual Worlds*. Paper presented at the ACADIA 2002 Conference: Thresholds between Physical and Virtual Pomona, CA.

Kroeber, A., & Kluckhohn, C. (1952). *Culture: A Critical Review of Concepts and Definitions*. New York: Vintage Books.

Laurel, B., Strickland, R., Tow, R. (1994). Placeholder: Landscape and Narrative in Virtual Environments. *ACM Computer Graphics Quarterly, 28*(2).

MacIntyre, B., Bolter, J.D., & Gandy, M. (2004). *Presence and the Aura of Meaningful Places*. Paper presented at the PRESENCE 2004 Conference: 7th Annual International Workshop on Presence, Valencia, Spain.

Mori, M. (1981). *The Buddha in the Robot* (C. S. Terry, Trans.). Tokyo: Kosei Pub. Co.

Mosaker, L. (2001). Visualising Historical Knowledge Using Virtual Reality Technology. *Digital Creativity, 12*(1), 15–25.

Nielsen, J. (1998). 2D is Better than 3D. *Jakob Nielsen's Alertbox*. Retrieved 12 February, 2010, from http://www.useit.com/alertbox/981115.html

Riegler, A. (2001). Virtual Science: Virtuality and Knowledge Acquisition in Science and Cognition. In A. Riegler (Ed.), *Virtual Reality: Cognitive Foundations, Technological Issues and Philosophical Implications*. Frankfurt am Main: Peter Lang.

Riva, G., Castelnuovo, G., Gaggioli, A., & Mantovani, F. (2002, October). *Towards a cultural approach to presence*. Paper presented at the PRESENCE 2002 conference: Fifth Annual International Workshop on Presence, Porto Portugal.

Riva, G., Waterworth, J.A., & Waterworth, E.L. (2004). The layers of presence: a bio-cultural approach to understanding presence in natural and mediated environments. *Cyberpsychology and Behavior, 7*(4), 402–416.

Robillard, G., Bouchard, S., Fournier, T., & Renaud, P. (2003). Anxiety and presence during VR immersion: a comparative study of the reactions of phobic and non-phobic participants in therapeutic virtual environments derived from computer games. *CyberPsychology and Behavior, 65*(5), 467–476.

Rykwert, J. (1996). Preface. In C. Melhuish (Ed.), *Architecture and Anthropology (Architectural Design)* (pp. 6). London: Academy Press.

Schiffer, M.B., & Miller, A.R. (1999). *The Material Life of Human Beings: Artifacts, Behaviour and Communication*. London: Routledge.

Schroeder, R. (1996). *Possible Worlds: The Social Dynamic of Virtual Reality Technology*. Boulder, CO: Westview Press.

Schroeder, R. (2002). *Copresence and interaction in virtual environments: an overview of the range of issues*. Paper presented at the Presence 2002 Conference: Fifth Annual International Workshop on Presence, Porto, Portugal.

Slater, M. (1999). Measuring presence: a response to the Witmer and Singer presence question- naire. *Presence: Teleoperators and Virtual Environments, 8*(5), 560–565.

Swinth, K., & Blascovich, J. (2002). *Perceiving and responding to others: human-human and human-computer social interaction in collaborative virtual environments*. Paper presented at the PRESENCE 2002 Conference: Fifth Annual International Workshop on Presence, Porto, Portugal.

The Free Online Dictionary, T.F.O. (n.d.). Virtual. *Dictionary.com* Retrieved 27 February 2010, from http://dictionary.reference.com/browse/Virtual

Thompson, C. (2004, 9 June 2004). The Undead Zone: Why realistic graphics make humans look creepy. *slate*. Retrieved 28 February, 2010, from http://slate.msn.com/id/2102086/

Tilley, C.Y. (1999). *Metaphor and Material Culture*. Oxford, UK; Malden, MA: Blackwell Publishers.

Tuan, Y.-F. (1992). Place and Culture: Analeptic for Individuality and the World's Indifference. In W. Franklin & M. Steiner (Eds.), *Mapping American Culture* (pp. 27–50). Iowa City, IA: University of Iowa Press.

UNESCO. (2005). Intangible Heritage. Retrieved 25 October, 2005, from http://www.unesco.org/culture/heritage/intangible/html_eng/index_en.shtml

Weckström, N. (2004). *Finding 'reality' in virtual environments*. Unpublished Masters, Arcada Polytechnic, Helsingfors/Esbo.

Chapter 5
Game–Style Interaction

5.1 Defining Games

A considerable amount of literature has argued that interactive engagement in a computer medium is best demonstrated by games (Aldrich 2004; Champion 2003; Laird 2001; Schroeder 2002). With this in mind, this chapter suggests certain techniques that virtual environments (especially cultural heritage ones) can learn from game design.

In order to understand what computer game design and interaction could offer to people who build virtual environments for tourism, heritage, and archaeology, we need to define the features and criteria of successful games and game–style interactivity.

One of the more concise reviews of game definitions is a paper by Juul (2001a). He offered the following definition of games, which is really more the listing of six criteria for a game to be a game.

> A game is a rule-based formal system with a variable and quantifiable outcome, where different outcomes are assigned different values, the player exerts effort in order to influence the outcome, the player feels attached to the outcome, and the consequences of the activity are optional and negotiable.

Juul believes these criteria are necessary and sufficient, and that only games have all six criteria. The criteria may well be sufficient, for they are certainly more comprehensive than earlier definitions, but it is arguable whether they are all necessary.

For this thesis, such a comprehensive definition is not necessary. This research is more interested in what it is about game environments that make them engaging, which is not the same as attempting to uncover the uniquely identifying features of games that no other activity, product, or process shares with them.

Part of the attraction of games is certainly due to their interactive and engaging nature, for they are interactive and entertaining sources of play as learning (Aldrich 2004, p. 240). Perhaps a more helpful definition for designers is the definition by Salen and Zimmerman (2003, p. 572), as it attempts to explain what

E. Champion, *Playing with the Past*, Human-Computer Interaction Series, DOI 10.1007/978-1-84996-501-9_5, © Springer-Verlag London Limited 2011

makes games entertaining. In their large tome on game design, they wrote the following often-quoted definition of a game:

> A game is a system in which players engage in an artificial conflict, defined by rules, that results in a quantifiable outcome.

While Salen and Zimmerman talk of a magic circle that separates (but not always clearly) the boundaries of a game from the real world, they seem to focus rather quickly on conflict (rather than the more generic terms of challenge and competition). They also discount games that may never have a final outcome (such as cricket), and do not mention the importance of strategy.

Here is a working definition of a computer game (different to Salen and Zimmerman); a game is a challenge that offers up the possibility of temporary or permanent tactical resolution without harmful outcomes to the real world situation of the participant.

5.2 Defining Game–Style Interaction

Mention of task or strategy is important; games typically challenge and develop procedural learning through the selection of various options with varying consequences. One common feature of successful games is that they may offer different strategies of accomplishing a goal: interaction often involves hybrid-learning practices.

In other words, clues, goals, and methods are often learnt, developed, or found via conversation, observation, by trial and error, or even a blend of some or all of these ways of learning. Therefore, games offer different ways of interacting in order to learn. However, since computer games are generally goal-based, they tend to emphasize procedural rather than prescriptive knowledge. That is, they provide clues and methods for learning how to solve a task rather than teach what is right or wrong, or what are true or false.

Computer games are hence orientated towards trial and error interaction. So when I talk of game–style interaction it could be understood to mean interaction geared towards solving a task (procedural interaction), or it could be understood to mean game genre interaction (the interaction you typically find in certain types or genres of games).

Another option could be to define game–style interaction as meaning the types of interface technology (such as joysticks, and consoles) that one finds in games. Console gamers have access to task-specific devices and interfaces not common to desktop personal computers.

However, these interface devices are either highly dedicated to a certain type of game, or different in degree rather than in kind to the standard PC interface. They may well have improved task-efficiency or ergonomics, but for many games, one can still use a keyboard and mouse. Hence, the success of games cannot be directly related to the use of dedicated gaming interface devices.

Since I am attempting to increase engagement in virtual environments in order to increase cultural learning, I intend using the phrase game–style interaction to describe interaction that uses the interactive elements commonly found in games.

5.2.1   Useful Features of Games

Games have context (user-based tasks), navigation reminders, inventories, records of interaction history (i.e. damage to surroundings), and social agency. Engaging virtual environments also require interaction geared towards a task, a goal. As noted by Amory (2003, p. 714):

> The development of a number of models to explore the relationships between educational theory and game design provides developers with a conceptual and practical framework that can support the development process. Also, well-crafted games appear to require appropriate puzzles integrated into strong story lines where graphics, sounds and technology are used to create an entertainment medium that could also champion learning objectives.

As in games, virtual environment users may prefer personalization. Further, just as the most popular games (excluding Tetris), require representations of opponents (social agents), so too do virtual environments. Games provide competition, and therefore challenge, a feature typically lacking in virtual environments.

Games are a familiar medium to users, and help train us how to learn and how to use props as cultural tools.

> Making content appealing to the end-learner may be the lesson that the e-learning industry needs to learn most of all… (Aldrich 2004, p. 7).

As users become engaged in the tasks, it is easier to observe them without damaging their level of engagement, especially as games traditionally have built-in evaluation mechanisms. Furthermore, games cater to learning curves of new users by advancing in complexity over time, and can be personalized.

The technological limitations of Internet-available virtual environments do not seem to have hindered the popularity of complex games. The most popular form of virtual environments is arguably the computer game. Nearly 75% of people under the age of 30 have played a computer game. Entertainment software is the fastest growing of all types of entertainment, outselling films, according to a paper by Bryce and Rutter (2001):

> It is estimated that almost three quarters of people under thirty have played a computer game, and the leisure software industry is estimated to be worth more than $6 billion in Europe making it a more lucrative market than [in] either the USA or Japan. In the USA, sales of games now outnumber sales of books and in the UK games are worth 80% more than video rentals. In the UK – which makes up more than half the European market – gaming software is not just significant in terms of consumption, as it also has an impressive development an export profile massively outperforming film and television.

Computer games are at least partially responsible for the giant leaps forward in computer graphics technology and related hardware, such as CD-ROMs (refer Laird 2001; Laird and van Lent 2000; Weckström 2004). Laird (2001, p. 70) compared the power of these game engines:

> … The original Playstation, released in 1995, renders 300,000 polygons per second, while Sega's Dreamcast, released in 1999, renders 3 million polygons per second. The Playstation 2 sets the current standard, rendering 66 million polygons per second, while projections

indicate the Xbox will render more than 100 million polygons per second. Thus, the images on today's $300 game consoles rival or surpass those available on the previous decade's $50,000 computers.

In terms of computing power, current game consoles also rival supercomputers of a decade or more, and they are used for AI research. Laird (2001, p. 70) argued:

> The impact of these improvements is evident in the complexity and realism of the environments underlying today's games, from detailed indoor rooms and corridors to vast outdoor landscapes. These games populate the environments with both human and computer controlled characters, making them a rich laboratory for artificial intelligence research into developing intelligent and social autonomous agents.
>
> Indeed, computer games offer a fitting subject for serious academic study, undergraduate education, and graduate student and faculty research...

Via computer games, we can further explore cognitive issues of memory recall, engagement, and the notion of 'flow'. For example, according to Bryce and Rutter (2001):

> Psychological presence in public gaming arenas is investigated by the use of the optimal experience or the flow framework (e.g., Csikszentmihalyi 1975)....
>
> **These aspects of the flow experience are intense involvement, clarity of goals and feedback, lack of self-consciousness, a balance between the challenge of the situation and the skills required to meet them, and a feeling of total control over the activity**. Preliminary research suggests that the psychological experience of gaming is consistent with the dimensions of the flow experience as outlined by Csikszentmihalyi. [Bold from original text].

Games are already being used in academic research, especially for Artificial Intelligence research. Laird and van Lent (2000, p. 1177) offered the following reasons:

> One attractive aspect of working in computer games is that there is no need to attempt a "Manhattan Project" approach with a monolithic project that attempts to create human-level intelligence all at once. Computer games provide an environment for continual, steady advancement and a series of increasingly difficult challenges. Just as computers have inexorably gotten faster, computer game environments are becoming more and more realistic worlds, requiring more and more complex behavior from their characters. Now is the time for AI researchers to jump in and ride the wave of computer games.

Game mods are modifications of games or creations of new game levels using the level editor that is downloadable or integral to many commercial games. Using this native tool set hobbyists can create professional-looking game levels either from scratch or using in-game assets. Importing of three-dimensional models, animations, and textures is also often possible. In recent years academics have also begun to create game mods; but for environmental visualization rather than for interactive entertainment. For example, Germanchis et al. (2007) of RMIT University, Melbourne created an interactive real-time visualization of the port of Queenscliff (in Melbourne Australia), using the editor available with the commercial game Far Cry (Fig. 5.1). Their purpose was to explore game engines as a visualization tool for multimedia cartography, not to use the game level for amusement.

Fig. 5.1 Virtual Queenscliff (Courtesy of William Cartwright and Tim Germanchis)

Further, games are an important if not essential part of human culture and cultural learning. If a virtual heritage environment is to aim for at least some degree of overview of a distinct cultural perspective, it must deal with at least the representation of how that culture uses the idea of play, and the idea of games. For example, W. Holmes wrote the following in 1907, quoted by Juul (2001b):

> The popular notion that games....are trivial in nature and of no particular significance as a subject of research soon gave way, under the well-conducted studies of Mr. Culin, to an adequate appreciation of their importance as an integral part of human culture.

5.2.2   Engaging Features of Games

Table 5.1 classifies the critical engaging features of games. Please note that it is difficult to separate game genres in terms of whether they involve the participant being socially embedded or physically embodied (for another taxonomy refer Crawford 1982; Salen and Zimmerman 2003).

There are two other features worthy of mention. The first is found in virtually all games. Rewards may be internal (game feedback), or external (awards and status conferred by other members of the gaming community). The second feature is found in virtually no games. Unlike games and game situations in real life, where playing may be changed due to in-game events, or referential (refers to past players), the continually interpretive phenomenon of cultural creation and transmission is typically faked or *baked on* in computer games. For example, instructions are often

Table 5.1 Engaging features of games

Features in game genres	Games test	Elements	Game feedback
Physically embodied: Combat games (usually involving aiming and moving), racing games (all usually have an element of social agency)	Hand eye co-ordination	An avatar to represent the player, dynamic environmental elements that are hostile or beneficial, metaphorical mortality or health	Collision causes sound, surface erosion of deformation, loss of points, end of game or level of game
Socially embedded: Racing games (against others–also involves some form of embodiment). Strategy games, Civilization-type world building games, interrogation or text-guessing games, riddles	Memory (spatial, procedural, and navigational)	Set roles procedures or levels of ability to complete tasks. Other players or scripted agents	Point system or change of status or power or equipment levels inside a game or (rarely) impostors are uncovered. There may be automated voiceovers on success or failure at completing tasks. Success may be compared to the success of other players
Challenging (hard fun): All game genres	Pattern matching, and puzzle solving. Predictive thinking and bluffing	Tasks, affordances, and constraints. Random events or options between players to vary strategies	Increasing complexity, number of puzzles, or situations to overcome Sometimes winning guesses or strategies increase equipment or status, sometimes more of the environment is uncovered. Can be time-based

delivered via a narrator or book during the introduction, they cannot be added to, layered, or otherwise modified.

However, what the table does indicate is that challenge and rewards are integral to most games but that the notion of hermeneutic inscription and interpretation is 'faked'. There is no hermeneutic richness either in the sense of being afforded rich interpretations of cultural frameworks to unravel and decipher, and is there the sense that one can express oneself symbolically through the creative modification and personalization of artifacts.

The mixture of affordances and constraints and different levels is designed to be challenging in the sense of 'hard fun'. It has to be difficult enough to be intriguing, but not too difficult to make the user give up in frustration. In addition, there are many rewards, new weapons, changes in levels, and revealed secrets. However, the game can hardly be considered hermeneutic, for the only way the worlds can be layered with anything approaching personalization and communication is through destruction and debris caused by the user's battles and vandalism.

5.3 Case Study: Heretic II

Games are activity-based rather than hermeneutic environments. To give an example of the limited hermeneutic capacity of games, let us examine the computer adventure game Heretic II.

Heretic II may appear analogous in form to virtual heritage environments, only it has added tasks, goals, and interactive features. In the game, the returning hero finds his town deserted except for the diseased and crazed survivors. His goal is to find the source of the virus and hence its cure.

Unfortunately, battling to escape the town he himself is infected. Time is now running out, and every so often, he too faints (often at the worst possible moment). He must explore various palaces and towns belonging to different races, identify doors, levers and portals in order to go further, gain more powerful weapons and other artifacts, find power-ups (metaphorical devices placed in the environment that boost the avatar's health and combat ability), and survive being attacked by various creatures with various diverse weapons and abilities.

The terrain can be outdoors or urban, and he must avoid bursts of flames, outdoor spaces (vultures will swoop on him), remaining in one place for too long (creatures will start tracking him), swamp, lava, and hostile creatures. Using Fencott's (1999) terminology, Heretic II contains attractors (phototropia via glints of light, which signify open spaces, excitement and freedom), repellers (a variety of alien creatures that guard 'power ups' and lurk near narrow passageways), and connectors (such as ropes and water portals and crates you can use as steps).

The sureties are the creatures that attack, power ups, water, land, lava. The many different types of combatants have special skills, weaknesses and proclivities. If left alone, they may also fight amongst themselves. Constraints include starting the game with only two weapons, the player's avatar faints at inopportune moments, every so often users have to follow certain paths, and so on. Affordances are the ropes, weapons, power-ups, levers tools buttons ledges rubble (closed doors) and sliding doors.

In our terms, Heretic II has dynamically attenuating physiological zones that record interaction history (via corpses and damaged walls that reveal he has passed this way before). Heretic II is based on artifact-related tasks to help direct the main character to the overall goal, and a mostly static two-dimensional map (though it indicates the player's position on the map). It also has avatar dialogue (though not in the interactive single player role).

Despite the rich detailing of environments, agents, and artifacts, Heretic II does not have a rich sense of cultural immersion for the same reasons as other main-stream computer games. The only goal is collecting artifacts for the vanquishing of others, social interaction is limited to violence, time spent on reflection is punished, and we do not develop any feeling for the perspectives of the local inhabitants as their actions are purely for fight or flight.

In short, the computer game gives us examples of interactive game elements, dynamic places, agency, artifacts, and an intertwined system of goals strategies and tasks. The user is to some extent embodied as a mortal object, and has been given a social identity through the introduction and via the pre-rendered cut-scenes.

5.4   Dynamic Places

To evaluate a virtual terrain with and without dynamic interactive features is an essential step in evaluation of place as opposed to cyberspace. With this in mind, one could create dynamic places (GIS-enabled database that stores and records localized events and occurrences); along with visual and audio cues indicating changes in climate flora fauna and terrain. In addition, parts of the environment could be harmful to the avatar's metaphorical health.

An environment could host a gradient of inhabitability, ranging from shelter and familiar territory, to a hostile world depending on task direction, artifacts carried and preservation of health points. The more aware and adeptly the user can navigate through the environment, the quicker their journey between tasks, and the less the health points that they will have lost.

During the night or during severe simulated climatic change (indicated by the sound of strong wind etc.), their health points may be drastically diminished and so they will be encouraged to look for shelter.

Creating dynamically changing environmental factors that have an effect on how people move through virtual environments could increase engagement and provide for experiences that are more memorable. Paths, changing light and obstacles may aid or impede navigation.

The dangers and opportunities of the environment could also be contextually related to the local cultural perspective and to the overall goal of the wayfinding. In tandem with metaphorical embodiment (i.e. a sense of mortality is symbolically represented), less skilful navigation could adversely affect metaphorical 'health points' (as borrowed from game design).

5.4.1 Dynamic Place Design: Unreal Palenque and Xibalba

An example of a dynamic place is a game level we created in Unreal Tournament, porting models from my earlier Palenque project (originally created in Adobe Atmosphere). When evaluating archaeology students and visualization experts in 2004, I had found that people typically move forward rather than walk around when navigating web-based virtual environments on a PC, so I wanted to see how peripheral projection may engage and encourage people to better explore their environment. I also required a faster and more powerful rendering engine, So in 2005 I organized a student project where my digital reconstruction of a Mayan city, Palenque, was ported to a game engine (Fig. 5.3).

Adobe Atmosphere was an online virtual world-type software program, and I used it to create the virtual environments and evaluate how different modes of interaction affected cultural understanding, but I will discuss the evaluation side as a case study in Chapter 7. Here I would just like to say that Adobe Atmosphere was slow and buggy and difficult to script navigational guides, add physics, or design reasonably fast games.

Unreal Tournament was not only much more powerful in creating vivid and detailed environments, it also featured ready-made interaction behaviors, 3D assets and game–style genres. The game engine allowed quick and easy use of current models (including avatars and flying birds), was significantly quicker, and could be used to project via several cameras at once (it has been used to run in a CAVE). Unfortunately the genres, assets and behaviors were typically to spawn (create) weapons, shoot people, and blow things up.

Over a mere 12 weeks, two of my students set about creating an engaging and dramatic retelling of the Mayan Creation myth, using my Palenque models, but also taking advantage of Unreal Tournament's more advanced features. In order to engage participants in the archaeological setting and acquaint them with the virtual environment the students devised two levels. One was Palenque (Fig. 5.2), with the recreated temple models and terrain. The other was Xibalba, the Mayan under-world, (similar to our notion of hell). Xibalba was modeled on the description in the Mayan book that recounts their Creation Myth, *The Popol Vuh*.

In order to explore the more dangerous (even volcanic) underworld, the player had to find a lightning stick by a magical tree, return to the ball court, and push the Mayan ball into the ceremonial hoop. If done correctly, the ball court would be rendered asunder, and the player would fall into the opening chasm, descending into Xibalba (Fig. 5.3).

To make the game more challenging, physical and immersive, we used a curved mirror and the CaveUT code developed by Jeffrey Jacobson, to project the environment *around* the player, onto a specially made black box, roughly 2.4 m^2 (not shown). The original idea was developed by Paul Bourke at the University of Western Australia, for economic projection in planetariums (Fig. 5.4). However, this idea also had immersive appeal for gaming. For very reasonable cost, one could project onto the front and sidewalls and the ceiling or floor just by projecting into the curved mirror (Fig. 5.5). Players stood up, and walked by stepping on an Arduino dance mat, and they navigated using a 3D joystick.

Fig. 5.2 Palenque in Unreal Tournament

Fig. 5.3 Unreal Tournament and Sensor Pads: artistic version of Xibalba

One interesting discovery of this project was the immersive aspect of projection that catered for peripheral vision. When people are surrounded by a large game space in three dimensions that is bigger than they are, and when they interact by

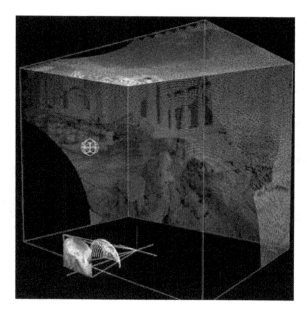

Fig. 5.4 Room projection using a curved mirror (Courtesy of Paul Bourke)

Fig. 5.5 Palenque prototype in Unreal Tournament projected via curved mirror

standing and moving (we used sensor pads so that they could move by physically raising and lowering their feet rather than using a mouse), the gameplay is enhanced. The scale of the place and the increased virtual relation to the actual physical embodiment of the visitor enhances the believability of the virtual characters, for the NPCs (Non-Playing Characters) develop a territorial spatial presence as they can now physically surround the player.

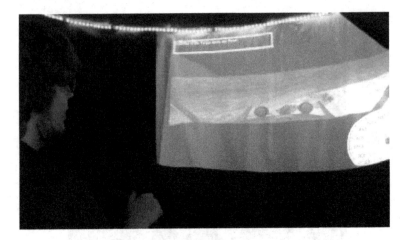

Fig. 5.6 Car racing inside a tent

5.4.2 Racing in a Tent: Spatial and Haptic Immersion

The next year, two other students developed interactive environments along with the physical interfaces, which created an even more engaging sense of spatial immersion and dynamic *placeness*. Firstly, they developed or modified interfaces to enhance the physical sense of immersion, including peripheral vision. A curved mirror created a larger and more wraparound display (Fig. 5.6). As will be briefly mentioned in Chapter 8, torque 3D had the capability for real-time terrain deformation, so it was possible in car racing games for the audience to change the car racing track before the player (driver) got to it.

The students modified a car racing demo built in the Torque engine and connected it to a digital massage chair placed beneath a salvaged truck seat. The player actually feels the terrain through a converted massage seat that is fed height-data of the terrain as the player drives over it (Fig. 5.7).

5.5 Constrained Tasks and Goals

Games are typically more than just virtual environments with dynamic places. A virtual environment could give people specific roles; allow them to choose roles, or allow them to move up or down the social ladder depending on how well they complete their socially defined tasks. Hence, the goal would be social progression. As Juul (2003) argued:

> The rules of a game add *meaning* and *enable actions* by setting up *differences* between potential moves and events.

Fig. 5.7 Massage chair

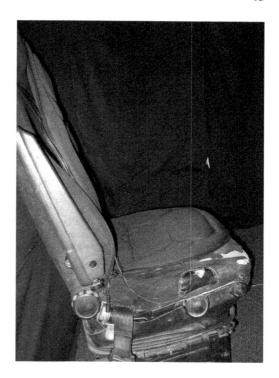

We have seen that games provide goals and tasks, but that these are typically violent in nature (especially towards the inhabitants). However, I suggest that there are at least three non-violent learning modes used in games that we could modify to help structure goals and tasks for virtual heritage environments. Three non-violent but possibly competitive interaction modes common to games are observing, exploring (trial and error), conversation (and trade). Sterelny (2003) wrote that modes of cultural learning are complex and usually hybrid but it may be helpful to sketch out a schematic of cultural learning through interaction (Table 5.2).

5.5.1 Interaction Modes in Palenque Using Adobe Atmosphere

In the following case study (Figs. 5.8 and 5.9), there are three different interaction modes. One mode is action based, and the participants had to push back slabs to find the hidden tomb (this was actually what happened in the discovery of the Tomb of Pakal under the Temple of Inscriptions). If they managed to push back the sarcophagus lid of Pakal when they reached the tomb, a portal appeared that took them to a reconstruction of Palenque's Ballcourt (the Mayan Ballcourt symbolized war, life and death, the growth of maize, and the victory of the Mayan ancestors over the Lords of the Underworld, Xibalba).

Table 5.2 Schematic of cultural learning

Interaction	Description
Observation	Inferred narrative: Through observing how agents or externs change in the environment, users may infer how to act or behave, or how the world is seen by the people who live there or by the designer of the world
	Exploring: The visitor can explore static or dynamic environments without having to navigate past obstructions or having to manipulate the environment or solve tasks. Typically, explorers learn in virtual environments by navigating through the environment, approaching objects, and observing what happens via pre-scripted triggered information or pre-recorded events
Trial and error (activity-based)	The aim is to investigate dynamic environments that involve risk or hindrance to the explorer. Typically, investigators learn by clicking on objects, or approaching objects, which may trigger information or pre-recorded events
	Reconfiguration: May include solving puzzles by clicking on certain objects or choosing certain combinations perhaps at certain times
	Detective work: Inspired to develop and test hunches in order to solve riddles
Conversation	Instruction: Guided instruction via avatars or embedded narratives
	Verbal pattern matching: one says or enters words for doors to open
	Conversation: One learns by talking to others (they are either real people represented by avatars or pre-scripted agents or AI controlled agents)
	Trading: Can be non-verbal but is still arguably a form of communication

The second mode was observation based only, and participants were asked to find artifacts located in the large and navigationally confusing Palace.

In the third mode, the three major temples of the Cross Group had scripted guides, representing a Mexican tour guide, King Pakal, and his son. Their movements and speech were proximity-based, and they got angry or fell over if participants ran into them. The goal was also to click and read information relating to the giant inscribed tablets in each of the Temples. At the end of the experiment people were asked to answer six questions for each interaction mode, to see if they had learnt and were able to extrapolate information from what they had seen.

Evaluations were conducted using a first year archaeology class of 43 students, and in the second stage, 24 more experienced participants who were either virtual environment designers or cultural historians with an interest in virtual heritage. In the third stage 10 IT-experienced people from Lonely Planet Publications (a travel publications company with a strong web-based presence), were tested. I also created four more imaginative and less authentic 'worlds' based on the cultural perspectives of the ancient Mayans in Palenque, Mexico. As part of the evaluation participants

If you hold down the shift key you can also fly to the top
MORE INFO
Early reconstruction work by Leopoldo Batres in the early 20th century.
He has unfortunately removed evidence of the true appearance of the pyramid, including its original height. It is now around 215 feet (65 m) high with five tiers.
Directly under the Pyramid of the Sun is a tunnel which leads to caves used for religious ceremonies.

original model for research purposes courtesy of Sociedad Planeta Vivo/Planeta Vivo Society
http://www.planetavivo.org

Fig. 5.8 Initial warm-up environment

Any time you want to see the INSTRUCTIONS-press your mouse in the 3D world and then press i on your keyboard.
Lord Pakal- your guide to the Hieroglyphic Stairs is waiting for you.
Chan-Bahlum your guide to the House A is waiting for you.
A Mexican guide will be your guide to the Oval Tablet. He is waiting for you.
PAKAL: Welcome to one of the most important artworks in Palenque.
PAKAL: Click on the stairs to find out more about them.

PAKAL: THAT HURT!!!

Fig. 5.9 A screenshot of the guide greeting the visitor at the Palace

The balcout symbolises this.
The carvings in Mayan temples also show this crack in the mountain

OK, you had enough time to answer!
Now it is time to end the adventure

You are standing on a caiman (a form of crocodile

The Mayans believe the earth grew out of a crack in the caiman's (or turtle's) back.
The balcout symbolises this.
The carvings in Mayan temples also show this crack in the mountain

Fig. 5.10 Fictional world setting using caiman and World-Tree

were also asked to rank the imaginative worlds against the archaeological worlds in terms of a range of 'presence' criteria.

In the Mayan 'Primal Mountain' World, fog was used in one world to convey a mythical setting and in the more archaeological environments glare was used at regular intervals to indicate where spiritually valuable artifacts were located (Fig. 5.10). They were asked to find the beginning of the world (the Mayan sacred Sky-Tree) and click on it for information. They were then asked to find any other people (there were two Mayan paddler gods paddling around the mountain). They were also asked if they noticed the mountain they were on was actually a giant crocodile (the Mayans believed the world was created from a crack in the back of a caiman or turtle). As an aside, not a single person said they had noticed unless it was pointed out to them or they had fallen off the mountain.

In the Mayan Village world (Fig. 5.11), a participant could select an avatar that was either one of four Western-style backpacking characters or an avatar in local Mayan dress. Photographs of real people available via the Lonely Planet Images database were mapped onto the face of the avatars. The Mayan avatars were also sized appropriately (less than 5 ft tall) and only by changing into that smaller avatar were participants able to explore the interior of the Mayan huts. The aim was to find the other participant by orientating their avatar via large Mayan carvings in the jungle and then find the village using the interface guides and the sound of music. If they walked straight into trees, their avatar slowed down and cried out in pain. Which objects they found and how quickly they found them was also automatically recorded. Participants were asked at the end the relative sizing of the avatars and the results were statistically compared to how well the participants answered other questions.

In the Mayan Cave world, when the avatar walks into the water, they automatically start swimming under water, blue fog appears and the sound of bubbling water

Fig. 5.11 Mayan Village

Fig. 5.12 Mayan Ballcourt world

drowns out the ambient Mayan music. If the participant does not keep pressing the forward arrow they slowly ascend back to the surface of the water. By finding, collecting and then dropping artifacts at a hidden shrine, a Mayan sky-snake appears and so does a portal that takes them back to the start.

In the Mayan Ballcourt world (Fig. 5.12), each participant turned into a Mayan ball player, and each was asked to try to get the rubber ball to touch the hoop. If they did so, thunder and lightning were triggered.

5.5.2 *Constrained Tasks in Journey to the West*

Another example of constrained tasks was our design of Journey to the West as a game level using the editor available in the inexpensive commercial game Neverwinter Nights. This design level was based upon a single chapter from the famous Chinese book, chapter 59, entailing the adventures of the four main characters, Monkey, Pigsy, Sandy and Monk Sanzang as they attempt to cross the Fiery Mountains on their journey west to recover Holy Scriptures for the Tang Emperor. On their way, they must convince the antagonist, Iron Fan Immortal (also known as Raksasi), to lend them her Plantain Fan in order to blow out the fires which block their passage west (Fig. 5.13). The game focused around the dealings of the main character; a being possessed of great physical and magical power, as he fights enemies and the elements to reach his goal. Players would recreate the adventures and deeds of Journey to the West (which had been translated from the original Chinese by one of the students), and in doing so, would learn the story as well.

Exploring the environment was required to find magical artifacts, monkey could transform into animal spirits, and the diary feature of Neverwinter Nights was used to unfold the story via journal entries that helped the player navigate through the game level. The end goal of the level was to advance the story to the next level. Loading screens for each level could also include relevant information such as the historical background (Fig. 5.14) or clues for navigation and level advancement.

There were some issues with the technology, Neverwinter Nights had some major bugs, contradictory or missing documentation, different versions and extensions conflicted with each other, and the game only ran on a PC with an extension pack.

Fig. 5.13 Journey to the West-Monkey encounters Raksasi (Iron Fan Immortal)

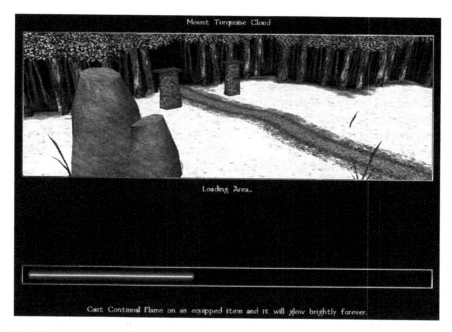

Fig. 5.14 Journey to the West Loading Screen

It also took a great deal of energy and effort to transform the Western medieval setting into a more appropriate Asian setting.

If we decided to recreate a similar Journey to the West adventure today, we would probably want to incorporate the many different cultural retellings of the story. We would also have to address the major issue: that the Chinese playtesters did not think the character was powerful enough (which creates several game balance issues), but that also their understanding of the original book was incorrect for they knew Journey to the West only through modern retellings, they had not read the original book. This would not be an essay task for how do you politely improve a foreign culture's popular but inaccurate understanding of their own literary classics?

5.6   Social Agency: Avatars Agents and Actors

Research indicates Social Presence is linked to a sense of interactivity. Wickens and Baker (1995, p. 515) suggested one of the five features of virtual environments was being 'ego-referenced', that is, from a user perspective rather than from a fixed-world perspective. Others have argued for virtual identities and Social Presence (Greeff and Lalioti 2001; Kelso et al. 1993; Schubert et al. 2000). Kelso et al. (1993, p. 2) described people as 'interactors' adding to the 'dramatic presence' of Social Presence and interactivity factors.

Introducing other users into a virtual environment only increases the feeling of presence when interaction with others is possible, there needs to be genuine interaction with these other actors (Regenbrecht and Schubert 2002; Schubert et al. 2000).

Here I should clarify a distinction between avatars, agents and actors. I will use actors as the generic term for users/participants in an interactive virtual environment, represented by three-dimensional characters ('avatars'). Agents are computer-scripted characters (sometimes called Non Playing Characters, or NPCs).

Many projects are now using agents (or bots) for interactive story telling in virtual environments (for example, http://www.eg.org/events/VAST2001/ or the conversational humanoid project, at the MIT Media Lab, http://gn.www.media.mit.edu/groups/gn/projects/humanoid/). Hence, computer-scripted agents could answer certain questions. They could also remember who passed by and what they did. They may have a limited ability to allow participants to leave messages for each other, which may aid Social Presence. Towell and Towell (1997) suggest that a sense of presence is evident even in 2D mediums, such as chat groups, because of the strong feeling of talking to other intelligent beings.

Tasks for actors could include, discovering secrets using artifacts and agent dialogue, collect information and or artifacts of interest. At higher levels of interactivity actors can leave messages via agents for future visitors.

Computer-scripted agents ('agents'), represented by avatars that users can talk to, gain information from, and that remember them, can give the user information on where artifacts are, and how where and when the artifacts can be used. Agents can give out tasks, increase realism, and help navigation. In addition, Behr et al. (2001) described an avatar that talks and moves, and acts as a guide, while visitors explore the virtual environment, but that is all it does (Mulholland and Collins 2002). Pape et al. (2001) also proposed creating a virtual guide for historic sites. Only none of these examples are very interactive or are used to evaluate user engagement. For example, not a single paper appears to have suggested using scripted agents as evaluation mechanisms for user engagement.

It is feasible that by using computer-scripted agents participants can gain a sense (to some degree) of Social Presence, awareness, and identity. The agents can also be used as navigational and task-related cues, and they can record conversation for evaluation of user engagement. For example, these agents could be capable of not only simple dialogue phrases that participants can engage with to find out information, the agents' memories of these conversations would allow us to evaluate the engagement of the participant in an environment. The agents could record the accuracy of the dialogue when people attempt to communicate with them. The users would thus need to learn what questions could be asked. The degree of recall efficiency by agents is related to the culturally appropriateness of the dialogue. It would also be very interesting to allow agents the facility over time to have their dialogue corrupted by alien (i.e. non-contextual) phrases of the participants.

5.6.1 Agency in a Marco Polo Game

I had mentioned in the previous chapter that some writers had argued that cultural immersion requires the perceived presence of other real social beings. Nonetheless, we do not have contextually based evaluation data on how embedded and culturally constrained visitors to a virtual heritage site need to be. For example, if we use our own language to communicate we will not be fully embedded in the recreated culture. Other visitors will almost certainly distract from the contextually situated embedded and embodied cultural experience. The premise that visitors require other real people in the virtual environment in order to feel Cultural Presence is thus unsubstantiated and highly problematic.

On the other hand, if the virtual environment contains a collection of artifacts that can be observed, interpreted, or understood as a coherent materialization by intelligent beings of a shared social system, this may be considered passive Cultural Presence. We can see culture, but we either cannot participate in it or with it due to a lack of culturally constrained creative understanding, or because the originators have long since passed away. Cultural presence, albeit in a weakened form, is possible in the absence of Social Presence. This is important, as so far, creating dynamically believable artificial characters that transmit explicit and engaging cultural knowledge is extremely difficult, and real people have trouble staying 'in character.'

However, it occurred to me that we could solve the Social Presence problem and the believable agents problem, by creating a situation where the authenticity of the player (and not the NPCs) is called into question (Fig. 5.15). In order to satisfy the NPCs that the player is a "local", the player has to satisfy questions and perform like the actual local characters (the scripted NPCs). Hence the player has to observe and mimic these artificial agents, for fear of being discovered. I have called this a cultural Turing test, but in fact it is a reversal of the Turing test, where a questioner has to determine from written answers if the writer is a human or a computer. Here the computer (through the artificial characters) is trying to determine if the human player is sufficiently artificial character-like.

Fig. 5.15 An Unreal bot (NPC) in Unreal Palenque game level

While the Palenque prototype game level in Unreal Tournament had default bots and wildlife, we decided to develop a new environment in the Half-Life 2: Source engine. The game scenario was the return of Marco Polo to Italy. In real life the bearded and much changed Marco Polo was not recognized by his family on his return from China, and so we imagined a hypothetical situation where an agent from Emperor Khan attempts to reach Italy before Marco Polo, impersonate him, and try infiltrate the local aristocracy to steal their cultural artifacts and scientific knowledge (the Emperor had apparently wanted Marco Polo to send him back wise men from Italy). With this scenario, and using bots that operated on Bayesian logic, the game engine could test the player's cultural knowledge, and track the player's spatial orientation and location, and ability to observe and mimic local knowledge in order to convince them he was actually Marco Polo.

5.7 Artifacts

Once designers have provided goals for participants in virtual environments, they will need to create interactive elements to enable and encourage participants to reach those goals. Fundamentally, there are three such interactive elements, social agency, modifiable artifacts, and dynamic environments.

If social behavior is an important way of transmitting cultural information in relation to artifacts (and externs), then what is required is some form of seemingly autonomous social agents, be they computer based or other participants. However, participants do not just learn about social agents through viewing how they are represented, participants also learn about them through how they interact with the environment. This interaction is via the manipulation of objects, and the creation of objects to manipulate other objects. In short, artifacts represent the transformative desires of the people that wield value and exchange them.

Designers of real and virtual environments also need to build on the relationship between patterns of inhabitation and usage of spatial artifacts, such as furnishings, in order to reveal the personal taste and habits of inhabitants (Beckmann 1998; Rapoport 1982).

Artifacts may also help represent the local physical affordances of the environment. There is a growing view that physical space and engagements need to address perceptions of appropriate or believable social behaviors (Schuemie et al. 2001). Also, there could be reactive artifacts (that respond to interaction in constrained and contextual ways), which may help indicate how, where and when to behave.

In a virtual environment that simulates a past culture, the ability to code and relay information through interactions with artifacts is surely as useful (if not more so) as interacting directly with computer-based agents. It is more authentic in the sense that more of our information of past people does actually come to us via inferences (which Schiffer call correlons), than through actual people or direct representations of people.

Meister (1998) claimed that too often buildings are perceived of as instantaneous products. Their relation to culture is also frequently simplified:

> We art historians too often speak of temples as if built by kings, but they are built for communities; as ritual instruments the use of which changes; one function of which is to web individuals and communities into a complicated and inconsistent social fabric through time. They survive by communities making use of them in a reciprocal relationship of self-preservation quite removed from agendas of historical conservation, Osymandias-like memorialization, or archaeological concerns. ...a temple is not one structure, nor of one period or even one community. It moves through time, collecting social lightening and resources. It must be repositioned constantly to survive.

According to recent research (Mosaker 2001), tourists want to share cultural perceptions and learn through doing, being told, observing, and asking. They wish to feel engaged in the activity, enjoy the spectacle, feel the pressure of time (the relative cultural idea of time–place), and understand the 'embedded' meaning of local cultural activity based on artifact.

Char Davies (2003), the artist who creates the virtual environment artwork Osmosis, wrote to me in to explain how virtual heritage should guide us towards different perspectives:

> I love old artifacts, particularly from really old civilizations. They're like a way of viewing the world through someone else's 5000-year-old eyes, a testament to small lives. I get the same from Outsider Art - people who've been dirt-poor manual labourers all their lives asserting that they have a mind, a way of looking at the world that's their's.
>
>   The kind of vague idea I have is about a crowded space filled with 'things' that represent people - lives - in the way the Sumerians would place worshipping figures in their temples to represent themselves praying in absentia. And the sounds would be those lives confirming their existence, the fact that they're as important as anyone else in the scheme of things! So I want to produce fairly happy sounds, not mournful wails that would sound like they're grieving over the fact that they're dead - more to evoke the kind of feeling I get when I go into the Egyptian Room in the British Museum, say. A satisfaction that these people have had a life, and that it's commemorated.

So even if the word 'culture' is a noun and not a verb, cultures are processes, not products. Cultures can only exist socially through artifacts, labeled by Sauer as 'agents of change' (Crang 1998). However, artifacts alone constitute only a fragment of the cultural process. To understand a cultural environment, one requires both artifacts, and an idea of the task that motivates people to use them.

For example, maps are interesting and revealing artifacts, yet they are often viewed as straightforward devices to locate and orientate. Yet they are not just instrumental artifacts but also epistemic ones with a long history: they have helped organize our knowledge of the world for many millennia.

Sterelny (2004, pp. 241–242) traced the ancestors of the map (cave paintings) back over 30,000 years:

> With the invention and elaboration of pictorial representation, humans came to be makers of specialised epistemic artefacts. It is very difficult to date the first appearance of specialised epistemic artefacts, but unmistakable, superbly executed paintings are over 30,000 years old (Mithen 1998). In Mithen's view, the use and elaboration of epistemic artefacts explains the extraordinary acceleration in both the richness and the variability of human

cultures over the last 50,000 years or so. He thinks our archaeological record shows the marks of a cognitive breakthrough.

Sterelny (2004, p. 241) wrote that maps are "tools for thinking". That means maps are epistemic artifacts, they are items that structure our knowledge outside of our minds. They are not just external to us but also portable, designed to function as representational resources.

Western notions of reality are thus only part of the features of cognitive mappings for other cultures. There are other social and cultural aspects to maps. While modern mapping professionals view the maps they make as an objective and accurate abstraction of reality, maps are actually culturally specific and socially constrained. They are designed via social conventions for a specific audience, and are abstracted to help people's cognitive mapping. One example of a cognitive map as a socially specific and culturally constrained artifact is the Aboriginal painting. These paintings are typically of landscapes, but they are not just aesthetic stylizations of landforms, they are also maps. They reveal specific and strategic but also mythical features of the surrounding land to each tribe.

There are of course functional reasons for maps, which typically plays an important practical part in navigating large virtual environments. Disorientation in virtual environments is a frequent and troubling issue for many users, an issue noted by various writers (Darken and Sibert 1996; Elvins 1997; Vinson 1999). Virtual environments, even those with Head Mounted Displays (HMDs) and motion tracking, lack many orientating features of the real world (Vinson 1999).

However, both Modjeska (1997) and Elvins (1997) argued that maps in virtual environments should serve merely as abstractions of reality. They both believed that navigation will be more usable if maps are similar to the way our spatial memory is created, recalled, and acted upon as part of a decision making process.

Rather than seeing wayfinding as a process, Elvins (1997, p. 1) saw wayfinding as a type of ability:

Wayfinding is "the ability to find a way to a particular location in an expedient manner and to recognize the destination when reached", i.e. navigating with spatial knowledge and a destination in mind.

There is also confusion in the literature over whether a cognitive map is the process by which people store navigational knowledge, or whether it is the instantaneous product of cognitive mapping, i.e. a cognitive map is formed in the mind on demand from cognitive mapping processes. Lagoudakis (1998), for example, seems to have defined a cognitive map as the former; but Soini (2001) defined it as the latter, 'a product of this [cognitive mapping] process at any point in time' (Soini 2001, pp. 227–228).

Medical research indicates that Soini is more likely to be correct; cognitive maps are created on demand as their elements are retrieved from different parts of the brain on demand. The researchers Wang et al. (2001, p. 191) wrote, "Space is represented in the mind not once but multiple times, not unified but segmented."

Soini further distinguished between the term 'mental map', as those maps that people draw when they are asked to sketch out their cognitive maps, and concept maps. Soini (2001, p. 229) defined a concept map as "a graphic system for understanding the relationship between concepts." Soini also defined symbol mapping as freehand mapping of places visited by selecting symbols that represent different personal meanings, such as 'nice', 'beautiful', and 'private'. She suggested there might be many interesting 'hybrid' ways of combining (and evaluating) these different types of mapping.

Billinghurst and Weghorst (1995) have previously evaluated engagement by qualitative and quantitative measurement of 'sketch maps'. Their research indicates that accuracy in sketching the virtual environment after the experience is directly related to engagement in the virtual environment.

Given her thorough investigation of the terms, I will follow Soini's definitions of mapping, and refer to a person's cognitive navigational knowledge as cognitive mapping, the image or schematic they process from their cognitive mapping processes on the fly as a cognitive map, and their drawn interpretation of their cognitive map as a mental map. Mental maps could include sketch maps, symbol maps, iconic maps (symbols with no specific personal connotations), or concept maps.

It is important to stress that cognitive maps are not the same as maps created by professional cartographers. Neural research by scientists on monkeys indicates that we remember locations in terms of salience (behavioral significance) not by what is actually there (Wang et al. 2001). Thus, the way we access these cognitive maps is typically not just via quantitative estimates and measurements but also in relation to personal attachments and perceptions (Billinghurst and Weghorst 1995). Raubal and Egenhofer (1998, pp. 895–896) reiterated the point that wayfinding is developed by habits and social practices along with image schemata, "recurring mental patterns that help people to structure space so that they know what to do with it."

Given this distinction, maps in virtual environments may be needed, and they are indeed capable of providing better affordances for cognitive mapping, but they also offer other advantages over real world maps, they can filter the experience. Being interactive, recordable, and dynamically personalizable, digital maps can gradually or contextually reveal the unknown, keep a personally relevant record of the past, or offer a shadowy gate to the future. A foreteller of what lies ahead, or what is a worthwhile digression or quicker way around a yet to be seen obstacle, real world maps help 'preview' possible and optimal journeys.

Yet digital maps used for previewing (wayfinding) can also be directional and proxemic. As users progress through the virtual environment, a digital map could improve in local accuracy. This feature is already used in certain types of games, and could help sustain mystery, but also reduce cognitive loading. For example, imagine that on entering a virtual environment for the first time, that the map is faded and only shows a very blurry concept of what is in the area, as found on maps by neighbors. As one explores the virtual environment, the map becomes more accurate.

Digital maps could also be related more closely to a sense of place. Consider a virtual environment with dynamic place elements that both afford and constrain progress. Changes in lighting could symbolize day and night. Nighttime could be the metaphorical resting time when a user needs to find a safe place to sleep (recharge). Coupled with an interactive digital map, the user could be induced to plan and record (via the map), all paths and journeys so that they do not fall into a stupor in a dangerous place (from which they cannot move or wake).

Any device for orientation will help users navigate through an environment, but an interactive digital map may further allow a graphical history of their virtual travels.

For example, Ramloll and Mowat (2001) created a virtual environment where participants could take in-scene snapshots of exit and entry points. They could retrieve these snapshots at any time and click on them to move to those specific locations. The writers reported that this function increased ease of navigation.

On the other hand, Nitsche and Thomas (2003) described a project that uses cinematic devices and teleporting assailants to confuse and hinder the participant's mental mapping of an environment. They believe these steps increase dramatic tension, and help make small environments appear larger (and hence more interesting for the participant).

Further, unlike typical conventional maps, digital maps can automatically filter information according to one's current position, individual preferences, or hidden (or targeted) events in a virtual environment. They can also be used like an inventory, to keep a reminder of what options or resources are currently accessible.

In the sense that maps can act as memory aids to wayfinding, they are also 'memory' maps, graphical travel diaries. Digital interactive maps can help orient, navigate, and recollect past episodes along a journey. Digital interactive maps can also 'remember'. Such memory maps could record vistas, landmarks, use of artifacts, and encounters; they can act as a form of pictorial diary. As an aid to memory recall, users may select, scale, and position thumbnail icons of events, encounters, or artifacts onto their map. For example, users could customize from a palette of icons (castles, houses, bridges, food sources etc.), and select, scale, and position these pictorial icons to remind them where they went, what they did, and where the safest routes are found.

Further, as artifacts, the way maps are used, personalized, and aged, are 'traces' of their 'life-history'. Maps are epistemic artifacts to aid perception and decision-making, but in being used, they reflect popular and annotated points. Most importantly for us, an interactive personalizable map could show where people went, and how effectively they avoided the areas dangerous to their metaphorical 'health' points in the above game–style scenario. While research indicates there is no one primary map, the same research does indicate that our cognitive mapping is multimodal and hierarchical. Given this, it seems reasonable to presume that a multimodal graphical mapping device that people indirectly customize (indirectly as the customization arises through task selection) will enable the navigation to be more intuitive and hence usable.

5.7.1 *Mapping to Aid Navigation for Egyptian Mythology*

The journal and map entries of games could be incorporated into educational puzzles and quests, but these have not yet been fully developed, as far as I know, by educationalists. In my teaching and research I have tried to approach these problems by thematically constraining the player, and by augmenting graphic gameplay with textual diaries using the built in tools of game editors. For example, using the game editor in Elder Scrolls III: Morrowind, (the predecessor to Oblivion), students were able to quickly

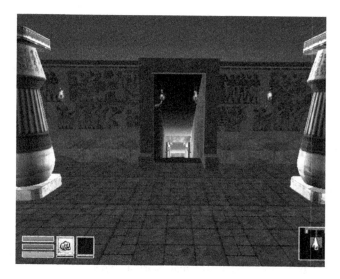

Fig. 5.16 Elder Scrolls III: Morrowind and the Egyptian Temple of the Gods

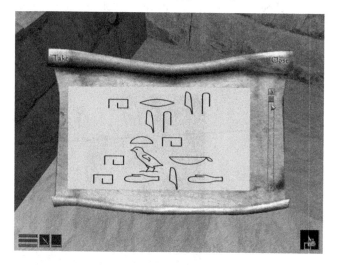

Fig. 5.17 Egyptian game glyphic inventory

develop a fictional Egyptian temple, with textual entries giving the player information on how to recreate the powers of individual Egyptian gods (Fig. 5.16).

We have seen that digital media can create mythic realms where cultural belief systems can appear to take on tangible form and power. Students used the Elder Scrolls III: Morrowind game level editor to build an archaeological game that gives the player Egyptian god-like powers if they can translate the hieroglyphs without enraging the mummies. In order to gain the mythical powers of the gods in the Egyptian Tomb prototype, they had to find and add the correct hieroglyph to their inventory map (Fig. 5.17).

Why would players want to learn the correct meaning of each hieroglyph? By correctly recounting and using the correct hieroglyph in the correct place, players could unlock secret hiding rooms. Appropriate use of journals, diaries and maps turns them into external cognitive artifacts. If these external cognitive artifacts are initially fragmented, and can be augmented dynamically by the player's intentions and activities, they may also act as evaluation devices.

5.7.2 *Mapping Through Drawing*

We have seen that games can teach spatial, hand-eye, detection, and strategic knowledge. Games can sometimes modify their own laws of nature, so traditional myths can appear to have the same validity as Western laws of physics. Due to the power of their specialized editors (designed to allow players to create and share their own game modifications), and their highly adaptable peripherals, games can help create relatively low-cost and thematic virtual experiences.

Even First Person Shooter games, environments where virtual life is violent and brutish and short, deliberately thwart and therefore help develop spatial awareness and in doing so, probably improve the cognitive mapping of players (a cognitive map being the real-time creation in our mind of specific and related places that we have previously visited). The actual maps in games are typically designed to help

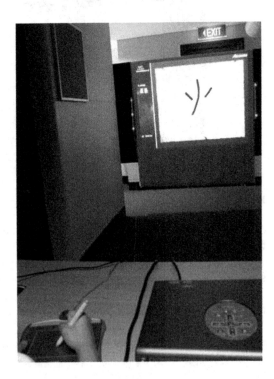

Fig. 5.18 Drawing game (Chinese writing language) using Torque 2D

players locate themselves in relation to hostile opponents, or to find their way out of disorientating spaces.

However, these maps can also function as an inventory of items collected, and sometimes as a symbol library. The previous example showed how the map could be used as an inventory collector and glyphic library, but maps can also teach the player rudiments of a current or past graphic language through drawing. The next image shows exactly this, students devised a writing game in Torque 2D, using a graphic table the player has to accurately trace over the Chinese symbol in order to progress through the game (Fig. 5.18). I see great potential here not just for educational games in general, but also for virtual heritage.

5.8 Game-Based Learning

In Table 5.3, we can see that instruction, observation, and trial and error as modes of learning are often found in games. However, the grey indicates that it is difficult to classify games according to the schematic modes of cultural learning, for cultural learning is often a hybrid mixture of learning modes. Further, games frequently blend modes, as can be seen in the right-hand column of Table 5.3.

On the other hand, it is possible to classify game devices (to create challenge or provide information) according to these cultural learning modes. The events used to tell stories (cut-scenes, voiceovers etc.) are typically not part of the gaming itself, but are devices to provide a background. So they may be used in virtual environments to recount historical events. However, they are not directly useful to virtual travel environments that cater for different modes of learning.

Travelers and tourists learn about places by going there, observing events, and being instructed by signs, guides and printed material. Such learning in games is typically before the start of the actual game, in the form of a textual introduction or voice-over. It is seldom part of the overall game-play itself. Game tutorials, on the other hand, are procedural. Some games offer short walkthroughs where users may practice learning to jump and sidestep, use weapons etc.. As contextually appropriate simulations, these games within games offer something real world tourism seldom encompasses, learning by doing.

5.8.1 Procedural Versus Prescriptive Learning

There is another important distinction between real world tourism and computer gaming. In the game world, we might read erosion and damage to detect whether we have been there before, but generally, we are meant to read place features in games in order to gauge where the affordances and constraints are most likely to be located.

To paraphrase Adams (2004), place features in games are designed to afford rather than entertain. It might depict a mood through genre conventions, (such as

Table 5.3 Interaction learning modes in games

Cultural learning	Game devices	Typical games
Instruction: Learn about the significance of a place by social learning (by people telling you or instructing you)	Cut-scenes, non-playing characters (NPC), notes found in the scene, the intro, and voiceovers	Being told what to do is anathema to gamers, as they typically want to act rather than to listen
Observation: Deduce cultural beliefs by inference from the properties of related artifacts (for example, properties in Japan near burial grounds are significantly cheaper than other housing areas) We can also learn about the significance of a place by how old or worn it appears	Watching other players, reading the game tutorial	*Myst* is similar to early interactive fiction but it also contains pictorial clues, so perhaps it can be called an observation game. That said, observation based learning is common to many types of games and perhaps most evident in Tetris and Space Invaders (they do not require instruction to learn how to play or the outcomes
Trial and error: Learn about a place through task-based activity there (for example, we learn a swimming pool is suitable for swimming)	Configurative challenges, puzzles, emergent behavior, randomly set selection triggers	Strategy games like Civilization
Hybrid: Learn through a mix of the above. We observe or read why or how people do things, we get some advice on what we are doing wrong or we overhear how or why other people do it, then we try out different strategies in order to most enjoy it, or most successfully complete the task	(Hybrid mix of above)	Even simplistic 3D shooter games often involve instruction (at start), observation (where enemies or affordances are), and trial and error (learning how and when to use weapons)

specific lighting, sound, scale and symbolic details), but place is a stage on which things are meant to happen in the present or indicate what will happen in the immediate future, not tell the stories of the past. These devices set the scene, rather than provide historically accurate information.

So how does one blend game–style interaction with virtual travel or heritage environments? Despite literature conflating narrative with environmental storytelling (Jenkins 2004), knowledge derived from observation of place features in games is typically procedural (Table 5.4), rather than prescriptive (Table 5.5). Gamers do not

Table 5.4 Procedural learning via social roles

Participant aims	Learning about an extant culture	Learning about a past cultural learning	Game genre
Adventurer: reach objective by 'reading' site without embodiment being threatened	Typically shallow hybrid of three types of cultural learning	More observation, as well as trial and error	The Qin or China game: escape the Forbidden City by solving puzzles. Or a 3D adventure game, Heretic II
Invader-God like figure: control or overcome inhabitants	Mix of observation and trial and error		Typical 3D first person shooters, black and white has god-like figure
Avoid being killed	(Hybrid mix of above but perhaps with more strategy than observation)	Uncovering and solving puzzles in order to return to own time	Civilization perhaps comes closest but it is a (isometrically viewed) game of socially constrained strategy with instruction rather than social conversation
Control or overcome invaders (this is a mirror image of Invaders profile)	(Hybrid mix of above)		Civilization perhaps comes closest but it is an isometrically viewed game of socially constrained strategy with instruction rather than social conversation

Table 5.5 Prescriptive learning via social roles

Participant aims	Learning about an extant culture	Learning about a past culture	Game genre
Tourist: Enjoy life of site from a safe and comfortable distance	Exploring and shallow modes of conversation	Instruction, shallow modes of observation	Extant: the new travel game genre, like Weekend in Capri
Traveler: Complete tasks using local affordances	Instruction, observation, and trial and error	Observation, and trial and error	A Past culture: The early Myst series
Archaeologist: Find what happened by examining material remains, geographical changes, epigraphy etc.		Intense observation and deduction. Some trial and error through scientific experiments	ArcDig. Perhaps murder mysteries or interactive fiction comes closest
Anthropologist: Understand the beliefs roles and relationships of inhabitants and their surrounds	Intense observation and conversation. Instruction depends on level of emic or etic immersion		Myst had elements of conversation but this is not typically a 3D game. The role the gamer plays in The Sims may be between this and the next category

learn what happened from observing features of place (shadows, openings, strange devices), they learn what to expect and where to move in case of trouble.

Likewise, in the real world, to travel through a country without outside resources we have to learn to 'read' the land, and solve local problems with local solutions. While tourists can learn from seeing how people do things, they themselves do not learn by doing but by watching the actions of others, by reading the interpretations of others, and by listening to others.

If we consider the two tables on cultural learning via social roles, it appears that travelers are closer to typical gaming roles than tourists are. Archaeologists are more akin to tourists, but they must actively interpret the place.

It may pay to tailor the virtual environment to the expected social role and objectives of the user, in terms of prescriptive learning as an archaeologist (detective), tourist (non-playing character or observer), or in terms of procedural learning aimed at the traveler (adventurer).

It may also be possible to learn about a virtual heritage environment as an inhabitant, but this suggests new game genres, for in games inhabitants tend to actually be displaced travelers suffering from amnesia (i.e. a hybrid of the social roles discussed). Traders may also be seen to be a hybrid of inhabitant, strategist, and adventurer.

When considering learning in relation to the particular social role and identity of the gamer, this schism becomes more apparent. There exists a degree of separation between games that develop procedural knowledge, and virtual environments' tendency to follow traditional pedagogy by presenting prescriptive knowledge.

Learning about different cultures usually involves a blend of instruction, observation, and trial and error. The separation of certain roles may be open to conjecture, for example, travelers and anthropologists both require some degree of prescriptive (historical) knowledge. These roles may be distinguished by the degree of emphasis placed on learning modes by these different social roles and identities. Generally, then, it appears that the roles and identities mentioned might be separated into those that learn by actively doing (by trial and error) and those that learn passively, by observing and by being instructed.

To separate tourist from travelers, the latter may be seen as akin to the adventurers–explorers found in computer games. An obvious example of this genre is the game example previously discussed, Heretic II. Progress in Heretic II is through procedural learning, knowledge learnt through trial and error. There is also as a degree of social instruction, 'as the last of your race, you need to do x', and a degree of observation, 'a key! There must be a lock nearby that I need to open...' but the learning in the game itself is generally through doing.

However, archaeology is usually attempting to uncover prescriptive knowledge, knowledge of events, what happened when, and who did what. Hence we could crudely separate games into those that attempt to unravel narrative (such as *Myst* and other types of interactive fiction), and those that allow interaction through doing (the competitive adventurer–explorer games). The former detective style games are much closer in spirit to the learning found in archaeology, while contextual travel (rather than commercial luxury tourism) is much closer to adventuring.

The strategy games where one tries to develop empires through selecting resources (and sometimes throwing dice), may be a blend of the above, as it incorporates procedural learning (via calculated risk taking), and prescriptive learning (by the game providing historical facts about the resources that may help player decisions). This type of game may expose the workings of previous civilizations, and it may incorporate historical events in the way it works out permutations of player decisions, but as a learning platform, it encounters the problem of how to separate fact from fiction for the player (Kirriemuir and McFarlane 2003; Squire and Barab 2004).

Having said historical learning tends towards prescriptive and not the procedural knowledge emphasized in games, one might wonder if game–style interaction would be of use in understanding other cultures. It appears games are often competitive and destructive, focused on doing and changing rather than understanding, recovering and preserving. The next section suggests possible solutions that are not necessarily competitive or destructive.

5.9   Game Genres and Cultural Learning

As well as providing a genre for affordances in virtual environments, game–style interaction may also offer some insight into cultural beliefs and behaviors (Champion 2004). Four examples of game–style interaction are described here, all involve procedural knowledge, with the last few particularly oriented towards understanding the contextual constraints, social identities and behaviors of the inhabitants.

5.9.1   Snakes and Ladders

The classic snakes and ladders metaphor can be applied to travel across time and space. In the case of Mayan archaeology, the inhabitants actually believed in portals that led to a sky world above, and to an underworld controlled by a lord of death. These portals were either sky-snakes or wells and cracks in the earth. Designers could use these metaphors to allow people to teleport across time and space. In many rendering engines, collisions are captured, and avatars have some degree of physics (collision, inertia). Borrowing from the 'Steal the Flag' games, different players with different characters (and hence different capabilities) could gain points or important items by sneaking up and colliding with others. I started developing such a game for Palenque using Adobe Atmosphere. The Mayan notion of portals, directional magic, different levels of living and dying, and celestial dimensions and oracles seemed an apt fit for such a game genre.

5.9.2 Different Perspectives per Player

In some game rendering engines available online, it is possible to be in one version of an environment while seeing a player in the same world even if they are at a different computer looking at a different version of the same world. While it may not immediately appear useful, by synchronizing the players but not the world an interesting scenario can be developed.

Each player can see each other but each player is trapped in their own perspectival version of the world (Fig. 5.19, image, temple and avatars by author, museum modeled by http://www.planetavivo.org). Only through other players describing their world to them can invisible (unsynchronized) objects appear to the players.

A simpler version of this game would be for players to have avatars invisible to themselves. In order to find out their social role, where they fit in and what they can do, it may be necessary for them to encounter other players in order to have their physical form described to them.

5.9.3 Role Playing

Perhaps the most powerful way of historical immersion is via role-playing. Although theatre provides a strong metaphor library for virtual environments, improvised theatre is more apt as it requires direct audience interaction while having

Fig. 5.19 Shared avatars with personal worlds

some plot guidelines. Participants could 'wake up' in social roles and social costumes, and have to gain information from local avatars as to what they look like, who they are, and their role and abilities in that culture.

Many traditions tell of changelings. Players could learn different ways of interacting with the world depending on the nature of their character's background and the location of that character. In the case of Mayan culture, everyone had spirits that wandered the world at night and fought battles with evil spirits from the bowels of the earth.

5.9.4   The Spy Game

Perhaps the most interesting and most promising metaphor in terms of cultural immersion would be that of the spy game. In this scenario, both scripted agents and players are given characters and agendas. Other agents or players are given the task of trying to find out who are the real inhabitants and who are the pretenders through the choice of words, how suspicious their movements or behaviors, or by how long they tarry in a spot without doing what they are supposed to do.

5.10   Issues of Time: Interaction Versus Historical Authenticity

We can avoid artifacts solely designed for conflict and destruction when we design virtual environments with Cultural Presence. Yet another factor that might conflict with interaction, and records of interaction history is that (virtual) tourists traditionally look for authenticity. Paradoxically this means a desire for an environment that is both authentic (untouched by crowds of tourists and tourist related industry), and amenable to tourism (replete with contemporary tourist resources and facilities).

Perhaps most importantly, if the virtual environment shows changes over time (something multimedia is brilliant for), historical accuracy needs to be aimed for, for educational reasons, but people also want autonomy. Virtual tourists want an opportunity to interact with history and to chose interpretations of the past, but as we advance in time towards the present the more factual the account of what happened, the less the opportunity for autonomy. Juul (2001a) wrote:

> There is an inherent conflict between the *now* of the interaction and the *past* or "*prior*" of the narrative. You can't have narration and interactivity at the same time; there is no such thing as a continuously interactive story.

We could examine historical games such as Close Combat or Civilization for ideas on how tourists could interact more meaningfully and entertainingly with history. However, games that perform the role of 'game-fictions' gain their engagement not from adherence to historical events but from their ability to depart from 'the historical record' (Atkins 2003; Jenkins 2004).

There are at least nine possible partial or complete solutions to this issue.

5.10.1 Ancillary Non-celebrity Characters

We could create ancillary characters that are not recorded in history, and allow people to take on their roles. Giving people the ability to 'augment' history with their own personal interaction history (fictions), the interactions they have with historical figures (henceforth referred to as 'celebrities'), could enhance or embellish the personality of the celebrities.

If the artificial intelligence deployed was highly sophisticated, the celebrity could remember past interactions, and get bored with routine actions of the ancillary characters, forcing the non-celebrities to attempt ever less likely interactions.

5.10.2 Autonomous Action, Immutable Results

We could allow participants a myriad of actions, as long as their actions achieved the right results (construct Stonehenge, invade Britain, take coffee beans from Arabia to Java, etc.). However, they have to take these coffee beans at the right time and to the right place.

A theory buzzing through the social sciences, memetics, talks of certain 'killer' ideas that takes on a life of their own, using people as carriers rather than as the progenitors. A meme is a popular self-serving cultural concept with no single owner, a cognitive equivalent to Dawkin's description of the 'selfish gene'.

Robert Aunger (2000) describes memes in his edited reader, *The Status of Memetics as a Science*. They are from a theory postulated by Richard Dawkins in his book *The Selfish Gene* (Jenkins 2004). This sort of option could simulate the spread of ideas in a memetic way, independent of individual intention, but socially inescapable and inexorable.

5.10.3 Groundhog Day

In the film Groundhog Day, the actor Bill Murray plays a weatherman caught in a time warp. No matter what he tries to do, he keeps waking up to the same morning. He eventually escapes the time warp by choosing a considerate and unselfish action for the first time in his life. In a similar fashion, a virtual heritage environment could allow participants to choose any action, but only one or a few would allow the historical plotline to move forward. Only the correct interactions would be recorded, although the number of times an actor chooses the wrong action could be counted.

5.10.4 Possible Worlds

This method would allow virtual participants interaction to change history with the result that participants find themselves in parallel possible worlds. This approach has been heavily used in science fiction (H.G. Well's *The Time Machine*, *Black Adder*, *Bill and Ted's Excellent Adventure*, *Dr Who*, *Star Trek*, the Canadian film *Possible Worlds* etc.). While fascinating from 'the what' if scenario point of view, this method may be less useful for teaching historical facts.

5.10.5 Diary of Emotional Development

The main narrative follows historical events but participants are given the opportunity to write down or otherwise record the emotional development and mental states of main character celebrities. Participants might also have the option of recording in multimodal form any events they think are crucial turning points.

While becoming the self-appointed scribes of history might be personally informative, participants are not likely to be highly engaged, as the interactivity is not varied and they do not contribute to the story. Perhaps the celebrities could punish those scribes who are too clumsy, forgetful, or inaccurate. The scribes' stories could be embedded into the virtual environment, and be commented on by other scribes.

5.10.6 Surfing Memetic Drift

Actors have to choose the successful memetic idea, social force, or artifact that changes the world in a significant way. Only if participants choose the correct object or idea can they advance through time and space. Each artifact may trigger other related events that also change history, so the actor can choose from a web of possible associations. If the actor chooses the wrong idea (for example, picks the turkey to represent the United States – the bald eagle as a symbol of America), they might have to endure a video of what happened before being told no, it never actually happened – start again. A database could record the participants' choices against reality, and against those of previous actors.

5.10.7 Augment History with Real World

It is possible to augment history with annotations of real-world visitation. One could use social agents as guides to trails left by previous visitors who deposit into secret caches videos, sound recordings, and images of the place as they visited it in the real world. Or perhaps their clues get washed around or moved by dynamic environmental forces, and the current participants have to match the 'clues' depicting real places, to where those places are or will be in the virtual travel environment.

For example, a young woman climbs the Himalayas. In the many cyber-cafes of Katmandu or from a PDA with GPS (a Global Positioning System), she could email audiovisuals of her path into the virtual environment, which her parents could follow from a computer in their own home. As they watch her photos, they could spin around in the related 3D context of the place she is visiting as it is now (perhaps fed by real-time climatic data) or as it used to be thousands of years ago.

5.10.8 Augmented Cultural Exchange

In a virtual environment, visitors could meet other visitors. The other visitors could be actual inhabitants of that site, academic authorities, computer generated characters, or even real people as virtual characters who deliberately give misleading accounts of the area and of themselves. The goal could be to identify who are the locals, authorities, and deceivers (agent based or human users), and what the truth actually is.

5.10.9 Dynamic Places

All of the above options are chronological in the typical sense, participants encounter problems, try to solve them, and travel through time as they do so in a forward motion. Yet the scientists' uncovering of the past (and hence the discovery of the content of virtual heritage environments), is looking backwards by thinking backwards. By uncovering fragments, scientists piece together what happened before and afterwards.

If participants find a germane and pivotal artifact, event or action, a portal opens and could take them to the associated past leading up to the creation of that object. Hence, the task is to find doors to the time before rather than to the time after. As people travel further back in time, less is known, and there are more potential interpretations of the era. This means that participants could interact more and more with the main narrative. Over time, the artifacts, and the records of the participants' own interaction history would become lost, turned into myth, or covered up by 'alternative' histories.

5.11 Game-Based Evaluation

Virtual environment designers have recently become very interested in computer games, and why they have succeeded so well, when conventional virtual environments have not. There has also been a boom in game design studies; to the extent game design academics have agreed the field requires more rigorous criticism and evaluation.

Surely the latest academic research is not required to explain why people want to play these games, for game technology is continually advancing? I am not convinced.

Could traditional HCI help create more enjoyable virtual environments or games? No, I don't think this is necessarily true either. My reason for both my answers is due in no small part to a paper I read some years ago by Malone (1982). This paper, *Heuristics for designing enjoyable user interfaces: Lessons from computer games*, was written nearly a quarter of a century ago, yet it has only recently resurfaced in the papers and theses of current game researchers.

The paper was an attempt to understand why games are "captivating" and how they can be "used to make other user interfaces interesting and enjoyable to use." In order to answer this question he set up three empirical studies (but only describes two), and takes away "motivational features" to see which features add the most to captivation. Malone asked eight groups of ten students to play a computer game (called Darts), and then another game (Hangman) but with one of eight features missing. He recorded how long played each game (completion time), their personal opinions (as to which game they preferred), and their gender.

Results indicated fantasy was more important than feedback (as long as it is appropriate to its audience). A preference for fantasy over performance feedback may surprise some, but it did not surprise me, for games are designed to appeal to the imagination rather than get a job done.

I was particularly interested by this simple method of evaluation. When I wished to evaluate user experience of virtual environments, I was faced with choosing people to compare two virtual environments against each other (subjective preference), or compare the task performance of two different user groups in two different environments. With the first method people typically lack experience in judging virtual environments against each other as it is such a new technology. With the second method I had to pray that that the testers' relevant demographic factors would be spread relatively evenly across the two groups.

In his second study, using a similar method, Malone found that explicit goals, score keeping, audio effects, and randomness were particularly important. These two studies were then followed in the paper by his claim that *challenge*, *fantasy*, and *curiosity* were the important ingredients that make games captivating and fun to use.

Malone explained that HCI traditionally seeks to improve software that is easy to learn and easy to master, but notes the founder of Atari said games are designed to be easy to learn but difficult to master. Malone argued that computer games are more like toys than other software applications, which in turn are more like tools. Unlike shopping web pages, or software designed for office use, games have goals but they do not have to have clear outcomes. They do however incorporate challenge and fantasy, and stimulate curiosity.

Challenge is defined as involving "a goal whose outcome is uncertain," as there is often variable difficulty level or multiple goals (potentially distributed over different levels). Fantasy incorporates emotionally appealing features, or well-mapped cognitive metaphors. Curiosity is seen as "optimal level of information complexity." It may incorporate randomness or contextual humor.

Malone was perceptive enough to realize that challenge is not merely about making things difficult, but also about making these barriers tantalizing to solve. When

I evaluated over 80 people and how they learn about the original inhabitants through exploring virtual reconstructions of archaeological sites, I asked the users if the environments were challenging without realizing this subtle distinction. The users were confused as to whether I meant challenging as in "this is difficult, I am not sure I can or want to complete it", or "this is really testing me but I really don't want to do anything else until I crack it." This second meaning of challenging is an important feature of a successful game, it affords *hard fun*.

Gestalt theory seems to be behind Malone's concept of curiosity as a motivating feature of games, he suggested users want to have 'well formed knowledge structures," that games deliberately suggest such knowledge but present the "knowledge structure" as incomplete, inconspicuous or unparsimonious (by this I think he means games provide red herrings or an overflow of potential clues).

Fantasy is the concept that I am least convinced by, not because it is not an important part of computer games, but because I am not convinced we can create a successful sense of fantasy merely through creating emotional triggers, connotations, and metaphors directed towards specific audiences. The fantasy element of complex game-worlds is not so easily circumscribed by heuristics, just as Malone did not convincingly explain why the boys rather than the girls enjoyed the digital fantasy of popping balloons, or how this trait could be best used in designing future games.

For example, two of the most popular computer games have been *The Elder Scrolls IV: Oblivion* (single player medieval-styled quest fantasy for game consoles and computers), and *World of Warcraft* (an online multiplayer role-playing fantasy). The degree to which players can choose their character attributes allows them to undertake the game using a myriad of skills and strategies in order to solve a variety of challenges. They do not buy these games because the games are programmed to have conditions and triggers, they do not play these games because the games are rule-based systems; they play these games because the games *challenge* them to change the world and to explore how these character roles embody and express aspects of their own personality.

What is also striking about these games is how they can motivate people without explicitly showing them what lies ahead. These games are mysterious knowledge structures that loom out of the dark, closed portals surrounded by long-lost instructions, or meeting grounds of conflict and competition where players do not actually know what happens next, only that there is the possibility of eventual success.

I suspect Malone's work has resurfaced for at least two important reasons. Firstly, writers have been arguing over the defining features of games, as they are attempting to build a critical research area that can describe and prescribe how to design games and how to improve them.

You may recall that Juul (2003) defined a game as "a rule-based formal system with a variable and quantifiable outcome, where different outcomes are assigned different values, the player exerts effort in order to influence the outcome, the player feels attached to the outcome, and the consequences of the activity are optional and negotiable." And you may also recall that Salen and Zimmerman (2003) wrote that "A game is a system in which players engage in an artificial conflict, defined by rules, that results in a quantifiable outcome."

Where is the fun in that? Definitions of computer games as systems do not address why users find games enjoyable. Despite being in relatively recent publications, these definitions do not directly lead us to producing better games (or, in my case, virtual environments), that users enjoy more. Malone's paper reminds us that games are not played *because* they are systems, so defining games in terms of rules-based systems does not shed any light on the user experience.

Secondly, the huge recent popularity of online multi-player worlds cannot be explained purely in terms of usefulness or usability. Many of these games are crying out for help from HCI specialists to design improved interfaces, they do not necessarily create entirely new forms of narrative or cinematic innovation, and yet they are still commercial successes.

Recent publications, such as a doctoral thesis by Federoff (2002), and papers by Jorgensen (2004), Desurvire et al. (2004), and Shneiderman (2004), have stressed the importance of Malone's paper in explaining the unique features of games, how they differ in the way they are experienced from other types of software, and how a new set of heuristics is needed to address these specific game features. Knickmeyer and Mateas (2005) have even described how the coding scheme of *Façade*, an interactive narrative game, was inspired by Malone's three categories.

Disseminating history, heritage, and cultural perspectives involves not just objective fact, but also communicating the unique context and intrinsic worth of situated perspectives, character motivations, traditions, rituals, mythologies, and communal beliefs. The more enjoyable these virtual environments can be, the more likely users will learn and be interested in learning.

Malone's paper reminded me that the quest is to create more challenging environments, (and challenge in the sense of a difficulty people wish to face, not wish to avoid). It also reinforced for me a subtle gap between games and other software in the way HCI could or should be used. Using the latest technology or quoting the latest research does not automatically ensure that the essential questions are being addressed.

5.12   Summary of Games–Style Interaction

Many virtual environments have aimed for realism rather than for meaningful interaction. Yet this may not be the most effective means of educating and engaging the public.

Material culture is not a collection of objects; it is an embodied and embedded snapshot of a dynamic world-view, an interface and depository to social ideas and beliefs. This interface of art and craft allows us to visualize our cultural understanding and transmit it to others for review and feedback. If culture is an interactive process of observation, instruction, and active participation, we need to know how we can meaningfully replicate this process in virtual environments. It may prove easier to evoke this world-view through vagueness and uncertainty rather than through clear and unbiased vision.

And we may gain some of these answers from a closer study of game–style interaction. Games are challenging, rewarding, and sometimes personalizable.

They also offer cues on how to help people navigate through virtual environments. The specific elements that make three-dimensional games engaging and believable rather than realistic may also be usefully applied to virtual heritage environments. However, games are typically not hermeneutic, and are based around procedural rather than prescriptive learning.

Unlike many games, virtual heritage environments also have a set narrative to tell. How do we allow the freedom of interaction and personalization along with the unveiling of history through one or more narratives? Can we infuse written history with multiple personal and cultural perspectives?

Virtual heritage requires an understanding of what is 'historical'. For example, an indigenous storyteller may well argue cultural understanding is based in minds more than in books. How do designers capture it and how do designers invoke the feeling of encountering it as something either new or familiar? Designers need to know how to create a sense of embodiment, and to what extent they need to constrain and embed the visitor as a social actor in a context that can be highly fragile, ephemeral, and intangible.

For virtual heritage projects, and for virtual environments to some extent, the central issue appears to be learning about others and how that can be supported via digital media. Cultural Presence involves learning intangible heritage information – how is this possible via digital media?

For creating a virtual environment with a notion of a 'place' (a region recognizable to a user as a culturally coded setting), merely identifiable or evocative virtual environments are not enough. A virtual environment must allow visitors to see as much as possible through the eyes of the original inhabitants. It must also suggest ideas of thematically related events, evidence of social autonomy, notions of territorial possession and shelter, and focal points of artifactual possession. In other words, the virtual environment must provide a perspective of a past culture to a user in a manner similar to that deduced by trained archaeologists and anthropologists from material remains (fossils, pottery shards, ruins, etc.).

There are certainly large gaps in the knowledge of what would make the experience more engaging and educational. The components of virtual environments could be tested to see how well they afford authenticity, realism, engagement or learning in virtual places. Evaluators could also test discernible change in learning or entertainment acquired using different types of interaction, or evaluate user preference or user ranking of presence criteria when presented with different types of virtual environments.

Yet we still do not have a full range of contextual evaluation methods. Virtual heritage is seldom evaluated since so many resources and so much prestige is built into what so often turns out to be a fixed (i.e. not alterable after the fact) product. More research is needed to determine which forms of interaction and type of depiction are more compelling, task-effective, useful for Cultural Presence, and optimal for learning purposes.

However, there are at least four major design criteria that such a prototype would need to aim for. These criteria are embodied and physically responsive places, socially embedded and challenging constrained tasks and goals, some degree of hermeneutic enrichment (interpretation offered through the situated use of artifacts), and an unobtrusive way of evaluating engagement.

I have suggested some examples featuring dynamic place elements, constrained tasks and goals, social agency, and contextual artifacts (using epistemic artifacts such as maps), that might point the way to at least partially addressing these criteria. Certainly some of the techniques used in computer games may help. The exploration of the environment can be traveler rather than tourist based (that is, the participant is given tasks to complete), and there may be design elements of game–style interaction that can also increase engagement in virtual heritage environments.

There is also the issue of moving through time while interacting (playing) with history. I suggested nine different methods of combining historical fact with game–style interaction, but there are certainly far more to be discovered. There are many possible solutions, and in the next chapter we will discuss virtual environments that take a particular interest in heritage content using game engines or inspired by game–style interaction.

References

Adams, E.W. (2004). The Philosophical Roots of Computer Game Design. Approximate Transcript of talk given at the 2004 Game Developers' Conference, [GDC]. Retrieved 27 April 2010, from http://www.designersnotebook.com/Lectures/Roots/roots.htm

Aldrich, C. (2004). *Simulations and the future of learning: an innovative (and perhaps revolutionary) approach to e-learning.* San Francisco, CA: Jossey-Bass.

Amory, A. (2003). *Another Country: Virtual Learning Spaces.* Paper presented at the World Conference on Educational Multimedia, Hypermedia and Telecommunications. Retrieved 26 April 2010, from http://www.ukzn.ac.za/ited/amory/edmedia2003.pdf

Atkins, B. (2003). *More than a game: the computer game as fictional form.* Manchester: Manchester University Press.

Aunger, R. (Ed.). (2000). *Darwinising culture: the status of memetics as a science.* Oxford; New York: Oxford University Press.

Beckmann, J. (1998). *The virtual dimension: architecture, representation, and crash culture.* New York: Princeton Architectural Press.

Behr, J., Fröhlich, T., Knöpfle, C., Kresse, W., Lutz, B., Reiners, D., et al. (2001). *The Digital Cathedral of Siena – Innovative Concepts for Interactive and Immersive Presentation of Cultural Heritage Sites.* Paper presented at the ICHIM 2001 conference, International Cultural Heritage Informatics Meeting, Milan.

Billinghurst, M., & Weghorst, S. (1995). *The Use of Sketch Maps to Measure Cognitive Maps of Virtual Environments.* VRAIS Proceedings of the Virtual Reality Annual International Symposium (VRAIS'95), Washington, DC, USA.

Bryce, J., & Rutter, J. (2001). *In the Game – In the Flow: Presence in Public Computer Gaming (Poster).* Paper presented at the Computer Games and Digital Textualities Conference. Retrieved 26 April 2010, from http://digiplay.info/Game.php

Champion, E. (2003, 11 – 14 February). *Applying Game Design Theory to Virtual Heritage Environments.* Paper presented at the 1st international conference on Computer graphics and interactive techniques in Australasia and South East Asia GRAPHITE '03, Melbourne.

Champion, E. (2004, February). *Heritage Role Playing – History as an Interactive Digital Game.* Paper presented at the Interactive Entertainment Workshop (IE2004), UTS, Sydney, NSW, Australia.

Crang, M. (1998). *Cultural geography.* London; New York: Routledge.

Crawford, C. (1982). *The Art of Computer Game Design.* Retrieved 30 April 2010, from http://www.vancouver.wsu.edu/fac/peabody/game-book/Coverpage.html

Darken, R.P., & Sibert, J.L. (1996). *Wayfinding Strategies and Behaviors in Large Virtual Worlds.* Paper presented at the SIGCHI conference on human factors in computing systems: Common ground, Vancouver, British Columbia, Canada.

Davies, C. (2003). Virtual Heritage. Email to author. Canada.

Desurvire, H., Caplan, M., & Toth, J.A. (2004). *Using Heuristics to Evaluate the Playability of Games*. Paper presented at the CHI '04 conference: extended abstracts on Human factors in computing systems.

Elvins, T. (1997). Virtually lost in virtual worlds-wayfinding without a cognitive map. *ACM Computer Graphics Quarterly, 31*(3), 15–17.

Federoff, M. (2002). *Heuristics and Usability Guidelines for the Creation and Evaluation of FUN in Video Games*. Unpublished Master of Science thesis, Indiana University, Indiana.

Fencott, C. (1999, 30 September). *Towards a Design Methodology for Virtual Environments*. Paper presented at the User Centered Design and Implementation of Virtual Environments-a one-day workshop at the King's Manor, University of York.

Germanchis, T., Cartwright, W., & Pettit, C. (2007). Virtual Queenscliff: A Computer Game Approach for Depicting Geography. In W. Cartwright, M. P. Peterson & G. Gartner (Eds.), *Multimedia Cartography* (2nd edition, pp. 359–368). Berlin; New York: Springer.

Greeff, M., & Lalioti, V. (2001). *Interactive Cultural Experiences using Virtual Identities*. Paper presented at the iCHIM2001 conference. Retrieved 30 April 2010, from http://www.makebelieve.gr/vl/Publications/ICHIM.pdf

Jenkins, H. (2004). Game Design as Narrative Architecture [Electronic Version]. *Electronic Book Review*, Online. Retrieved 30 April 2010, from http://www.electronicbookreview.com/thread/firstperson/lazzi-fair

Jorgensen, A. (2004). *Marrying HCI/Usability and computer games: a preliminary look*. Paper presented at the NordiCHI '04 conference: Proceedings of the third Nordic conference on Human-computer interaction.

Juul, J. (2001a). Games telling stories? A brief note on games and narratives. *Game Studies, The International Journal of Computer Game Research, 1*(1).

Juul, J. (2001b). The repeatedly lost art of studying games. Review of Elliott M. Avedon & Brian Sutton-Smith (Ed.). The Study of Games New York: Wiley 1971 [Electronic Version]. *Game Studies, The International Journal of Computer Game Research*, n.p. Retrieved 30 April 2010, from http://www.gamestudies.org/0101/juul-review/

Juul, J. (2003). *The Game, the Player, the World: Looking for a Heart of Gameness*. Paper presented at the *Level Up: Digital Games Research Conference Proceedings*, Utrecht.

Kelso, M.T., Weyhrauch, P., & Bates, J. (1993). Dramatic presence. *Presence: Teleoperators and Virtual Environments, 2*(1), n.p.

Kirriemuir, J.K., & McFarlane, A. (2003). *Use of Computer and Video Games in the Classroom*. Paper presented at the Level Up Digital Games Research Conference, The Netherlands.

Knickmeyer, R.L., & Mateas, M. (2005). *Preliminary evaluation of the interactive drama/facade*. Paper presented at the CHI '05: Human factors in computing system conference (extended abstracts).

Lagoudakis, M.G. (1998). Spatial Knowledge in Humans, Animals and Robots. Retrieved 30 April 2010, from http://www.cs.duke.edu/~mgl/papers.html

Laird, J.E. (2001). Using computer game to develop advanced AI. *Computer, 34*(7), 70–75.

Laird, J.E., & van Lent, M. (2000). *Human-Level AI's Killer Application: Interactive Computer Games*. Paper presented at the Proceedings of the Seventeenth National Conference on Artificial Intelligence and Twelfth Conference on Innovative Applications of Artificial Intelligence. Retrieved 27 April 2010, from http://ai.eecs.umich.edu/people/laird/papers/AAAI-00.pdf

Malone, T.W. (1982). Heuristics for designing enjoyable user interfaces: Lessons from computer games. In *Proceedings of the 1982 conference on Human factors in computing systems* (pp. 63–68). Gaithersburg, MD, ACM Press.

Meister, M.W. (1998). *The Getty Project: Self-Preservation and the Life of Temples*. Paper presented at the ACSAA Symposium. Retrieved 28 April 2010, from http://dept.arth.upenn.edu/meister/acsaa.html

Modjeska, D. (1997). *Navigation in Electronic Worlds: Research Review for Depth Oral Exam*. Unpublished Ph.D. thesis, University of Toronto, Toronto.

Mosaker, L. (2001). Visualising historical knowledge using virtual reality technology. *Digital Creativity, 12*(1), 15–25.

Mulholland, P., & Collins, T. (2002). *Using Digital Narratives to Support the Collaborative Learning and Exploration of Cultural Heritage*. Paper presented at the International Workshop on Database and Expert Systems Applications (DEXA'02), Aix-en-Provence, France.

Nitsche, M., & Thomas, M. (2003). *Stories in Space: The Concept of the Story Map*. Paper presented at the Second Conference on Virtual Storytelling ICVS '03, Berlin.

Pape, D., Anstey, J., D'Souza, S., DeFanti, D., Roussou, M., & Gaitatzes, A. (2001, 30 May–1 June 2001). *Shared Miletus: Towards a Networked Virtual History Museum*. Paper presented at the International Conference on Augmented, Virtual Environments and Three-Dimensional Imaging (ICAV3D), Mykonos, Greece.

Ramloll, R., & Mowat, D. (2001). *Wayfinding in Virtual Environments using an Interactive Spatial Cognitive Map*. Paper presented at the Fifth International Visualisation 2001 conference, IV2001 Proceedings, London.

Rapoport, A. (1982). *The meaning of the built environment: a nonverbal communication approach*. Beverly Hills, CA: Sage Publications.

Raubal, M., & Egenhofer, M. (1998). Comparing the complexity of wayfinding tasks in built environments. *Environment and Planning B, 25*(6), 895–913.

Regenbrecht, H., & Schubert, T. (2002). Real and illusory interactions enhance presence in virtual environments. *Presence: Teleoperators and Virtual Environments, 11*(4), 425–434.

Salen, K., & Zimmerman, E. (2003). *Rules of play: game design fundamentals*. Cambridge, MA: MIT Press.

Schroeder, R. (2002). *Copresence and interaction in virtual environments: an overview of the range of issues*. Paper presented at the Presence 2002 Conference: Fifth Annual International Workshop on Presence, Porto, Portugal.

Schubert, T., Regenbrecht, H., & Friedmann, F. (2000). *Real and Illusory Interaction Enhance Presence in Virtual Environments*. Paper presented at the Presence 2000. Third International Workshop on Presence. Retrieved 28 April 2010, from http://www.temple.edu/ispr/prev_conferences/proceedings/98–99-2000/2000/Schubert,%20Regenbrecht,%20Friedmann.pdf

Schuemie, M.J., van der Straaten, P., Krijn, M., & van der Mast, C.A.P.G. (2001). Research on presence in virtual reality: a survey. *CyberPsychology and Behavior, 4*(2), 183–201.

Shneiderman, B. (2004). Designing for fun: how can we design user interfaces to be more fun? *Interactions, 11*(5), 48–50.

Soini, K. (2001). Exploring human dimensions of multifunctional landscapes through mapping and map-making. *Landscape and Urban Planning, 57*(3–4), 225–239.

Squire, K., & Barab, S.A. (2004). *Replaying History*. Paper presented at the 2004 International Conference of the Learning Sciences, Los Angeles, CA.

Sterelny, K. (2003). *Cognitive Load and Human Decision, or, Three Ways of Rolling the Rock Up Hill*. Paper presented at the Innateness Workshop. Retrieved 28 April 2010, from http://www.victoria.ac.nz/hppi/staff/publications/sheffield.pdf

Sterelny, K. (2004). Externalism, epistemic artefacts and the extended mind. In R. Schantz (Ed.), *The Externalist Challenge. New Studies on Cognition and Intentionality* (pp. 239–254). Berlin & New York: de Gruyter.

Towell, J.F., & Towell, E.R. (1997). Presence in text-based networked virtual environments or "MUDS,". *Presence: Teleoperators and Virtual Environments, 6*(5), 590–595.

Vinson, N.G. (1999). *Design Guidelines for Landmarks to Support Navigation in Virtual Environments*. Paper presented at the SIGCHI conference on Human factors in computing systems: the CHI is the limit, Pittsburgh, PA.

Wang, H., Johnson, T.R., & Zhang, J. (2001). *The Mind's Views of Space*. Paper presented at the 3rd International Conference of Cognitive Science, Beijing: China.

Weckström, N. (2004). *Finding 'reality' in virtual environments*. Unpublished Masters, Arcada Polytechnic, Helsingfors/Esbo.

Wickens, C.D., & Baker, P. (1995). Cognitive issues in virtual reality. In W. Barfield & T. Furness (Eds). *Virtual environments and advanced interface design* (pp. 514–541). Oxford: Oxford University Press.

Chapter 6
Playing with the Past

6.1 What Is Virtual Heritage?

Visualization has been defined as "to form a mental image of something incapable of being viewed or not at that moment visible... (Collins Dictionary)...a tool or method for interpreting image data fed into a computer and for generating images from complex multi-dimensional data sets" (McCormick et al. 1987).

So the point of virtual heritage might be to visualize a culture through its artifacts. Virtual heritage is thus a 'visualization' or 'recreation' of culture. In virtual heritage projects, the aim is typically to "recreate" or "reconstruct" the past through three-dimensional modeling, animation, and panorama photographs. In some advanced cases, objects are laser-scanned, and accurate textures of what used to be there are applied to the resulting digital models.

Why would we do that? For many reasons, for when a culture is no longer with us, when a culture is so ingrained that we do not normally notice or appreciate it, or when the remains of a society or civilization are currently inaccessible or scattered.

It may now seem to us that virtual heritage is simply the recreation of what used to be there. Yet what used to be 'there' was more than a collection of objects. Those objects had specific meaning to the cultural perceptions of the land's traditional inhabitants.

In the article entitled *Lost worlds become virtual heritage*, Chan (2007) defined the goal of virtual heritage in terms of intangible heritage:

Virtual heritage technology aims to recreate a three-dimensional navigable world and also to provide something much less tangible – a sense of look and feel.

However, the above goal does not explain the importance of heritage. Consider another definition of virtual heritage, by Stone and Ojika (2000):

[It is]...the use of computer-based interactive technologies to record, preserve, or recreate artifacts, sites and actors of historic, artistic, religious, and cultural significance and to deliver the results openly to a global audience in such a way as to provide formative educational experiences through electronic manipulations of time and space.

E. Champion, *Playing with the Past*, Human-Computer Interaction Series, DOI 10.1007/978-1-84996-501-9_6, © Springer-Verlag London Limited 2011

So the purpose of virtual heritage is to record, preserve and recreate objects and processes of cultural significance. According to Stone and Ojika, it should present the results transparently to the public, preferably globally as well as locally. They also suggested it should attempt to provide a learning experience. However, we may have to modify this definition. For example, virtual heritage projects cover cultural significance in terms of both time and space, but both together are not necessary features, so this feature is descriptive rather than prescriptive.

Another omission with the above definition regards the presentation of and inter-action with specific cultural *beliefs*. ICOMOS, UNESCO, and other organizations are moving towards including within the scope of heritage the preservation and communication of intangible heritage, which include cultural beliefs (similar or dissimilar to our own). There is also the need to aim for authenticity of reproduc-tion, scholastic rigor, and sensitivity to the needs of both audience and the share-holders of the original and remaining content.

Three international charters deal with the subject of cultural heritage, and they stress the importance of communicating cultural significance. The ICOMOS Burra Charter (1999) defines cultural significance as involving "aesthetic, historic, scien-tific, social or spiritual value for past, present or future generations. Cultural signifi-cance is embodied in the place itself, its fabric, setting, use, associations, meanings, records, related places and related objects."

More recently, the London Charter (Beacham et al. 2003) aims to create rigorous guidelines for the use of 3D technology in the creation of virtual heritage. It recom-mends that 3D visualization methods are applied with scholarly rigor, and "accu-rately convey to users distinctions between evidence and hypothesis, and between different levels of probability." The last principle says "consideration should be given to the ways in which the outcomes of 3D visualization work could contribute to the wider study, understanding, interpretation and management of cultural heri-tage assets."

The Ename ICOMOS Charter (ICOMOS 2007) suggested that the aim of digital media (and by extension, virtual heritage), is to facilitate understanding and appre-ciation, communicate, safeguard, and respect the authenticity, as well as contribute to, promote inclusiveness, and develop technical guidelines for cultural heritage sites. The Ename charter defines a Cultural Heritage Site as "a place, locality, natural landscape, settlement area, architectural complex, archaeological site, or standing structure that is recognized and often legally protected as a place of historical and cultural significance."

In previous writings I suggested that one prevalent feature of New Media is the development of user-centered, personalizable data, not constrained by one type of hardware device (Champion 2006). However I don't believe that realism is the predominant driving force behind entertainment media. For example, while Serviss (2005, p. 5) argued that 60 frames per second was already achievable by the game console PlayStation 2, he noted the real advances in the near future will be player customization and the ability to experience emotions via these environments. The increasing emphasis of new media on user-customization and personalization leads me to suggest that the purpose of virtual heritage is to re-examine the user experience that digital media can provide to better understand and experience tangible and intangible cultural heritage.

Given the above, I suggest five major aims. Firstly, virtual heritage should aim to carefully capture objects and processes of cultural significance. Secondly it should present this information as accurately, authentically, and engagingly as possible. Thirdly, it should attempt to distribute in a sensitive, safe and durable manner the project to as wide and long-term an audience as possible. Fourthly, it must aim to provide an effective and inspirational learning environment that best communicates the intended learning goals. Fifthly, it should attempt to carefully evaluate its effectiveness in regards to the above four aims in order to improve both the project, and virtual heritage in general.

6.2 The Problem of Culture

If the cultural geographer Yi-Fu Tuan is to be believed, culture is that which is not seen. He wrote that "Seeing what is not there lies at the foundation of all human culture" (Tuan 1998). He has further defined culture as a shared form of escapism. Such a definition raises an interesting paradox for the visualization of past cultures. How do we see what is not there?

There are many issues in the presentation of culture. One is the definition of culture itself, the second issue is to understand how culture is transmitted, and the third is how to transmit this cultural knowledge to people from another culture. In the case of virtual heritage, a fourth also arises, exactly how could this specific cultural knowledge be transmitted digitally?

Research has indicated that the general public does not want realism but entertaining immersion. Various researchers have suggested that virtual environments (specifically heritage environments) often lack several features that would make them more engaging to the general public.

> ..[The] archaeological use of VR is at present all about the creation of pictures...Only after they have been generated does attention turn to the uses to which such models can be put. (Gillings 2002, p. 17)

Both Gillings and I suggest it is not a lack of realism but a lack of meaningful content, which impedes the enjoyment of virtual heritage. I call it the 'Indiana Jones' dilemma. On the one hand, adventure films have popularized archaeology as an interactive and engaging pursuit. On the other hand, they and computer games typically destroy the very object of admiration. Digital media can recreate both objects and activities, but what sort of activity is both engaging and educational? How can we both significantly preserve and meaningfully communicate the past?

The following 11 case studies are selective examples from an escalating field of projects. They represent game-inspired projects in terms of interactivity or technology, and are not meant to cover the whole spectrum of virtual heritage research. They do however provide an idea of the range of possible content, technology and interactivity. For example, the first project was designed using beta software, but is available to anyone with a PC and an Internet browser. The last project was shown in a complex, expensive and unique installation and was by invitation only.

6.3 Virtual Heritage Case Studies

6.3.1 *Art History in Online Worlds: Santa Maria, Italy*

The following project by Dr. Glenn Gunhouse was an online taught assignment using Blink 3D. Gunhouse teaches Western art, as well as Roman art and architecture. Before they were taken off the market, he used Adobe Atmosphere and then Blink 3D. He has explained his process for designing this church in the journal *VR in the Schools* (Gunhouse 2007).

The image shows a 3D model of the thirteenth-century church of Santa Maria ad Cryptas, near Fossa, Italy (Fig. 6.1). Gunhouse designed the architectural model with AC3D, applied his own photographs of the frescoes to its walls, and created the web-accessible 3D model with Blink 3D. The environment was chat-enabled, so that he could meet students in the space and talk with them when required.

The assignment started from problems in asking student to decide the spatial arrangement of frescos in the church from photographs they were given. They typically followed the numbering of the photographs without trying to understand the

Fig. 6.1 Blink3D (Courtesy of Glenn Gunhouse)

spatial arrangement of the church. He first suggested that students create a 3D paper prototype of the church, and results appeared to improve in terms of spatial layout but not in terms of the description of the frescos. His second solution was to build a 3D model in AC3D, assign four light points in Giles to create the light maps and export the 3D model, jpgs, and light maps as a web-enabled environment available via the Blink 3D web plug-in. Now the students could walk through the virtual church and discuss with each other where the frescos belonged. Gunhouse noted that the students using the 3D online model delivered clearly improved reports to those students who only had access to photographs.

So as a pedagogical tool method, the use of 3D online environments appears to have been successful. And any determined art historian without extensive 3D and scripting experience could follow the process Gunhouse described in his paper. However there is a catch and it is to do with the technology.

Blink 3D was based on the Ogre 3D rendering engine, added simple JavaScript behaviors, and created stand alone environments or plug-ins that could be viewed via a web browser on a PC. It was designed to be easy to use and quick to create with, and was a spiritual successor to Adobe Atmosphere. The features sounded impressive, including AGEIA PhysX™ Physics Engine, ambient and positional 3D sound, DirectX 9.0 and Open GL (but did not run on Macs), a choice between extended JavaScript (BlinkScript) or default behaviors, a programmable Graphical User Interface, animation tracks, distance spot and point lighting, mesh Level of Detail (LOD) support, and the ability to read and write XML documents.

I still believe it was a great idea; it was built on a stable, cross-platform and free real-time rendering engine (Ogre 3D) that had both Open GL and Direct 3D support. However the engine is not for the fainthearted, and Pelican Crossing (who made Blink 3D) modified it to run in a web browser and they made it available to the general public who could now either use built-in behaviors or create and attach simple JavaScript scripts. However, in practice it did not appear to be so intuitive to use and suffered (like so many of these technologies) from mysterious bugs. It followed the tragic fate of Adobe Atmosphere, and is no longer available, so Gunhouse is now converting his models from Adobe Atmosphere and Blink 3D to Unity.

6.3.2 Virtual Forbidden City, China

The Forbidden City in China was off-limits to foreigners for over five centuries until the Chinese government turned it into a public museum in 1925 (IBM 2008). In 2005 IBM with the assistance of the Palace Museum in Beijing began a 3 year project to recreate an online simulation of the Forbidden City, available to both English-speaking and Chinese-speaking audiences (Fig. 6.2). It is a true multiplayer world, where visitors can meet and talk to each other or post comments and questions in an online forum. As at 30 April 2010 there were well over 300,000 site registrations. It runs on Mac, Windows and Linux.

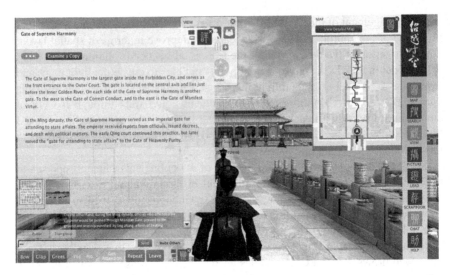

Fig. 6.2 Virtual Forbidden City, China (Courtesy of IBM)

According to John Tolva via his Ascent Stage Blog, who works for IBM and worked on this project (as well as the Eternal Egypt and the Heritage Museum multimedia websites), it is a "Participatory Cultural Environment to stress the importance of a space alive with people – other visitors who you can interact with and, if possible, computer-controlled representations of historic persons" (Tolva 2006). He then writes "Though 3D representation is widespread in the field of cultural heritage (primarily for preservation), this kind of multi-user, education-focused cultural worlds does not exist."

The environment apparently runs on Torque from Garage Games, and is a 275 MB download for Mac users (Schonfeld 2008). The interface is relatively intuitive, and the information pages that fade in and out are useful, and the map is very helpful considering the size of the simulation. However, you do need a reasonably fast computer, and the right Internet ports open if you are to play it, and to see other people and chat to them.

6.3.3 Dordrecht Monastery, The Netherlands

Dordrecht Monastery (Fig. 6.3) is a culturally significant monument, for the Kingdom of the Netherlands began there in 1572. In 2007 the city archives invited the games company Paladin Studio to create an interactive 3D visualization of the Monastery, and show how the buildings changed over the centuries, (today only some of the foundations exist).

Dylan Nagel, who is a cofounder of Paladin Studios, trained as an archaeologist and his postgraduate thesis project was an online 3D visualization of the major buildings of the Mayan city of Palenque, in Mexico. He worked for the games

Fig. 6.3 Dordrecht Monastery, The Netherlands (Courtesy of Dylan Nagel, Paladin Studios)

industry and then worked for Quest 3D in the Netherlands, before starting Paladin Studios. Perhaps that explains why this model is such a good showcase of Quest 3D, it won the Quest 3D Award in 2008. Fixed camera paths allow the visitor to follow predetermined overhead views of the building, or click buttons to go backwards and forwards in time. There is HDR lighting, and background singing but no avatars. The "Hof van Dordrecht 3D" simulation can also be viewed on YouTube (Paladin Studios 2007).

6.3.4 Urban Design and Virtual Sambor, Cambodia

Virtual Sambor Prei Kuk is an online virtual heritage site of a seventh century temple complex created by Professor Yehuda Kalay's Digital Design Research Group at the University of California, Berkeley. The download file is 100 MB, created using Garage Game's Torque game engine. Kalay has categorized this virtual heritage environment as an immersive, interactive, web-enabled, multi user virtual environment (MUVE). He describes MUVES as follows (Kalay n.d.):

> MUVEs are a new media vehicle that has the ability to communicate cultural heritage experience in a way that is a cross between filmmaking, video games, and architectural design. Unlike a film, it allows the observer to be an active participant in the experience. Unlike video games, its objective is to teach, rather than entertain. And unlike architectural design, it models – in addition to the built environment – also the people who inhabited the site, and their rituals.

The visitor can chose one of four avatars (two male, two female) and can choose to wave their hand, pray, switch from first person to third person, open or close the map, jump, or chat from the keyboard (although I did not see other people in the

Fig. 6.4 Virtual Sambor – the market (Courtesy of Yehuda Kalay)

virtual environment to chat to, perhaps this was due to technical issues or merely visiting at the wrong time). The main scene (Fig. 6.4) is of the market, with live and dead animals, and NPCs (Non Playing Characters) carrying out their daily tasks. There are many NPCs but perhaps because of their numbers, they have a low polygon count (they don't look highly realistic or detailed). Some of the animals appear to be 3D and some appear to be alpha facing 2D pictures.

There is a 5 min YouTube video (University of California 2009) that usefully explains the significance and rituals of the site using in-game footage, and I'd recommend watching this before entering the virtual environment, as there are less navigational cues and information inside Virtual Sambor. One thing of note, the video explains the major buildings have fine even exquisite detail but it seems hard to capture in the virtual environment (Fig. 6.5). Close up detailed photos, panoramas or secondary camera views would be a worthwhile addition.

The chief priest (Fig. 6.6) makes an offering of red and blue lotus leaves, and burns incense and makes food offerings in the main shrine (which would be out of bounds for real world tourists). It would be interesting if the visitor's avatar when inside a sacred space in Virtual Sambor could interfere with the ritual and passage around the shrine causing the priest and other NPCs to react to this. I'd suggest this is a kind of intangible bounding box: there are invisible cultural demarcations in rituals and using NPCs that can detect when these boundaries are violated by interlopers would help emphasize the local cultural affordances and constraints.

Fig. 6.5 Virtual Sambor – tower (Courtesy of Yehuda Kalay)

Fig. 6.6 Virtual Sambor – ritual (Courtesy of Yehuda Kalay)

6.3.5 *FAS Palace, Mesopotamia*

A project team consisting of members of UCLA's Cuneiform Digital Library Initiative (CDLI), the Federation of American Scientists (FAS) and the Walters Art Museum (WAM) created *Discover Babylon*, a visualization of ancient Mesopotamia

(Lucey-Roper 2006). One major aim of the project was to reach "non-traditional museum visitors." It was developed as a museum kiosk project and as a PC game to be played at home.

The player travels back in time to a Neo-Assyrian palace. As you can see in the interface (Fig. 6.7) there is a camera with a set battery life that acts as a time constraint. The goal is to capture (via the camera) as many artifacts as possible before the camera batteries run out. The reward for a successful "capture" is an information popup box that appears with more information on the artifact. It is deliberately short and simple because of the time and cognitive demands on a typical museum visitor. The kiosk was designed specifically for the Walter Art Museum's Ancient Near Eastern Art Gallery.

The home PC version was designed to be longer, requiring knowledge of the museum, and visiting not one but three time periods; the Uruk Period (3300–3000 BC); the Ur III period (2100–2000 BC), and the Neo-Assyrian period (1000–600 BC). (Federation of American Scientists n.d.). The interaction modes were "observation, reading or completing challenges." The primary problem is a time traveler called Dexter, "who has figured out how to travel back in time, accidentally and unknowingly wreaking havoc with the fabric of time." In searching for Dexter (in order to fix time), the players find themselves appear as a different character in each game level. For example, if they appear as a scribe, they are tested on their scribe knowledge.

An in-world tool (or in my terminology, an external cognitive artifact) was also developed, called My Learning Assistant, a graphical PDA that records information

Fig. 6.7 Palace Kalhu, Assyria (Courtesy of Federation of American Scientists)

and provides clues. Further, the game developers declared they would capture information, logged results of "where the player has gone, what was found to be interesting, challenging or boring, and what questions were asked" could also be retrieved (with the player's permission). The 218.8 MB Windows XP game can be downloaded from the FAS website (http://fas.org/babylon/the-game).

Feedback from users appeared to be highly positive but there were some usability issues. They would have preferred mouse interaction, being able to use any keyboard (not just a full desktop keyboard), alignment between the keyboard conventions and computer games (the S key did not take the avatar backwards but spun them around 180 degrees), and being able to change from third person (the game default) to first person (to enhance the sense of immersion or to help with examination of artifacts and with general navigation).

6.3.6   Culture and History Inside a Game: Palestine and Italy

Global Conflicts: Palestine is an award-winning game in an award winning series; it was voted PcZone Indie Game of The Month award in 2007 and won a BETT award in 2010 (Fig. 6.8). At time of writing (in 2010) it was also relatively inexpensive; US$15 for one license, $75 for a class set of 30, and $120 for a school set of 250. For our purposes it is also relatively unique; there are not very many commercial educational computer games that focus on learning about different cultures, are designed to complement classroom learning, and are part of a series made by a company (Serious Games Interactive) dedicated to serious games. Available in Danish or English versions, the PC or Mac game demo can be downloaded from their website (http://www.globalconflicts.eu).

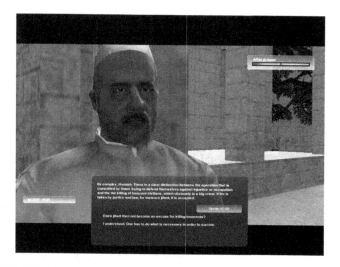

Fig. 6.8 Global Conflicts: Palestine – dialogue with Imam (Courtesy of Serious Games Interactive)

The gameplay is relatively straightforward: the player takes on the role of a journalist and their mission is to interview different sources from both points of view (pro-Israeli and pro-Palestinian). Interviewing means approaching characters and choosing questions or replies in the dialogue box that appears. The goal is to find the right quotes to make a great story (as rated by the game's editor). In order to collect and assemble the quotes (using the quote button), the player must decide which story and informants to believe (such as how Palestinian terrorists suspects are treated by the Israeli Defensive Force). Serious Games Interactive also suggest students aged 13–20 could play the game and in small groups afterwards discuss their viewpoint, write an essay, and rate other student essays in the online forum (Serious Games Interactive n.d.).

The reviews I have seen are mostly positive. One review noted it was not as polished as mainstream commercial games, but was relatively rare in being a thought provoking experience (Clare 2007). I thought the review raised an interesting point: how there was no humor in the game but that it may have added to the character depth of the NPCs (Non-Playing Characters). I wonder if humor was deemed too dangerous or may have had an adverse affect on class learning and on the dramatic impact. Incidentally, the technical or user interface faults raised by reviewers (Clare 2007; Grabowski 2007) can be explained away by the technology. Serious Games Interactive was one of the first major commercial players to use the rendering engine Unity, and creating graphical user interfaces and animated characters in Unity was much more challenging than it is now.

Actually the game reminds me of a totally different approach. Rather than taking a fledging game engine and pushing it as far as it could (then) go, the Australian collective selectparks modified a commercial game, Half Life 1, using the limitations of the game to chilling dramatic effect. Their game level was called *Escape from Woomera*; depicting the Woomera Detention Centre in Australia for asylum seekers, refugees or illegal aliens.

Trying to find a sentient NPC that could teach you (the player) how to escape the camp (if you could not gain asylum) was an exercise in frustration, and the lack of artificial intelligence and expressiveness of the many NPCs wandering aimlessly around heightened one's feeling of depression and loneliness. The game level featured in the national newspapers and drew scathing criticism from the then Minister of Immigration for receiving federal (i.e. national) funding from the Australia Council's New Media Arts Board (Nicholls 2003). Despite its education potential, I don't believe it was designed for classroom learning, and it was single player only. The Half-Life game is now archived but can still be downloaded (selectparks 2007).

Returning to Denmark, how did Serious Games Interactive modify their game series? With the Uganda game, they added a way of conveying the NPC's stress, so you could convince NPCs when you pressure them (a device similar perhaps to the Bribe wheel in *Elder Scrolls IV: Oblivion*). So the change is perhaps a matter of degree.

However Serious Games Interactive changed tack with their latest game, *Playing History: The Plague* (Fig. 6.9). Like their earlier games, the game's website features a free demo download (Serious Games Interactive 2010). However it is designed for a much younger market, and is decidedly more amusing. The introduction to the

Fig. 6.9 Playing with history dialogue (Courtesy of Serious Games Interactive)

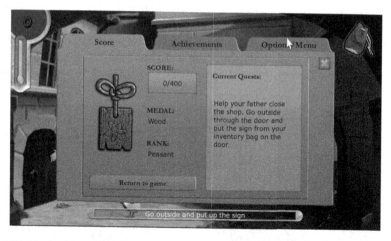

Fig. 6.10 Playing history interface screen (Courtesy of Serious Games Interactive)

game is by a cute-looking and Renaissance-clothed rat, I wonder if they ever thought of telling the story from a rat's point of view.

In terms of gameplay, although still point-and-click and text-dialogue-based, one can now also collect artifacts and leave them (via mouse drag and drop) in the environment (Fig. 6.10). And the rewards (or achievements) are now carried around with the player in an inventory (rather than determined at the end of the level (as in Global Conflicts: Palestine).

The educational goal behind the design of the game, according to Simon Egenfeldt-Nielsen (the Director of Serious Games Interactive), is to turn students into active players rather than passive consumers of historical events (Egenfeldt-Nielsen 2010).

He wrote that the game's solution to the problem of how one can interact with history, that is, how to change what is already changed, is to allow players to save one family but they cannot prevent the entire plague. He described this as creating a "little history."

6.3.7 Virtual Egyptian Temple

Apart from *Escape to Woomera* and *FarCry: Queenscliff*, I have not so far covered commercial game engines that have been modded by academics to create game-mods (Fig. 6.11). However, Unreal Tournament can perhaps lay claim to being the foremost game modder for academics in cultural heritage, architectural visualization, artificial intelligence simulations, and even 3D multi-user worlds hosted by videoconferencing software such as Skype.

Unreal Tournament was also the game engine that Jeffrey Jacobson used to create CaveUT (Jacobson et al. 2005). Basically, CaveUT recreates the CAVE designed by the Electronic Visualization Lab at the University of Chicago (Cruz-Neira et al. 1993), but at a much reduced price through using a commercial game engine.

A CAVE is a four to six wall virtual environment display, each wall being a projected screen, when set up as cube, the participant feels they are surrounded in a virtual room. Traditional CAVES are expensive, fragile and difficult to produce content for (Henden et al. 2008; Jacobson and Preussner 2010) but using Unreal Tournament, we can create different views of the same game or virtual environment,

Fig. 6.11 Virtual Egyptian Temple, Courtyard, Egypt (Courtesy of Jeffrey Jacobson)

Fig. 6.12 Virtual Egyptian Temple, Earth Theatre, (Courtesy of Jeffrey Jacobson)

and project these views onto separate walls, floor and ceiling, Or we can project them onto a curved surface to surround the viewer, for example the Earth Theatre at the Carnegie Museum of Natural History (Fig. 6.12).

Jacobson's nonprofit organization, PublicVR (http://publicVR.org) creates and hosts various virtual heritage projects, but the Virtual Egyptian Temple (Troche and Jacobson 2010) is perhaps their most famous, being hosted permanently at the Carnegie Museum of Natural History's Earth Theatre. The environment can be downloaded for free from the PublicVR site, and runs inside Unreal Tournament on a Mac or PC. A booklet is available as a free download and teaching tool as well.

The model is based on the ruins of the Temple of Horus at Edfu and other examples, so it is representative of a New Kingdom Egyptian Temple per se, in order to better function as a teaching tool for younger students (Jacobson and Holden 2007). The other intentional derivation from specific historical accuracy (as explained in the booklet) is to make the hieroglyphs larger (so they are more legible) and to include only the "essential details" and not model all of the spaces from the entire site. A game was also developed using the model entitled *Gates of Horus*, to play the game you must collect information and correctly answer a priest's questions before you are allowed into the inner sanctuary.

The Virtual Egypt Temple is one of the longest running virtual heritage projects that I know of. The first version (from 1993) ran in VRML and was hosted at the Guggenheim museum. For the above Unreal Tournament version, PublicVR hope to enhance the lighting, add more objects from artifacts available in the Walton Hall of Egyptology (also at the Carnegie Museum), change the wall coloring, and incorporate ambient music composed for the temple. PublicVR have also ported the site to Unity so it can now also run inside a web browser but at the time of writing this web version has not been publicly released.

6.3.8 Dome Visualization: Mawson's Hut, Antarctica

Peter Morse and Paul Bourke embarked on a project to visualize an historic site in Antarctica, Cape Denison. Mawson's Huts stand there, testament to the Douglas Mawson-led Australasian Antarctic Expedition of 1911–1914. The site is rarely visited and features some of the strongest winds on the planet, katabatic winds (Loewe 1950; Parish and Wendler 1991). The project shown here is a combination of panoramic bubbles and a 3D digital environment, the hemispherical dome here (Fig. 6.13) presents a spherical panoramic photograph (or bubble) of a real room in one of the real Mawson's Huts. I will discuss the panoramic bubbles in Chapter 7; here I would like to concentrate on the type of environment that runs the project.

The iDome is a hemispherical dome, which can be made out of fiberglass, steel, or another material that can be fashioned into a smooth spherical surface. At the bottom of the iDome is a hole through which the projector projects onto a curved mirror (similar to the security mirrors found on the walls of shops). In his effort to find an economical alternative to fisheye projection, Bourke (2005, 2006, 2008) proposed projecting onto a curved mirror instead. The mirror reflects a rendering of the virtual environment back onto the inside of the iDome. A warping algorithm ensures the image on the hemispherical dome surface appears natural and undistorted for the viewer. Four cameras in a game engine like Unity (used here) create the render textures which are then mapped to a fisheye which is then warped so it will appear correct when used with a curved mirror. Though this was devised for planetariums, Bourke's warping code has implications for immersive gaming (and heritage) applications.

Heritage is not the primary use for iDomes; they feature strongly in mining environment disaster training and scientific simulations. However, my first experience of similar technology was a game running inside an Elumens Vision station (sometime around 2002); it featured a trial version of Blueberry3D, a visualization package that in

Fig. 6.13 Mawson's Hut reconstruction in an iDome (Courtesy of Paul Bourke and Peter Morse)

this case featured a small car with exaggerated physics that you could drive over a large forested island. I found that experience highly immersive (even though many early Visionstations' field of view was 150 or 160 degrees, not 180 degrees), and Bourke's newer iDomes are considerably cheaper and higher quality. Bourke (2009, Bourke and Felinto 2010) has also shown game engines running inside the iDome, Source game engine screenshots converted to fisheye projections, and virtual environments using Blender 3D and Unity (the real-time rendering engine used for this project).

For driving and cycling games, involving a seated avatar and user, or for displaying panoramas and panoramic movies, the iDome is a great fit. However, to fully utilize the dome I feel that standing and moving interaction without using a desk, or mouse or keyboard would be more interesting even though this probably would mean a larger radius and/or raising the iDome so the line of sight lines up with the back of the dome.

Secondly, there is a sweet spot factor; more than one user may not get the best view. And this leads to my third point; there is a challenging issue for collaborative virtual environments. If we return to the image (Fig. 6.13), one might wonder why both of the men are pointing, and what they are pointing at. It is probably to provide focal direction for the photograph, and demonstrate how immersive the experience can be. Yet due to the curvature of the iDome neither person would be able to see what the other person is pointing at.

In a planetarium one could use a pointer or magic wand. I am sure there will also be workarounds and innovative solutions for these smaller projection environments, but it provides a good example of how cutting-edge display systems can create interaction headaches of their own that is not immediately evident in photographs or even in videos. If a mouse is used to navigate in the mixed environment of panorama and 3D world, this may also create some user interface issues if the participant is required to click on something in the screen.

6.3.9 Heritage Tour: Macquarie Lighthouse, Australia

The next virtual heritage environment was Eric Fassbender's Ph.D. project which evaluated the effect of music on learning in a virtual environment (Fassbender and Richards 2008). So the initial aim was not virtual heritage per se, but it involved several interesting features.

Not only was the musical setting a key part of the environment, the technology was a commercial role-playing game mod (*Elder Scrolls IV: Oblivion*), but run inside Macquarie University's 'Reality Center'. The Reality Center is a three-projector system, which projects the virtual environment onto a semi-cylindrical screen canvas, covering 160 degrees of the visual field.

The main model in the environment is a simulation of the university's icon, Macquarie Lighthouse, Australia's first lighthouse. It was designed by convict Francis Greenway and completed in 1818 before it had to be rebuilt several decades later. In the game level mod, a fictional descendent of the first lighthouse keeper

Fig. 6.14 Macquarie Lighthouse in Oblivion (Courtesy of Eric Fassbender)

greets visitors inside the environment, and provides information about the historical background of the lighthouse. The related image (Fig. 6.14) shows a pilot-tester viewing the environment, and listening to the lighthouse character (whose facial appearance and lip synchronization was created using Oblivion's level editor) delivering the history of the lighthouse.

Seventy-two participants (local undergraduate students) were tested in Experiment 1 but tests were conducted individually, they viewed a nearly 12 min video with different music as background and a control group without any music. Participants then answered a post-test questionnaire, which included a multi-choice test on information recall (dates, names, events, etc.), and questions about feelings of immersion (how much did you lose track of time, how much did you forget about yourself/problems, etc.), and some biographical information was requested (such as musical experience, and game-playing experience). Results from Experiment 1 (Richards et al. 2008) indicated that lower pitch and slower tempo of background music may improve learning (but not significantly so), and that the Oblivion music (which is part of the game level) helped learning significantly more than if there was no background music. A second round of experiments was conducted, and results are currently only available in the Ph.D. thesis (Fassbender 2009) on http://www. VirSchool.com or from the Macquarie University Library.

Experiment 2 involved half the participants using the Reality Center, and half using a three-monitor desktop setup and music was played or not played in either the first or second half of the video. Results showed that the number of historical facts remembered correctly from the three-monitor display system were higher than from the expensive and complex Reality Center system. This was completely counter to the initial hypothesis, leading Fassbender (2009) to suggest the VR system may have contributed to cognitive overload affecting the participants. This suggestion is based on research by Sweller (1988) and Clarke et al. (2005).

I am not totally sure why a game level was used to create what is in a sense a pre-rendered video, but the researchers saw interactivity as a possible confounding factor. What is clear here is the difficulty inherent in evaluating learning in an interactive virtual environment. However, the project does demonstrate the power and flexibility of modern commercial games and their ability to act as virtual environments and display on high-end virtual environment technology. For apart from being restricted (unnecessarily) by the game developers to being single-player, the Elder Scrolls IV Construction set (which is bundled with the *Elder Scrolls IV: Oblivion* game), is a powerful and very easy to use level editor. For example, the game engine also created automatic lip-synching for the NPC (Non Player Character) avatar to narrate the history of the Lighthouse, based on voice files recorded and edited specifically for the project.

6.3.10 Panoramic Explorations: PLACE-Hampi, India

The following project PLACE-Hampi (Fig. 6.15) was commissioned for France India year in 2006 and installed in the Opera House, Lille, France (Fig. 6.16). It was then shown at Martin Gropius Bau, Berlin (2007), ZKM, Karlsruhe (2008), Shanghai Museum of Science and Technology (2008) and the Immigration Museum, Melbourne (2008–2010).

The project is based upon 360-degree stereo pair panoramas (taken by a custom built pair of cameras, one for the left eye and one for the right eye) of the most significant archaeological, historical and sacred locations found at the World

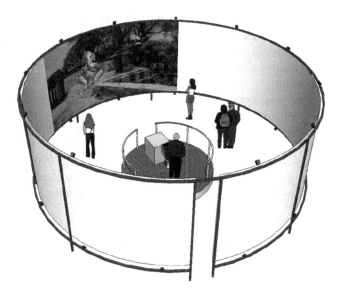

Fig. 6.15 PLACE-Hampi (Courtesy of Sarah Kenderdine and Jeffrey Shaw)

Fig. 6.16 PLACE-Hampi, Opera House, Lille (Courtesy of Sarah Kenderdine and Jeffrey Shaw)

Heritage site Vijayanagara (Hampi), South India (Kenderdine and de Kruiff n.d.; Kenderdine et al. 2008, 2009).

From over 100 panoramas taken on site, 18 were chosen. 3D computer generated characters were inserted into the panoramas. These animated deities (with movement take from motion capture) comprise a series of 'vignettes' and were conceived to visualize aspects of the Ramayana (an ancient Sanskrit epic) and the relationship between Hampi and Kishkindha (the home of the monkeys in this epic). Ambisonic sound recordings (which can cover 360 degrees) were also taken at the location of each of the 18 Hampi panoramas and classical Carnatic music was incorporated into the environment.

PLACE-Hampi was conceived and created by Sarah Kenderdine and Jeffrey Shaw together with John Gollings and Paul Doornbusch, Dr. L. Subramaniam, Paprikaas Animation Studio and support from the Archaeological Survey of India. Produced by the UNSW iCinema Research Centre in collaboration with Epidemic Paris, ZKM Karlsruhe, Archaeological, Survey of India, Lille3000, and Museum Victoria. It was financially supported under the Australian Research Council's Linkage funding scheme and the Australia Council's Synapse funding scheme.

6.3.11 Performance and Archaeology: Spaces of Mjalnar, Malta

The final case study presented here also ran inside the AVIE (The Advanced Visualisation and Interaction Environment) at iCinema, University of New South Wales,

Fig. 6.17 Spaces of Mjalnar from above (Courtesy of Bernadette Flynn)

Australia (Fig. 6.17: images are copyright of Bernadette Flynn, the photographer was Heidrun Lohr). The project Spaces of Mnajdra by Bernadette Flynn was the production evidence for a doctoral thesis and a continuing research project that investigated somatic knowledge (Flynn 2007b). Flynn defined somatic knowledge as "personal experiential perception" and the work was inspired by writings on phenomenology by the archaeologist Christopher Tilley (1994, 2004).

My reading of Tilley's argument is that traditional forms of archaeological discourse such as books and maps are abstract representations. Being representations they shield us from a direct experiencing of what they describe. Thus Tilley argued that to understand the past we have to physically explore the sites themselves, and attempt to understand via direct sensory experience how sites and artifacts relate to each other and how we relate to the sites. According to Tilley the irony of traditional approaches in archaeology lies in the exclusion of this human aspect, thus ensuring that what is documented fails to address how people might have moved and interacted with their material culture.

The prehistoric Mnajdra temples of South East Malta are one of the oldest megalithic structures in the world (3600 BC–2500 BC). The temples were captured by high-resolution panoramas that were assembled into a virtual environment and projected onto the walls of the AVIE (Advanced Visualisation and Interaction Environment) at iCinema, University of New South Wales (UNSW), Sydney Australia. The AVIE is a 360-degree stereoscopic immersive interactive visualization environment with motion and shape tracking systems and a multi-channel audio system.

Although I have not seen it firsthand, my understanding is that Spaces of Mjalnar, Malta (with funding from Heritage Malta) had the objective of conveying the direct bodily experiencing of a remote and sacred heritage site without mediation

Fig. 6.18 Spaces of Mjalnar from the user's perspective (Courtesy of Bernadette Flynn)

by computer peripherals in order to facilitate an "authenticity of experience" (Flynn 2007a). To facilitate this more direct form of interaction the project incorporated two input methods; a sensory wand attached to a pedestal so that users could explore the 3D space, and camera tracking of the participants' outlines. There was some freedom of movement; the participants could move freely within the space (Fig. 6.18). The wand revealed details on the walls that otherwise could not be seen and it could also rotate 3D artifacts (such as pots and figurines).

As participants moved their outline was tracked by infrared camera mounted in the ceiling and images of the original temple appearance were projected inside the captured outline. The captured outlines changed in scale, revealing the original corbelled roof construction, architectural details, and the low relief markings. At significant doorways an in-world performer moved inside the participants' shadows, inviting participants to adopt particular ways of moving though the space.

The launch and project evaluations ran from 21 to 23 February 2010, invited participants were members of the Maltese community, new media and heritage specialists or performers. There were three participants for each 1 hour session although the actual in-world time was of 30 minutes duration. Some preliminary observations are noted below but a more comprehensive account as well as the extended results will be made available in Flynn's doctoral thesis.

At an early design stage Flynn had planned to use 3D motion tracking with gesture recognition. However, the constraints of the available technology resulted in 2D tracking based on position location, which ironically proved to be more useful to the project. Participants were now freer in their range of movements and were no longer confined to certain gesture patterns. Users reported a strong sense of presence ('of being there') along with an observable bond with their shadows and the effect of their shadows in the visual reconstruction. It became evident to Flynn that the sense of presence 'of being there' was due to the immersive visualization of the surround panoramas augmented by the kinetic aspect of navigation.

Initially Flynn had considered the users as three individual participants. However, the evaluations highlighted the importance of the collaborative process within the group. The distinction between different users also varied considerably from those keen to map out all the interactive possibilities immediately, to those that wanted a slower, more open-ended meandering method of navigation. Some users took this further and resisted taking an active navigational role. A few participants even requested seats so that they could have a spectator-only role while watching others move within the AVIE space.

6.4 Summary

As I wrote at the start of this chapter, the projects discussed hopefully show at least some of the range of technologies, issues and creative solutions that can all lay some form of claim to being virtual heritage. Some of the projects use game engines while others use expensive and dedicated virtual reality systems. One or two are game levels. Some run in web browsers or as stand-alone applications on computers, others require specialized virtual reality centers. Most are academic and free for non-commercial use, but some are or were run as museum or art-gallery installations, and others are sold commercially. They are not included here as exemplars of best or worst practice, but hopefully reveal the myriad of ways one can interact with past civilizations, remote cultural sites, heritage issues and historical information.

Discussing these projects has also allowed me to reflect on my theoretical arguments raised in the earlier chapters. For example, apart from Macquarie Lighthouse all feature some level of interactivity (Table 6.1). Yet most are visualization-orientated rather than games per se. The Serious Games Interactive offerings are arguably hermeneutic in that they are designed for classroom discussion and debate, but still, the conversation takes place *outside* of the interactive environment, and the interactivity is pre-scripted narrative available via point and click.

I still believe that games are rule-finding interactive challenges, requiring judgment, priority selection, and direction towards goal completion. The affordances and constraints in games offer themselves directly to digitally mediated cultural learning, and so do the fantastical situations and role-playing. Yet thematic affordances and constraints are few in the examples mentioned, and dynamic place-making is also not a regular occurrence. There is some use of artifact-based interaction as well as maps to help navigation, understanding, and recall of completed tasks and past events, but there is scant evidence of atmospheric interaction with the environment, rituals, and people behavior.

Some projects show the development of thematically designed peripherals and large-scale displays but there are still usability challenges and interaction design issues. For example, how do the participants know whether they have visited, experienced

Table 6.1 Comparison of case studies

Case study	Visualization-based	Activity-based	Hermeneutic inside	Hermeneutic outside
Santa Maria ad Cryptas Fossa	Yes			
Virtual Forbidden City, China	Yes	Social chat		
Dordrecht Monastery, The Netherlands	Yes			
Virtual Sambor, Cambodia	Yes	Social chat		
FAS Palace, Mesopotamia	Yes	Collect items		
SGI: Global Conflicts: Palestine and Playing History	Yes	Take notes or collect items	Reflective judgment	Discussion
Virtual Egyptian Temple	Yes			Variant has teacher guide
Mawson's Hut, Antarctica	Yes			
Macquarie Lighthouse, Australia	Yes			Test
Place-Hampi, India	Yes	Outside world		
Spaces of Mjalnar, Malta	Yes (could be more so)	Movement, wand		

and understood the major events, stories, and situations? How does the designer know the type of interaction made available was most appropriate both to audience and to the culture depicted? How can they ensure that participants achieved the envisaged learning goals and understood the distinctions between the hypothetical, fictional or historically accurate components? Did the participants learn more from the experience than from watching a documentary or reading a book?

Most examples could go further in including audience participation: even though designing interaction for many users is difficult. So I would suggest that more research is required on providing learning situations for collaborative but dispersed audiences, there is still room for user-driven rather than instructor-driven interaction, and we need to investigate how we can break the magic circle (Champion and Jacobson 2008) so the audience becomes involved, and the player feels included in a larger social setting.

References

Australia ICOMOS. (1999). *The Burra Charter (The Australia ICOMOS charter for the conservation of places of cultural significance)*. Retrieved 10 May 2010, from http://australia.icomos. org/publications/charters/

Beacham, R., Niccolucci, F., Denard, H., Hermon, S., & Bentkowska-Kafel, A. (2009). *The London Charter For The Computer-Based Visualisation Of Cultural Heritage* (Charter No. 2.1). London: King's College, London).

Bourke, P. (2005). *Using a Spherical Mirror for Projection into Immersive Environments*. Paper presented at the Graphite (ACM SIGGRAPH) Conference. ACM SIGGRAPH, Dunedin, New Zealand.

Bourke, P. (2006, 2007). *Immersive Gaming: A Low Cost Projection Environment*. Paper presented at the DIME 2006 Conference, Bangkok Thailand.

Bourke, P. (2008, Unknown). FAQ: Spherical Mirror Projection for Hemispherical Dome Projection. Retrieved 25 March 2008, from http://local.wasp.uwa.edu.au/~pbourke/projection/domemirror/faq.html

Bourke, P. (2009, 11–13 May). *iDome: Immersive Gaming with the Unity Game Engine*. Paper presented at the Computer Games Multimedia & Allied Technology 09 (CGAT09) Conference, Amara Singapore.

Bourke, P.D., & Felinto, D.Q. (2010, April). *Blender and Immersive Gaming in a Hemispherical Dome*. Paper presented at the Computer Games and Allied Technology 10 Conference (CGAT10), Singapore.

Champion, E. (2006, 15 March). *Explorative Shadow Realms of Uncertain Histories*. Paper presented at the New Heritage Conference: Cultural Heritage and New Media. Theme: Beyond verisimilitude; interpretation of cultural heritage through new media, University of Hong Kong.

Champion, E.M., & Jacobson, J. (2008, 10–12 December). *Sharing the Magic Circle with Spatially Inclusive Games*. Paper presented at the SIGGRAPH Asia Conference, Singapore.

Chan, M.J. (2007, 8 May). Lost Worlds Become Virtual Heritage. *Science and Space*. Retrieved 12 June 2007, from http://edition.cnn.com/2007/TECH/science/05/08/Virtual_Heritage/index.html

Clare, O. (2007). Global Conflicts: Palestine Review [Electronic Version]. *eurogamer*. Retrieved 10 May 2010, from http://www.eurogamer.net/articles/global-conflicts-palestine-review

Clarke, T., Ayres, P., & Sweller, J. (2005). The impact of sequencing and prior knowledge on learning mathematics through spreadsheet applications. *Educational Technology Research and Development, 53*(3), 15–24.

Cruz-Neira, C., Sandin, D.J., & DeFanti, T.A. (1993). Surround-screen projection-based virtual reality: the design and implementation of the CAVE. *Proceedings of the 20th annual conference on computer graphics and interactive techniques* (pp. 135–142): ACM.

Egenfeldt-Nielsen, S. (2010). Playing History – the future of game-based learning is here. *Future of game-based Learning: Discussions, ideas and thoughts on the future of game-based learning*. Retrieved 10 May 2010, from http://egenfeldt.eu/blog/?p=80

Fassbender, E. (2009). *VirSchool – The Effect of Music on Memory for Facts Learned in a Virtual Environment*. Unpublished Ph.D. thesis, Macquarie University, Sydney.

Fassbender, E., & Richards, D. (2008). Using a Dance Pad to Navigate through the Virtual Heritage Environment of Macquarie Lighthouse, Sydney. *Virtual Systems and Multimedia, Lecture Notes in Computer Science*, 1–12.

Federation of American Scientists. (n.d.). Discover Babylon. Retrieved 10 May 2010, from http://fas.org/babylon/

Flynn, B. (2007a, 23–26 September). *Digital Knowledge as Archaeological Spatial Praxis*. Paper presented at the Virtual Systems and Multimedia (VSMM) Conference: Exchange and Experience in Space and Place, Brisbane Australia.

Flynn, B. (2007b, 18–20 October 2006). *Somatic Knowledge and Simulated Spaces*. Paper presented at the Archaologie und Computer 2006 Conference: Workshop 11, Vienna.

Gillings, M. (2002). Virtual archaeologies and the hyper-real. In P. Fisher & D. Unwin (Eds.), *Virtual Reality in Geography* (Vol. 17–32). London and New York: Taylor & Francis.

Grabowski, D. (2007). Global Conflicts: Palestine Review [Electronic Version]. *pc.gamezone*. Retrieved 10 May 2010, from http://pc.gamezone.com/gzreviews/r32950.htm

Gunhouse, G. (2007). Using Blink 3D to teach medieval church decoration. *VR in the Schools, 6*(2), 17–20.

Henden, C., Jacobson, J., & Champion, E. (2008, 25–27 September). *A Surround Display Warp-Mesh Utility to Enhance Player Engagement*. Paper presented at the ICEC: International Conference on Entertainment Computing, Pittsburgh, PA.

IBM. (2008). The Virtual Forbidden City [Electronic Version]. *Ideas from IBM*. Retrieved 30 April 2010, from http://www.ibm.com/ibm/ideasfromibm/us/forbiddencity/20081013/resources/IFI_10132008.pdf

ICOMOS. (2007). *The ICOMOS Charter for the Interpretation and Presentation of Cultural Heritage Sites*. Retrieved 27 March 2007. from http://www.enamecharter.org/downloads/ICOMOS_Ename_Charter_ENG_16-03-07.pdf

Jacobson, J., & Holden, L. (2007). Virtual Heritage: Living in the Past [Electronic Version]. *Techné: Research in Philosophy and Technology, 10: 3 (Spring)*. Retrieved 10 May 2010, from http://scholar.lib.vt.edu/ejournals/SPT/v10n3/

Jacobson, J., Le Renard, M., Lugrin, J.-L., & Cavazza, M. (2005). *The CaveUT System: Immersive Entertainment Based on a Game Engine*. Proceedings of the 2005 ACM SIGCHI International Conference on Advances in computer entertainment technology, ACM, 2005, Valencia, Spain, p. 187.

Jacobson, J., & Preussner, G. (2010, 29 June to 2 July). *Visually Immersive Theater with CaveUT*. Paper presented at the World Conference on Educational Multimedia, Hypermedia and Telecommunications (ED-MEDIA2010), Toronto, Canada.

Kalay, Y. (n.d.). Digital Modeling of Tangible and Intangible Cultural Heritage. Retrieved 30 April 2010, from http://steel.ced.berkeley.edu/research/sambor/?p=26

Kenderdine, S., & de Kruiff, A. (n.d.). PLACE-HAMPI: inhabiting the cultural imaginary. Retrieved 10 May, 2010, from http://www.place-hampi.museum/

Kenderdine, S., Shaw, J., Favero, D.D., & Brown, N. (2008). Place-Hampi: Co-Evolutionary Narrative and Augmented Stereographic Panoramas, Vijayanagara, India. In Y. E. Kalay, T. Kvan & J. Affleck (Eds.), *New Heritage: New Media and Cultural Heritage* (pp. 276–294). London and New York: Routledge.

Kenderdine, S., Shaw, J., & Kocsis, A. (2009, November). *Dramaturgies of PLACE: Evaluation, Embodiment and Performance in PLACE-Hampi*. Paper presented at the DIMEA/ACE Conference (5th Advances in Computer Entertainment Technology Conference and 3rd Digital Interactive Media Entertainment and Arts Conference), Athens.

Loewe, F. (1950). A note on katabatic winds at the coasts of Adélieland and King George V land. *Pure and Applied Geophysics, 16*(3), 159–162.

Lucey-Roper, M. (2006). *Discover Babylon: Creating A Vivid User Experience By Exploiting Features Of Video Games And Uniting Museum And Library Collections*. Paper presented at the Museums and the Web 2006. Retrieved 30 April 2010, from http://www.archimuse.com/mw2006/papers/lucey-roper/lucey-roper.html

McCormick, B.H., DeFanti, T.A., & Brown, M.D. (1987). Visualization in scientific computing – A synopsis. *IEEE Computer Graphics and Applications, 7*(7), 61–70.

Nicholls, S. (2003, 30 April). Ruddock Fury over Woomera Computer Game. *The Age*. Retrieved 10 May 2010, from http://www.theage.com.au/articles/2003/04/29/1051381948773.html

Paladin Studios. (2007, 9 November). Hof van Dordrecht 3D. Retrieved 30 April 2010, from http://www.youtube.com/watch?v=u4h66vdXNTw

Parish, T., R., & Wendler, G. (1991). The katabatic wind regime at Adelie Land, Antarctica. *International Journal of Climatology, 11*(1), 97–107.

Richards, D., Fassbender, E., Bilgin, A., & Thompson, W.F. (2008). An investigation of the role of background music in IVWs for learning. *ALT-J: Research in Learning Technology, 16*(3), 231–244.

Schonfeld, E. (2008). Real World Got You Down? IBM Invites You To A Virtual Forbidden City. *Techcrunch*. Retrieved 30 April 2010, from http://techcrunch.com/2008/10/10/real-world-got-you-down-ibm-invites-you-to-a-virtual-forbidden-city/

Selectparks. (2007). Escape from Woomera. Retrieved 10 May 2010, from http://www.selectparks.net/archive/escapefromwoomera/

Serious Games Interactive. (2010, n.d.). Playing History. Retrieved 10 May 2010, from http://www.playinghistory.eu/

Serious Games Interactive. (n.d., n.d.). FAQ. Retrieved 10 May 2010, from http://www.globalconflicts.eu/faq

Serviss, B. (2005). Escaping the world: High and low resolution in gaming. *IEEE MultiMedia, 12*(4), 4–8.

Stone, R., & Ojika, T. (2000). Virtual heritage: what next? *Multimedia, IEEE, 7*(2), 73–74.

Sweller, J. (1988). Cognitive load during problem solving: Effects on learning. *Cognitive Science, 12*(2), 257–285.

Tilley, C. (1994). *A Phenomenology of Landscape: Places, Paths and Monuments*. Oxford: Berg Publishers.

Tilley, C. (2004). *The Materiality of Stone: Explorations in Landscape Phenomenology*. Oxford: Berg Publishers.

Tolva, J. (2006, 17 June). The Forbidden City: Beyond Space and Time. *Ascent Stage: China Virtual Worlds*. Retrieved 30 April 2010, from http://www.ascentstage.com/archives/2006/06/the_forbidden_c.html

Troche, J., & Jacobson, J. (2010). *An Exemplar of Ptolemaic Egyptian Temples*. Paper presented at the Computer Applications in Archaeology (CAA) Conference: Fusion of Cultures. Retrieved 10 May 2010, from http://www.caa2010.org/

Tuan, Y.-F. (1998). *Escapism*. Baltimore, MD: Johns Hopkins University Press.

University of California, B. (2009, 17 March). Virtual Sambor Prei Kuk by UCB. Retrieved 30 April 2010, from http://www.youtube.com/watch?v=ojTTcHWTVQo

Chapter 7
Augmenting the Present With the Past

7.1 What Is Augmented Reality?

The spectrum of virtual reality was explained in conference papers by Paul Milgram and others (Drascic and Milgram 1996; Milgram and Kishino 1994). In the later paper they defined augmented reality as "augmenting natural feedback to the operator with simulated cues" but they also noted that it has been defined as "a form of virtual reality where the participant's head-mounted display is transparent, allowing a clear view of the real world."

Ron Azuma (1997) has also written a survey on augmented reality (AR), contrasting it with Virtual Environments (VE) and virtual reality (VR). Azuma argued that with VE technology the user is immersed in a virtual environment and cannot see the real world, while AR supplements the real world, by superimposing virtual objects on the real world, or compositing virtual objects on the real world. Azuma's definition says that augmented reality combines real and virtual, is interactive in real time, and is registered in 3D (Azuma 2005). This definition appears to be fairly standard in the academic literature, it was taken up by a more recent survey paper on evaluation in AR (Dünser et al. 2008).

A similar definition by Andersen and Qvortrup (2004, pp. 1–2) also hinges on the importance of 3D registration:

> ...The user' view point is mapped into the coordinate system of a virtual world, so that he sees what he would have seen had he been located at a certain point in the virtual world. In augmented reality, the mapping works the other way round: the user's position and orientation is now the point of departure, and the virtual world is presented in such a way that the user sees what he would have seen had the virtual object been located at a certain position in the real world.

However, the perspective of Michael May's article in the same book appears to differ. For May (1996, pp. 213–214), "traditional graphic signs are already a form of *augmented reality*, a way of drawing and writing directly on the reality of the environment, even though it is not as safe and efficient as electronic computer-supported forms." May also talked about graphical directions as a form of augmented reality even though it is not computer-generated, and how directional sound can functions as a "virtual acoustic display" when used to help with direction during emergencies

E. Champion, *Playing with the Past*, Human-Computer Interaction Series, DOI 10.1007/978-1-84996-501-9_7, © Springer-Verlag London Limited 2011

on ships, trains and aircraft. Another chapter in the same book took yet another approach. Kjeldskov (2004) wrote that "In contrast with virtual reality, augmented reality facilitates mobility in the real world as well as a close relationship between physical space and virtual objects."

In their book *Stepping into Virtual Reality* (Gutiérrez et al. 2008, pp. 7–8), the authors referred to Milgram's famous paper when they suggested that augmented reality and augmented virtuality are mixed reality. Mixed reality lies between virtual reality (where "everything one can perceive is artificial; the user is isolated from the real world") and "real reality" (where there is "no computer generated stimuli").

To these three authors augmented reality meant "most things are real" and this is the conventional explanation. For someone creating the digital material, the explanation makes sense but surely it depends also on what the user perceives as real or important? In the early pioneering stages of augmented reality the augmented part is often clumsy and obvious, but in the near future the augmented reality components may actually seem as real or even more real than the real components. This is due to improvements in projection technology, occlusion, 3D registration and computing power, but issues such as user satisfaction and collaborative work between say HMD wearers with non-HMD wearers remain (Azuma 2005; Azuma et al. 2001).

So I suggest there are at least three factors, the actual (designed) augmenting additions, the perceived augmenting components, and the perceived synthesis of these components. A design team may create a consummate augmented reality environment, but there is no guarantee all end-users will fully understand and appreciate it, and that the end result is worth the cost, complexity, appearance and weight of additional equipment.

At the risk of appearing pedantic, augmented implies a subjectively pleasing result. To augment something does not mean merely to add x to y, but to improve y. In some of the earlier academic papers augmented reality is also defined as *enriching* reality (Feiner et al. 1997). Yet the subject, i.e. the end user, is the only person who can judge this hence it is a subjective (and thus variable) judgment. Yet augmented reality is typically viewed as describing technical components, not elements of a subjectively successful immersive experience. So this leads me to prefer the term mixed reality over augmented reality or augmented virtuality.

Another problem lies with the last term, augmented virtuality. Although it is a fascinating concept and area of research to be discussed later in this chapter, literal explanation of the term raise issues from the point of view of the end user. It would literally mean to augment the sense of *nearly* being there, of augmenting an *approximation* of "being there". Imagine asking an end user "Did the extra technology which you may or may not have noticed feel additional to the overall system, and help immerse you more in the sensation of being *virtually* there"? To be immersed in a virtual world is to forego the direct sensation of being in a simulation in favor of feeling, thinking, and believing that one is surrounded by reality. To consider the degree to which something augments the feeling of "realness" is to ask people to hold the contradictory thoughts that both the virtual reality is real, and that it is not real enough because it can be augmented.

It is also clear that the word "reality" can be problematic but it is unlikely that we can move away from using this term. So for now I'll merely suggest that the term "Augmented reality" will become more and more redundant. As technology improves, deciding whether a mixed reality environment is augmented reality or augmented virtuality is pointless. It should depend on the end user and not on the designer, but the end user may have trouble discerning digital simulations *are* digital simulations. The end user should surely also be the one to judge whether the augmented components or the virtual components are in the majority (and this decision may depend not on the percentage of real versus virtual creations, but also whether the real objects or the virtual objects are more prominent in the display, in their symbolic and emotive connotations, or in terms of their interactive importance). Surely the more valuable question is whether the integration of the digitally simulated and the real work together in synergy.

To be fair, Ron Azuma appears to be sensitive to these criticisms. In more recent publications, Azuma (2004; Azuma et al. 2001) has stressed that augmented reality can involve different senses and augmented reality *supplements* reality. The notion of augmentation as necessarily improving reality seems to have faded into the background.

To return to the introduction to their book *Stepping Into Virtual Reality*, the editors Gutiérrez, Vexo and Thalmann (2008, pp. 7–8) wrote "In augmented reality, most of the objects are real." This simple and lucid definition makes sense when used to contrast with augmented virtuality (where most of the content is generated by a computer). However, it does raise some interesting issues. Who decides whether a screen has more virtual or more real components? Is it the percentage of pixels, the significant elements to act on the user's feeling that there is a world (or that they are in a virtual environment, or that virtual objects are in a real world)?

Perhaps success depends on how successfully the virtual and real objects can be distinguished by the end-user? If the goal is to create synergy of real and virtual (by augmenting reality or by augmenting virtuality), is it necessary or even desirable that an end user can and does distinguish what was real or virtual in the AR or AV?

Given these problems, it seems to me that though the above definition sounds like it is judged by the end-user, it is really an operational definition, not a subjective judgment by the end-user. Which brings us back to the initial problem: if the end-user doesn't experience an *augmented* reality, is it really AR?

Perhaps if we add in May's use of sound as a form of augmented reality (to act as local direction guides for people lost in a ship's corridors during an emergency), the issue becomes clearer. For an acoustically augmented reality, being able to distinguish between created and already existing sounds may be useful for an emergency, but is not useful when the created sound is meant to improve (augment) one's feeling of immersion in a place. Hence, I suggest that mixed reality may be a less confusing term: harmonizing the different types of reality for the enjoyment and understanding of the end-user is surely more important than the technical distinction as to whether the virtual or real-world media occupies more screen-space. Another issue, as we shall see, is that layered virtuality over the camera windows of portable devices is often called augmented reality, when there is no 3D registration of virtual objects and real space.

And as a side note, there are issues apart from how to define augmented reality or augmented virtuality. Writers have raised the potential problems of identity theft, health issues, and unwanted visual or aural advertising (Brandon 2010; Eaton 2009; Kirkpatrick 2009; Zacharias 2010). There are also interesting challenges for usability (Sterling 2009), as well as an escalating need for "hardware, software and legal standards" (Lamantia 2009).

Applied to virtual heritage, some pertinent issues could be the cost and fragility of HMDs and portable equipment, usability issues in training, evaluation issues (one cannot stand behind the end-user to see how they are going and what they are doing), and lighting and shadow issues. There is also an increased risk of end-users with HMDs accidentally walking into fragile artifacts due to cognitive loading, heavy equipment affecting their balance and coordination, or through having their view partially obscured by the HMD. For portable devices there could be the added issue of processor and graphic limitations when augmented reality is required for large and detailed heritage sites. First, though, I will outline just a few of the different types and modes of mixed reality (augmented reality and augmented virtuality), before discussing some implications for virtual heritage projects.

7.2   Blends of Augmented Reality and Augmented Virtuality

7.2.1   Inserted Walk-About Reality, University of South Australia

In 2000 The Wearable Computer Lab at the University of South Australia published a paper (Thomas et al. 2000) on a very interesting project, ARQuake (Figs. 7.1 and 7.2). They had previously written papers on wearable computing with augmented reality for terrestrial navigation, but now they were demonstrating its potential on campus using monsters from the computer game Quake (hence the name). I find this an interesting project not only for the technical achievements, but also because the participant's interaction can be seen (or at least guessed at) by others on the campus.

7.2.2   Overlaid Walk-About Reality, Columbia University

At Columbia University, Steven Feiner's Computer Graphics and User Interfaces Lab, Columbia University developed augmented reality equipment for "exploring the urban environment" (i.e. heritage tours around their university). This image of

Fig. 7.1 ARQuake (Courtesy of Bruce Thomas)

Fig. 7.2 HMD screenshot of monsters on campus (Courtesy of Bruce Thomas)

their Mobile AR backpack dates to 1997, and shows the hardware used in the paper (Feiner et al. 1997). There is also additional early work on guided tours using multimedia such as video in their 1999 paper entitled Situated Documentaries (Hollerer et al. 1999). Apart from the tracked see-through Head Mounted Display (Fig. 7.3), the project incorporated sound and a hand-held pen computer that added additional information.

This paper included images from an Augmented Reality tour of the Bloomingdale Asylum, which occupied Columbia's current campus in the 19th century. The above image (Fig. 7.4) shows a 3D virtual model of the main building of Bloomingdale Asylum, recreated at its original location, near Columbia's current Low Library.

Fig. 7.3 Early AR system
(Courtesy of Steven Feiner)

Fig. 7.4 Asylum (Courtesy of Steve Feiner)

This image was shot directly through the head-tracked, optical see-through, head-worn display used in the project. They have also investigated collaborative archaeology work using augmented reality.

7.2.3   Bubbled Reality Example 3: Mawson's Huts, Antarctica

I have mentioned the content of this virtual heritage project in Chapter 6. Here I wish to discuss the interesting use of technology and whether it is a form of mixed reality. Thanks to fine weather (which is unusual for this windy stretch of Antarctica), and the use of camera technology capable of 360-degree spherical panoramas and video, the virtual environment featured here (Fig. 7.5) includes textures, a 3D model of the existing hut and environment, interior and exterior shots, taken directly from the site (P. Bourke 2009). Incidentally, Frank Hurley (a famous Australian photographer) was on the 1911–1913 expedition and took exquisite (but fragile) photographs and stereoscopic plates.

In this virtual environment are embedded blue-tinted spherical panoramic bubbles that one can walk into, and as one walks into them their opacity increases to fill the screen (Fig. 7.6), when one walks away from their centre they slowly fade out. This allows the combination of photo-realistic panoramas with digital simulations of the terrain without the two competing with and obscuring each other.

Fig. 7.5 Mawson's Hut Exterior (Courtesy of Paul Bourke and Peter Morse)

Fig. 7.6 Mawson's Hut Interior (Courtesy of Paul Bourke and Peter Morse)

7.3   Other Types of Mixed Reality

7.3.1   Data-Streamed Virtual Reality

Layar is one of several companies and technologies that display real-time digital information on top of the real world as seen through the camera of a mobile phone or similar portable device. Layar uses data from the camera, compass and GPS to calculate your location and field of view to overlay location information over the camera view (Fig. 7.7).

Layar call this augmented reality even though the virtual 3D objects are layered *over* and not inserted into the 3D real world when seen on the camera of the phone or PDA. Their explanation (Layar 2010) is "We augment the real world as seen through your mobile phone, based on your location." However, I don't think this fits the traditional view of augmented reality, that all virtual and real objects and spaces have accurate 3D registration, one cannot be layered over the other, they must appear to the user even when moving to coexist in time and space. Other products that appear to take the more user-location based approach to the defining of augmented reality include Wikitude and Acrossair's *New York Nearest Subway* iPhone application (Byrne 2010; Kirkpatrick 2009) as well as Metaio, which in future might include recognition systems such as Google Goggles (Byrne 2010).

Kirkpatrick calls the typical device display for this mode of augmented reality an "enchanted window" and he defines augmented reality as "the technology of layering information on top of our naked view of the world." Byrne added that the

Fig. 7.7 Layar Augmented
Reality on a Phone (Courtesy
of Layar)

technology is still in a development stage; there are issues due to limitations in GPS
and compass accuracy on mobile devices such as the iPhone. Further, GPS doesn't
tell the device how to handle occlusion so "You may see augmented reality information about a building that is close to your position but obscured by another building."
However, accuracy may not always be the main goal for these developers. Byrne
also wrote "according to Claire Boonstra, one of the co-founders of Layar, the next
step for mobile AR is moving from 'functional AR to experience AR'."

7.3.2 Augmented Virtuality

The next example is perhaps not true augmented virtuality, because the real world
information is available as a screen overlay, and as far as I can tell, the spatial information is plan view (i.e. it can see on the plan what one is looking at, but not
whether the user is looking up or down). So there is no 3D integration of real world

objects with virtual world objects. However it is still interesting, for it adds real world information of heritage buildings to a Second Life environment, where a virtual world avatar represents the end-user (Fig. 7.8).

The creator of this mixed reality environment, Philippe Kerremans, goes by the Second Life avatar name Louis Platini, and the company website is named after his Second Life name. He released a white paper entitled "Virtual Tourism in Bruges" (Platini 2007), which explained how he sees the technology address issues in the market. Milgram and Kishino (1994) wrote a paper where they talked about a ""window-on-the-world" (WoW), AR to refer to display systems where computer generated images are either analogically or digitally overlaid onto live or stored video images." The Platini example is perhaps the converse, it can be considered to be a "(real) World-on-the-window."

It is worth noting that the Augmented Environments Lab (AEL) at Georgia Institute of Technology also managed to create augmented reality using Second Life. For someone using a HMD, Second Life characters scenes or objects can appear and interact with them in the real world. The AR Second Life client software is available from their website (Augmented Environments Lab 2010).

Fig. 7.8 Virtual World with Real World Information (Courtesy of Philippe Kerremans)

7.3.3 Audio Augmented Reality

The project *34 North, 118 West* was "an historic fiction set in downtown Los Angeles, using GPS to deliver sound" and shown at two arts festivals.

According to an online article by Jeremy Hight (2003):

> The project "34 North 118 West" utilizes technology and the physical navigation of a city simultaneously to forge a new construct. The narrative is embedded in the city itself as well as the city is read. The story world becomes one of juxtaposition, of overlap, of layers appearing and falling away. Place becomes a multi-tiered and malleable concept beyond that of setting and detail to establish a fictive place, a narrative world. The effect is a text and sound based virtual reality, a non-passive movement, a being in two places at once with eyes open.

This project also used GPS and a laptop computer (Fig. 7.9), but the journey was augmented by audio rather than by a visual virtual environment. A map indicated some of the hot spots ("data triggers") that activated the recordings, but others were not indicated: they were discovered on the journey. The desolate background of the real world Los Angeles helped create the ambience to the story, and although I said it was a fiction, the narrative was based on transcripts of Latino women who toiled there as railroad workers in the 1940s.

Although it is not as technically advanced as the visual augmented reality projects discussed at the start of the chapter, it lends itself more to social collaboration (even a see-through HMD creates more of a wall between the user and bystanders), for the map display is a physical artifact that can be shared, while bystanders can be asked for help in guessing where the hidden narrative hotspots might be. Hight has also told me that they wanted people to feel immersed in the "now" of the real place, to look around and not down, so the project team decided to not use a HMD.

Fig. 7.9 34 North by 118 West (Courtesy of James Hight)

7.3.4 Participant and Audience-Augmented Virtuality

In 2006 I supervised an honors student in the area of biofeedback and gaming. Andrew Dekker's thesis project examined how biofeedback could enhance gameplay. So far biofeedback has been used in virtual environments for exercise and for meditation, but it can also be used for visceral entertainment (Gilleade et al. 2005). In our quest to develop cinematic background effects derived from changes in the player's physiological states, Andrew created sockets to connect a meditation game's biosensors to the Source game engine (Dekker and Champion 2007). This was to allow the player's biofeedback to dynamically change a popular mod of Half-Life 2, the zombie level Ravenholm. With the biofeedback input, as the player becomes more excited, the music changes, the cinematic shaders change and even the AI of the zombies is affected.

Using a cheap commercial biosensor interface, and with access to the software development kit, Andrew incorporated the player's biofeedback (heartrate variability, skin response and heartbeat) at regular intervals back into the game level. As shown here (Fig. 7.10), the shaders of the game would change to white or red (or whatever the designer thought cinematically related to increased or decreased stress levels), and the higher the readings, the higher the rate of spawning of the monsters.

The changing effects in the pilot study could amplify the player's fear and horror. This is however only the first step, biofeedback can be also fine-tuned in order to seek out and capitalize on particular phobic triggers, to dynamically adjust as people become less scared, or even to help create a very anti-social social game. Ethically problematic, and therefore intriguing, a multiplayer game using biofeedback could

Fig. 7.10 Biofeedback in gameplay changes the shaders and NPCs

enable players to seek out their opponents' phobic weaknesses, and continually bombard them with the elements that most terrify them.

Would it be possible to affect current players of games and virtual worlds using the biofeedback of past players? An undergraduate student group signed up to one of my project ideas, testing out biofeedback on gameplay. I suggested recreating the Minotaur myth of Knossos using a game engine. Using a head mounted display, plastic sword (its position would be tracked), and 3D joystick, the player has to navigate through a labyrinth and kill the Minotaur. Spatially located recordings of previous player heartbeats could be used and amplified to increase the tension and drama. In other words, as the player passes by locations in the labyrinth where previous players' biofeedback was recorded, they would hear the heartbeat of the player at that point. The aim was thus to see if their biofeedback is directly affected by this "echo".

We were allowed access to plans and panoramas of the real Knossos, but the area under the palace was too small for the experience so the students created a larger labyrinth for the game level. They also spoke to academic psychologists on what was required, and then built their own device (Fig. 7.11). They looked at various game editors and settled on Unreal Tournament. The game featured a head mounted display, because the device we bought had quite a delay, which I thought would be excellent for increasing the suspense for the player, when they heard sounds behind them. Unfortunately, the students did not continue with the project, but I intend to resurrect it at a later date. I should also mention that to heighten the feeling of being in an underground labyrinth, as the player virtually approached the end of a corridor, electric fans would rotate and blow from the direction of the new corridor in the labyrinth.

If games were actually rendered as the foreground of live and dynamic content, ambient audience interaction could also be utilized. For example, at the University

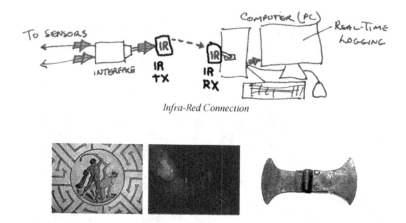

Fig. 7.11 Biosensor for Past Player Biofeedback For Minotaur Game

of Queensland I supervised a group of students (Bonnii Weeks and Jonathan Barrett), who built an ambient form of audience interaction, initially inspired by an interpretation of *MechWarrior*. The main aims were to more fully spatially immerse the player, while involving and not distancing the audience (Champion and Jacobson 2008).

In their game installation the player sits on a hydraulic chair with gameplay-driven force feedback, surrounded by the game environment projected via a curved mirror onto the inside of a dome or tent). The initial breakthrough of using a curved mirror had been developed by Paul Bourke at the University of Western Australia (Bourke 2005). We merely adapted the technology to new types of surround display to utilize peripheral vision, which increases engagement in gameplay (especially for car racing games). A large surround display also allowed better viewing for an audience, in an attempt to break down the magic circle (Fig. 7.12).

In the next phase of the project we had also planned to have the red lights (shown in Fig. 7.12) hooked up to the player's biofeedback or their "game-health". This would allow the audience to see how well the player was doing before deforming the terrain in real-time. This would mean just as the player began to calm down successfully after steep hills or pitted ground, the audience could redesign the landscape obstacles.

The students and I had also talked about a potential Greek god role for the audience; at certain key times they could move their hand over a sandpit. The camera (located above) above the real sandpit would track the movement and depth and then tell the game logic to redefine the sand, soil or sea, causing havoc for the (hero) player. We could easily further complicate this scenario. The audience and the player could share some amount of interaction, directly, or indirectly, but they may not exactly know what is pre-rendered, and what is interactive, or who is consciously, accidentally, or subconsciously controlling the interaction.

Fig. 7.12 Gameplay Augmented By Audience

These research projects are only initial investigations, but aspects of them could also be incorporated into a layered combination of social happening and game-play. Biofeedback and improvements in facial tracking could see real-time facial and bodily expression in games; which could also open up new dramatic possibilities in games and digital media in general. For example, the audience may only sometimes see player behavior or player events as they happen, perhaps sometimes they see past player actions (*phantomas*). We had already employed ghosts (badly video-taped actors inserted into a temple-scene), although they had no physics or collision, they could cause different parts of the game events to change dramatically.

What are the implications for virtual heritage? Non-playing characters' moods or abilities could be affected (perhaps infected is a better word), by biofeedback of the players they can encounter. Science fiction writers have already predicted this for at least four decades, for example, P. K. Dick (1964) has written of scenarios where people start developing traits of each other in reality or in virtual reality. And many religions from Mayan to Christian are based on some related notion of aura. Perhaps in-world visualization or auralization of the feedback when shown to the player would change the player's actual feedback. Could we also accumulate and share biofeedback across social groups? Would it destroy any bonding effect or create a sense of community? So there are still ethical issues to be explored, especially if one wanted to see if designers could *cultivate* biofeedback in order to control behavior (*civitas*).

7.4 Augmented Reality and Virtual Heritage

There are several notable uses of augmented reality for virtual heritage, apart from the case studies mentioned earlier in this chapter. Noh, Sunar and Pan (2009) have surveyed the potential of augmented reality for virtual heritage. A more recent and comprehensive review by Papagiannakis et al. (2008) focused on mobile augmented reality for virtual heritage. For them a major challenge is usability: "Machines that fit the human environment, instead of forcing humans to enter theirs, will make using a computer as refreshing as taking a walk in the woods." However they noted that there are still issues such as accurate tracking and registration, ruggedness, computing power, weight, networking, and social acceptance.

They are part of the MIRA Lab in Geneva. For their virtual Pompeii project, one could wander around the real Pompeii, listen to audio commentary, and through the HMD display see computer generated ancient Romans go about their business (Papagiannakis et al. 2005). What I found remarkable was the handling of occlusion: if the virtual character is located behind a stone table, you only see that part of their body that would be obscured by the table if they had been a real object located in the real world.

The ARToolkit, arguably one of the most important AR tools for researchers, has been used for museum exhibitions (Woods et al. 2004). Implementations of the software include the eyeMagic virtual storybook for children. To someone wearing a HMD, 3D computer characters appear to pop out of a book when the pages are opened. Other famous uses of augmented reality for cultural heritage include The Virtual Showcase and ARCHEOGUIDE.

The Virtual Showcase (Ledermann 2010) is unusual in that it appears to be a conventional museum display. The glass display cabinet can accommodate real objects while computer-generated objects can also be projected inside using a half-silvered mirror. The ARToolkit can be used in tandem with the Virtual Showcase for head tracking. I have not spoken to the inventors but I am guessing the Virtual Showcase is a variant of Pepper's ghost (a magic trick using an angled mirror to project objects so that they appear to float in the air).

Another famous case in virtual heritage research is the ARCHEOGUIDE project, which was set in the Ancient Greek site of Olympia (Dähne and Karigiannis 2002; Vlahakis et al. 2003). The augmented reality system placed complete virtual temples on top of the broken temple ruins of Olympia today as seen from the viewer's HMD. The researchers compared the HMD system with PDA and pen computer devices, and found issues of wearability (attractiveness and weight), and there were other usability issues (such as the pen-computer display was difficult to read in bright sunlight). In general though, the researchers found general acceptance and enthusiasm for the devices.

Given that there are already successful projects using augmented reality, what other innovative situations could we develop with the present technology? For example, imagine two users, each with see-through HMDs. They can see each other, and each person also has an augmented display. What if they were acting inside a role-playing game, and one person saw the mixed reality (and the clothing of the other person) from one cultural perspective, and the other saw the mixed reality (and the clothing of the other user) from another perspective? Using language and gestures perhaps they could start to see what the other person was seeing.

Perhaps this is too complex, but another scenario could be: person one sees the cultural and historical implications of what person two does, but person two does not see these implications. Or perhaps person one sees the future implications of what person two does in the virtual environment. That is to say, they look at the same virtual environment but at different times and eras.

7.5 Summary

According to the editorial introduction in their book *Virtual Applications: Applications with Virtual Inhabited 3D Worlds,* Andersen and Qvortrup (Andersen and Qvortrup 2004) differentiate virtual reality and augmented reality in terms of the coordinate system, and we have seen how early Azuma papers talked about the importance of 3D registration. This I might call the traditional *spatial* definition of augmented reality. There is however also an *information-based* definition: augmented reality adds information to reality. A similar information-based definition (by Roger Rice) is even more user-centric (Shute 2009):

> When I talk about AR, I try to expand the definition a little bit. Usually, when you talk to someone about augmented reality, the first thing that comes to mind is overlaying 3D graphics on a video stream. I think though, that it should more properly be any media that is specific to your location and the context of what you are doing (or want to do)... augmenting or enhancing your specific reality.

There is definitely a trend to move away from using a traditional see-through HMD, external database and separate fiducial markers. The increasing power, ubiquity and accessibility of phones and webcams have seen the development of new products such as In-Place Augmented Reality (Bergig et al. 2010). The markers are more like barcodes, and the information for the viewing device (camera or PDA) is incorporated into the printed image, for example a topographical map could appear in the phone's camera window as a 3D landform. Arguably this is not strict augmented reality though and the writers themselves call it dual perception, for you have two images, the printed topography on a sheet of paper, and the 3D landscape model occluding the real map when viewed from the camera window. Perhaps *In-place* is not the best word, for the augmented display is separate to the original image and any sense of 'place' is created from viewing the camera or phone displaying the printed image, you don't see the augmentation through viewing the printed image directly. It is still a laudable advance in technology, because here the instructions to the viewing device on how to augment do not require an external database or markers, as they are encoded into the image itself.

This is why I have mentioned here some case studies that are not traditionally defined as augmented reality or even as augmented reality, the definition of the term is under threat not because it is losing its significance but because it is actually becoming a genuine information and entertainment phenomenon.

There are also many different methods available to create augmented reality or augmented virtuality, and we have seen as one interesting distinction that projects can be based around the viewer position or the virtual world position. However, for interactive virtual heritage purposes I predominantly see three modes, head-based (i.e. HMD), screen-based (as in wall-sized display or computer monitor), and device-based (such as a PDA or smart phone whether it is an iPhone, Droid or other hand-sized device).

For all three, movement, collaboration and interaction raise interesting design challenges. For example, imagine standing on a hilltop in a Tunisian desert. On a circular fog screen that surrounds you is projected changing visualizations of past settlements, Roman, Bedouin, and French etc. Although the real present and the simulated past now appear to co-exist, how could you interact with the display? Would text or audio be incorporated, and could it change if you move your body or your line of sight? Could others individually interact with it without destroying the viewing for the general audience?

For any of the display types, if you can move through a virtual heritage site with augmented reality, how do you simultaneously experience and interact with the device or display? Can the experience be shared with others in anyway? Can the user experience be easily recorded for a future occasion when someone wants to relive the experience but no longer has the equipment, or wishes to retrace their steps or share the experience with others?

For general augmented reality applications, technical problems include the speed and processing power required to update the synthesized environment in real-time, the resolution and field of view of affordable HMDs, 3D registration issues of real world and virtual world spaces and objects, occlusion of these objects, cheap and effective real-time tracking of the participants, and integrating different lighting and shadows. Writers such as Sterling (2009) have also warned of interaction design problems. There are other end-user problems: potential privacy and identity theft issues, potential health consequences such as visual strain and Binocular Dysphoria) and there are also social factors. Participants could become disorientated, or feel cut off from the outside world or from others (who don't have the equipment or are not experiencing the same thing in the same virtual time or space).

That said, as each year passes I am more and more convinced of the advantages of augmented reality and augmented virtuality for virtual heritage. Modeling buildings and artifacts is a time-consuming process, and synthesizing the real world with digital media has immediate advantages in cost, saving of resources, and authenticity. For although the real present world is *not* always more authentic than a digitally recreated past one, I suggest it is usually more authentic. And traveling through a pristine real world heritage site with information media that augments your experience is surely preferably to modifying the real site with signs, labels and billboards for the convenience of tourists.

References

Andersen, P.B., & Qvortrup, L. (2004). Introduction. In P. B. Andersen & L. Qvortrup (Eds.), *Virtual Applications: Applications with Virtual Inhabited 3D Worlds* (pp. 1–5). London: Springer-Verlag.

Augmented Environments Lab. (2010). Using the AR Second Life Client. Retrieved 10 May, 2010, from http://www.augmentedenvironments.org/lab/research/arsecondlife/using-the-ar-second-life-client/

Azuma, R. (1997). A Survey of Augmented Reality. *Presence: Teleoperators and Virtual Environments* (August), 355–385.

Azuma, R. (2004). *Overview of augmented reality*. Paper presented at the ACM SIGGRAPH 2004 Conference: Course Notes.

Azuma, R. (2005, 8 May). Registration Errors in Augmented Reality. Retrieved 10 May, 2010, from http://www.cs.unc.edu/~azuma/azuma_AR.html

Azuma, R., Baillot, Y., Behringer, R., Feiner, S., Julier, S., & Macintyre, B. (2001). Recent advances in augmented reality. *Computer Graphics and Applications, IEEE, 21*(6), 34–47.

Bergig, O., Hagbi, N., El-Sana, J., Kedem, K., & Billinghurst, M. (2010). In-Place Augmented Reality [Electronic Version]. *Virtual Reality*. Retrieved 28 April 2010, from http://dx.doi.org/10.1007/s10055–010–0158–6

Bourke, P. (2005, 29 November–2 December). *Spherical mirror: a new approach to hemispherical dome projection*. Paper presented at the 3rd International Conference on Computer Graphics and Interactive Techniques in Australasia and South East Asia, Dunedin, New Zealand.

Bourke, P. (2009). *iDome: Immersive gaming with the Unity game engine*. Paper presented at the Computer Games Multimedia & Allied Technology 09 (CGAT09) Conference, Amara Singapore.

Brandon, J. (2010). Augmented Reality Past, Present and Future: How It Impacts Our Lives. *digital trends*. Retrieved 10 May, 2010, from http://www.digitaltrends.com/features/ge-augmented-reality-iphone-app-past-present-and-future-how-it-impacts-our-lives/

Byrne, C. (2010). Augmented Reality: the next generation [Electronic Version]. *Venture Beat*. Retrieved 10 May 2010, from http://venturebeat.com/2010/01/27/augmented-reality-the-next-generation/

Champion, E.M., & Jacobson, J. (2008, 10–12 December). *Sharing the Magic Circle With Spatially Inclusive Games*. Paper presented at the SIGGRAPH Asia Conference, Singapore.

Dähne, P., & Karigiannis, J. N. . (2002). *Archeoguide: System Architecture of a Mobile Outdoor Augmented Reality System*. Paper presented at the Proceedings of the 1st International Symposium on Mixed and Augmented Reality. Retrieved 7 May 2010, from http://portal.acm.org/citation.cfm?id=854948#

Dekker, A., & Champion, E. (2007, 24–28 September). *Please Biofeed the Zombies: Enhancing the Gameplay and Display of a Horror Game Using Biofeedback*. Paper presented at the Third International Conference of the Digital Games Research Association (DiGRA), Tokyo Japan.

Dick, P.K. (1964). *The Three Stigmata of Palmer Eldritch* (2007 ed.). Kent: Orion Publishing Group.

Drascic, D., & Milgram, P. (1996). *Steroscopic Displays and Virtual Reality Systems*. Paper presented at the SPIE: Perceptual Issues in Augmented Reality Conference, San Jose California.

Dünser, A., Grasset, R., & Billinghurst, M. (2008). *A survey of evaluation techniques used in augmented reality studies*. Paper presented at the ACM SIGGRAPH ASIA 2008 courses. Retrieved 7 May 2010, from http://portal.acm.org/citation.cfm?id=1508049#

Eaton, K. (2009, 26 August). Three Unexpected Dangers of Augmented Reality. Retrieved 10 May, 2010, from http://www.fastcompany.com/blog/kit-eaton/technomix/three-unexpected-dangers-augmented-reality

Feiner, S., MacIntyre, B., Hollerer, T., & Webster, A. (1997, 13–14 October). *A touring machine: prototyping 3D mobile augmented reality systems for exploring the urban environment*. Paper presented at the First International Symposium on Wearable Computers, Washington D.C.

Feiner, S., MacIntyre, B., & Seligmann, D. (1993). Knowledge-Based Augmented Reality. *Communicatons of the ACM, 36*(7), 53–62.

Gilleade, K., Dix, A., & Allanson, J. (2005). *Affective Videogames and Modes of Affective Gaming: Assist Me, Challenge Me, Emote Me* Paper presented at the Digra 2005 Conference, Vancouver, Canada.

Gutiérrez, M.A., Vexo, F., & Thalmann, D. (2008). *Stepping into virtual reality*. London: Springer-Verlag.

Hight, J. (2003). Narrative Archaeology [Electronic Version]. *Streetnotes*. Retrieved 19 April 2010, from http://www.xcp.bfn.org/hight.html

Hollerer, T., Feiner, S., & Pavlik, J. (1999, 18–19 October). *Situated documentaries: embedding multimedia presentations in the real world*. Paper presented at the ISWC '99 Conference: Proceedings of the 3rd IEEE International Symposium on Wearable Computers, San Francisco.

Kirkpatrick, M. (2009). Augmented Reality: 5 Barriers to a Web That's Everywhere [Electronic Version]. *readwriteweb*. Retrieved 10 May 2010, from http://www.readwriteweb.com/archives/augmented_reality_five_barriers_to_a_web_thats_eve.php

Kjeldskov, J. (2004). Lessons From Being There: Interface Design for Mobile Augmented Reality. In P. B. Andersen & L. Qvortrup (Eds.), *Virtual Applications: Applications With Virtual Inhabited 3D Worlds* (pp. 159–188). London: Springer-Verlag.

Lamantia, J. (2009). Inside Out: Interaction Design for Augmented Reality [Electronic Version]. Retrieved 10 May, 2010, from http://www.uxmatters.com/mt/archives/2009/08/inside-out-interaction-design-for-augmented-reality.php

Layar. (2010). What is Layar? Retrieved 10 May, 2010, from http://site.layar.com/download/layar/

Ledermann, F. (2010). The Virtual Showcase: An innovative augmented reality display system [Electronic Version], from http://studierstube.icg.tu-graz.ac.at/virtualshowcase/

May, W.D. (1996). *Edges of reality: mind vs. computer*. New York: Insight Books.

Milgram, P., & Kishino, F. (1994). A Taxonomy of Mixed Reality Visual Displays. *IEICE Transactions on Information Systems, E77-D*(12).

Noh, Z., Sunar, M.S., & Pan, Z. (2009). A Review on Augmented Reality for Virtual Heritage System. In M. Chang (Ed.), *Edutainment 2009* (pp. 50–69). Berlin Heidelberg: Springer-Verlag.

Papagiannakis, G., Schertenleib, S., O'Kennedy, B., Arevalo-Poizat, M., Magnenat-Thalmann, N., Stoddart, A., et al. (2005). Mixing virtual and real scenes in the site of ancient Pompeii. *Computer Animation and Virtual Worlds, 16*(1), 11–24.

Papagiannakis, G., Singh, G., & Magnenat-Thalmann, N. (2008). A survey of mobile and wireless technologies for augmented reality systems. *Comput. Animat. Virtual Worlds, 19*(1), 3–22.

Platini, L. (2007). Virtual Tourism in Bruges: The Travel Guide (PDF). Retrieved 30 April, 2010, from http://www.louisplatini.com/sl/files/Virtual%20Tourism%20in%20Bruges.pdf

Shute, T. (2009). Is it "OMG Finally" for Augmented Reality?: Interview with Robert Rice [Electronic Version]. *Ugotrade: Augmented Realities in "World 2.0"*. Retrieved 10 May 2010, from http://www.ugotrade.com/2009/01/17/is-it-"omg-finally"-for-augmented-reality-inter-view-with-robert-rice/

Sterling, B. (2009). Augmented Reality: the magic problem [Electronic Version]. *WIRED*. Retrieved 30 April 2010, from http://www.wired.com/beyond_the_beyond/2009/09/augmented-reality-the-magic-problem/

Thomas, B., Close, B., Donoghue, J., Squires, J., de, B., Phillip, Morris, M., et al. (2000). *ARQuake: An Outdoor/Indoor Augmented Reality First Person Application*. Paper presented at the Fourth International Symposium on Wearable Computers (ISWC'00) Conference, Atlanta Georgia.

Vlahakis, V., Karigiannis, J., & Ioannidis, N. (2003). Augmented Reality Touring of Archaeological Sites with the ARCHEOGUIDE System [Electronic Version]. *Cultivate Interactive*. Retrieved 1 May 2010, from http://www.cultivate-int.org/issue9/archeoguide/index.html

Woods, E., Billinghurst, M., Looser, J., Aldridge, G., Brown, D., Garrie, B., et al. (2004). *Augmenting the science centre and museum experience*. Paper presented at the 2nd international conference on Computer Graphics and Interactive Techniques in Australasia and South East Asia, Singapore.

Zacharias, N. (2010). 5 REAL PROBLEMS IN AN AUGMENTED WORLD [Electronic Version]. *Digitally Numb*, 2010. Retrieved 19 February 2010, from http://digitallynumb.com/post/399172973/augmented-reality

Chapter 8
Evaluating Virtual Heritage

8.1 Testing That Which Is Not Yet Fully Tested

...Researchers and commentators have not yet begun to grapple with the question: What does it actually mean to describe something as virtually real? It is my contention that until they do the unique potential VR has to change the way we approach, study and think about the physical world will not be fully exploited...archaeological use of VR is at present all about the creation of pictures. (Gillings 2002, p. 17).

There has so far been little research into evaluation best suited for assessing and improving the experience and learning of participants in a virtual environment (Bowman et al. 1999), and even less work done on virtual heritage environments (Bowman et al. 1999; Mosaker 2001; Roussou 2004). There are many usability techniques in related fields, in Presence studies, in Human–Computer Interaction research, and even in Ethnography. Yet the particular issues and demands of digital simulations of past cultures (Fig. 8.1) or exotic places necessitate specific and careful examination of user needs, technical feasibility studies, and appropriate content on a case-by-case basis.

There is already a large body of work on how artifacts and sites are best recorded and preserved. It is self-explanatory that virtual heritage environments are concerned not just with recording and preserving but also with transmitting cultural information.

There is also evaluation of user-experiences in museums, and via their websites (Goldman and Wadman 2002). Yet this work tends to focus on travel information, not travel experience, and certainly not on the cultural learning experience itself. There is still work to be done on what is cultural information, how it can be interactively experienced, how it is best experienced and learnt, and how to determine the strengths and weaknesses of a virtual heritage environment's ability to provide a cultural learning experience.

Fig. 8.1 Dr. Jeffrey Jacobson of PublicVR.org, testing his CAVEUT screens

8.2 Evaluating Cultural Learning

You may recall the following definitions (although open to argument) made at the start of this book.

Culture: Culture expresses shared beliefs and ritualized habits of social agents towards each other and their environment via artifacts and language. Cultural behavior is a subset of social behavior (behavior between two or more people), where behavior is governed by or understood in terms of a cultural setting involving the constrained use of artifacts.

Cultural learning could be summarized as learning through observation, instruction, or by trial and error. Therefore, there are two major ways of transmitting culture: through other social agents (through the language actions and reactions of other people), and through artifacts, (the objects created and modified by people). The former seems necessary for understanding a culture natively (from the inside as vicarious experience), and the latter seems necessary for extending cultural knowledge or developing cultural awareness of alterity (from the outside as observation or as extrapolated experience). The notion of cultural learning as a spectrum covering awareness to understanding, and nativity to alterity is also important for evaluation, even though it is seldom made (Champion and Dave 2002; Relph 1976).

Virtual heritage projects are a subset of virtual environments, so it may be helpful to study how the latter are evaluated. Many evaluations of virtual environments measure a sense of 'presence'. Presence is often defined along the lines of: the subjective sensation that one is 'present' in a three-dimensional environment that is mediated by digital technology. Presence has also often been described as the sensation of 'being there' in a virtual environment. 'Being there' is usually tested as a combination of factors: Social Presence, engagement, negative feelings, spatial presence etc. in a virtual environment (Slater 1999).

8.3 Virtual Heritage Evaluation

A further dimension of presence often mentioned in conjunction with multi-user environments is the notion of co-presence or Social Presence. There is disagreement in the Presence Research community over these terms (http://www.presence-connect.org).

Co-presence can only take place within a system where you have the sense of being in another place or environment other than the one you are physically in and being there with another person. This differs, in my view, from Social Presence.

Social Presence is rather the degree to which a person experiencing a virtual environment feels part of potential or actual social interaction with at least one other being also capable of social interaction and/or the degree to which they see social interaction (mutually perceived and understood) between two or more intelligent beings. Cultural Presence, on the other hand, is the feeling of being in the presence of a similar or distinctly different cultural belief system.

As described in Chapter 4, this notion is relatively new to virtual heritage environments but lends itself to their unique requirements for evaluation. For this definition specifies a goal, to measure the change in understanding of another cultural perspective different to one's own. Further, we need to measure the significance of that change in perspective and in knowledge, and the effectiveness of the tools and methods required to effect this change.

It must be stressed that this measure of change would be evaluated from at least two different viewpoints, the etic and the emic viewpoint. Etic means an outsider's (a stranger's) view of a culture. More specifically, it is used to describe the anthropologist's method of describing cultures from their own external cultural perspective. Emic means the converse, an insider's (a local's) view of their own culture's inter-relationship of concepts and meanings. In anthropology, it is used to describe the relevance and meaning of concepts and categories from within the same cultural perspective.

When we judge the strength of Cultural Presence, our judgment can be etic or emic. Cultural Presence may cover a spectrum of understanding and viewpoint (from etic to emic) with varying intensity. It may be felt, understood, or entered unselfconsciously, empathized with, or observed but not understood.

8.4 What Types of Evaluation Are There?

8.4.1 Expert Testing

Expert testing is usually done via cognitive walkthroughs or heuristic review. A cognitive walkthrough is a sequence stepped through by reviewers (Van House et al. 1996). While it is preferable to have cognitive walkthroughs undertaken by domain experts (visualization experts, archaeologists, or cultural historians), who then suggest ways of improving the intended design, it can be difficult to obtain such a range of expertise.

(Nielsen n.d.) defined heuristics as "a usability engineering method for finding the usability problems in a user interface design so that they can be attended to as part of an iterative design process." There are indeed heuristics for web-design, but they are based on a long history of creating HTML pages. Usability standards for evaluating not just usability but also usefulness for three-dimensional environments are still some time away.

8.4.2 Content and Media Comparison Studies

In a similar manner, it is very difficult to compare virtual environments with other media, few are comparable, few have the same objectives, and few mediums have the same constraints or public expectations (Christiansson 2001). Until there is a significant and substantial collection of virtual environments with similar aims and objectives, it may prove fruitless to attempt content comparison reviews, even if there have been cross-media presence surveys (Lessiter et al. 2001).

8.4.3 Physiological Testing

In their summary of presence evaluation measures, the International Society for Presence Research wrote that there have been several papers in presence studies on capturing presence using physiological measures (International Society for Presence Research 2003). However, presence may not directly equate to physical or physically observed mental changes (Schlögl et al. 2002), and it certainly does not directly tell us whether virtual heritage environments are causing changes in cultural awareness and learning.

Although it can be non-invasive, results can be unclear, as mentioned by Meehan et al. (2002). Slater (2003) also highlighted a typical problem with this form of testing:

> The problem with using physiological measures directly as a measure of presence is that it is not clear what the response should be in mundane situations. The expected physiological response to a stressful VE is one thing, but what is the expected response to being in, for example, a virtual simulation of an ordinary hotel room, just like one you've stayed in dozens of times before, where nothing out of the ordinary is happening?

8.4.4 Task Performance

Tasks are often set to record the participant's performance in solving them, in order to ascertain the degree of usability of the project. The term 'usability' has achieved a great deal of fame via the website of Jakob Nielsen (2003). He defines usability as having five components: learnability; efficiency; memorability; errors (how many and how severe); and (subjective) satisfaction.

He also mentions there are other factors, such as the highly important factor of utility; does it do what users want? Nielsen's suggestion for basic user testing is to test the project with representative users, and ask them to perform tasks. One could rephrase the above as an evaluation of effectiveness (how well the user achieves the goals they set out to achieve using the system), efficiency (the resources consumed in order to achieve their goals), and satisfaction (how the user feels about their use of the system).

Typical virtual environment usability research (Bowman et al. 1998) tests one audience (say ten people), with three different techniques to solve a certain number of tasks (such as navigation or object manipulation). When evaluating task performance against technique selection, the permutations may become overly complex. The tests were conducted using simple environments. Hence, the complex interdependent features of the environments may produce significantly different results. These specific results may thus not be generally applicable and test usability, not usefulness. Are there discrepancies between usefulness and usability? Would contextual constraints be useful or educational for users?

8.4.5 Surveys/Questionnaires

There are several issues with questionnaires. Slater (2004) has both used them and criticized them. He has argued in the past that one can evaluate presence through asking subjects to rate their feeling of being in another place, but he now believes their value is negligible. Questionnaires interrupt the engagement of participants so they are used at the end of the experience rather than during the experience itself, but this relies on memory recall and a succinct understanding of what actually happened (Slater 1999).

In addition, Presence criteria are usually evaluated using questionnaires, but large test audience numbers are not always available to the designers of virtual heritage environments. Some researchers also use a Prequestionnaire to gain demographic data and an idea of user expectations (Kim 1999). Many surveys and questionnaires used for virtual heritage projects are Likert-based questions; often asking participants to rate their answers from strongly agree to strongly disagree across a 5 or 7 number range.

The use of Likert scales has recently been debated when applied to Presence research (Gardner and Martin 2007; Slater 2004; Slater and Garau 2007) and the debate also applies to virtual heritage. The Gardner and Martin paper questions in particular the use of Likert scales for it often leads to "lumpy" data, but there is also the problem of how respondents can rank their responses to technology they may have never used before (and only used in a test environment), across a range of, say, 5 or 7 numerical values.

To compound the problem, some researchers divide the overall numbers to gain an average response. My "agree" is now considered the same numerical value as "your agree", which is worth one number less than another's "strongly agree" and so on. Yet Göb et al. (2007) point out that Likert scales are supposed to be used as ordinal numbers (numbers that rank) not as cardinal numbers (numbers that can be counted). So how can they be averaged?

8.4.6 Ethnographic Evaluation

An alternative method, as suggested by the International Society for Presence Research (2003), is an ethnographic approach. For example, in a no longer online article entitled *Ethnography and information architecture*, Rettig (2000) argued that information design tools were very similar to those used in archaeological and anthropological research.

These tools are observation (shadowing, people watching, examining 'artifacts'); interviews (contextual, storytelling); sampling (randomly, users are asked to sample events); and self-reporting (users take pictures or keep journals etc.). There are also a growing number of papers in applying discourse analysis and ethnographic observation on multi-user online game environments such as MUDs (Manninen 2003). The danger is that one could be evaluating Social Presence (how effective the virtual environment is at supporting social communication), rather than Cultural Presence (and how well it supports learning different cultural perspectives).

8.5 Evaluating Virtual Heritage Environments

Virtual heritage environments are designed for an end user, but it is not always clear what the end user requires. (Pletinck 2003, Slide 10) answered this point:

> What does the user want? Experience the past....in an accessible way....with scientific accuracy....through sustainable techniques...linked with the community.

People intending to travel to a site may have different requirements to people just exploring a virtual environment (Fig. 8.2). Designers may want to use virtual environments in different ways; used offsite to understand a past, imagined, or present site, inspire them to visit the real-world site through past, present, or imagined depictions, create as background for an online community, or use onsite to augment the experience. Which features are necessary not just for efficient usability, but also for onsite and offsite usefulness?

While the diagram (Fig. 8.3) may suggest virtual tourist and heritage environments have much in common (and indeed they do), it also highlights their differences. The former is more focused on travel information, while the latter is concerned with travel experience.

Fig. 8.2 A tourist attempts to explore a Virtual Heritage Exhibit at Sydney Custom House

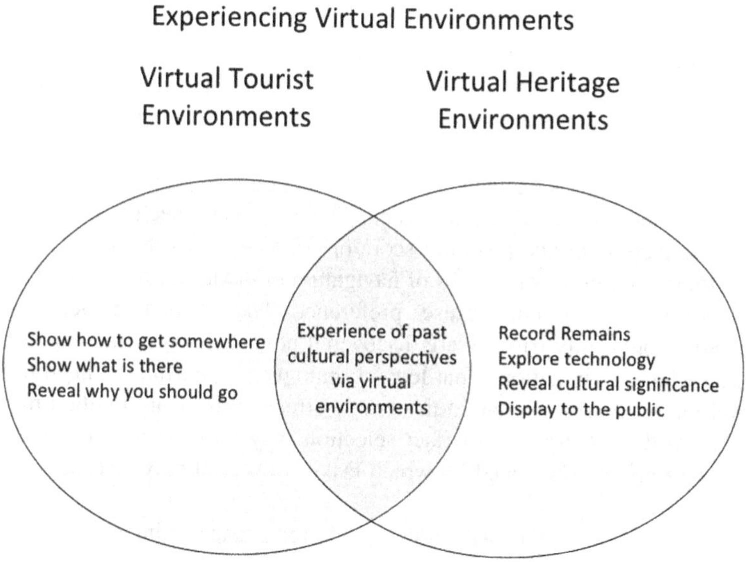

Experiencing Virtual Environments

Virtual Tourist Environments

Virtual Heritage Environments

Show how to get somewhere
Show what is there
Reveal why you should go

Experience of past
cultural perspectives
via virtual
environments

Record Remains
Explore technology
Reveal cultural significance
Display to the public

Fig. 8.3 Diagram of travel and tourism in a virtual environment

This is an important distinction. An evaluation of virtual heritage projects by Mosaker (2001) indicates interactivity and personalization may be more important than realism. Yet virtual heritage projects do not typically involve carefully modulated and monitored levels of interactivity. Hence, we do not know which method of interactivity is most appropriate, for varying audiences, mediums, or recreated objects.

8.5.1 Task Performance and Game Evaluation

I have argued that game–style evaluation may help us assess user performance without interrupting their enjoyment of the virtual environment. Unfortunately, this seems a relatively new area for research, as a paucity of literature exists so far on this subject. Case studies of learning via game–style simulations exist (Aldrich 2004), as well as descriptions of how we learn via video games (Gee 2003), so it seems only a matter of time before performance evaluation can be conducted contextually and indirectly.

Being able to monitor user performance, and what they prefer to select or solve without disturbing their engagement in the experience could be included in virtual heritage environments. For example, in games, data is gathered by innate interactive mechanisms (chat logs, health points, completion of the memento map, and the final state of the inventory of artifacts).

Such data could be compared against results from a pre-experience and post-experience user evaluation questionnaire to determine if we can gain user feedback on cultural immersion in virtual heritage environments without their enjoyment being curtailed, and without them being forced to participate in laboratory interviews or complete survey forms.

One possible long-term solution is to create a database that records user-interaction. This interaction is to be with artifacts (objects in the virtual environment), the places users visit (a record of places changing with the passage of time and use), and dialogue (interaction) with agents (avatars of computer-simulated people) that users meet.

We could use the mechanisms outlined in Chapter 6 to evaluate indirectly both task performance and user engagement. Through such mechanisms we could assess effectiveness by the resulting score or collected artifacts gained or lost by users in their attempt to solve tasks of navigation or dexterity. A record of options selected by users may indicate user preference. The extent to which a map is uncovered or proximity triggers are discovered next to items of information may indicate preferred navigation. Chat logs of dialogues with avatars linked to artificial intelligence databases may indicate how effective users are in eliciting information from the 'chat-bots'. Artifact selection may indicate user knowledge of what is appropriate. The speed by which tasks are solved may also help indicate user satisfaction.

Further, in test conditions we could provide for a range of interaction tools. We could evaluate their 'preferability' at the end of the evaluation by recording which tools are selected by users for the next would-be stage of the virtual environment. This method could be called 'evaluation via exit selection'.

We could also evaluate task performance tied to changes in physiology where deliberate control of the later is required in order to navigate or manipulate objects. For example, Char Davies' artistic work *Osmosis* uses breathing to rise or lower oneself (Davies 1998).

We now have the possibility of adopting biosensors (that are already appearing in commercial games) for virtual environments. Biosensors used in a research-setting offer up a range of interesting possibilities for evaluation and contextual interaction. Still, there are specific issues with evaluating say Cultural Presence that are not addressed by physiological testing. It is not clear how awareness of Cultural Presence in a virtual environment can be indirectly ascertained. Changes in brain state, heartbeat, or skin temperatures do not necessarily mean the participant is either increasingly aware of Cultural Presence, or is increasingly knowledgeable regards a new cultural perspective.

8.5.2 Statistical Methods Suitable for Virtual Heritage Projects

Gabbard et al. (1999, p. 41) wrote:

> Clearly, performing usability evaluation on non-traditional interactive systems requires new approaches, techniques, and insights. While VE evaluation at its highest level retains the same goals and conceptual foundation as its GUI predecessors, the practical matter of performing actual evaluations can be quite different.

Firstly, as virtual environments, one would expect virtual heritage environments to be open to similar statistical evaluation and such evaluation to be presented at related conferences and in relevant journals. There are conferences that cover the design and development of Virtual Heritage environments (VSMM, VAST), effective and usable museum learning experiences, (VSMM and iCHIM conference proceedings), HCI methods and evaluations, and the notion of presence in virtual environments (especially papers from the International Society of Presence Research conference proceedings).

In particular, Virtual Systems and Multimedia (VSMM) Conferences have special sections devoted to Virtual Heritage. Yet of the papers and articles that explain they use statistical methods, few of these papers evaluate the learning of the participants; none of them evaluate Cultural Presence and understanding as discussed in this book.

For example, in the Virtual Systems and Multimedia (VSMM) 2003 proceedings, of 93 papers, 12 papers describing virtual heritage projects appeared complete enough to have been subjected to user testing and inferential statistics, yet none of them mentioned statistical evaluation or even comprehensive user testing. There were however two virtual environments that had non-heritage content, that conducted user testing, (Lee et al. 2004; Thwaites 2003).

The Thwaites paper tested 44 subjects, with a Likert scale questionnaire and open-ended questions, on a Char Davies Virtual Reality art work, but the questions concerned issues of transparency, feeling affected, self-awareness, navigation, or feeling ill, no questions related to culture or learning. There was no statistical calculation mentioned (which is understandable, given the experimental and aesthetic focus of the work). The Lee and Kim paper used a Likert questionnaire with ANOVA statistical method, on whether explicit descriptors, traces or affordances were subjectively considered to help create the sense of a more interactive environment. The content, however, was not related to virtual heritage, and purely for the sake of the experimental design.

In the Virtual Systems and Multimedia (VSMM) 2004 proceedings (Thwaites 2004), of 169 papers, 18 papers with virtual heritage content appeared complete enough to have conducted testing and inferential statistics on the user experience. Apart from the author's own paper, three papers said that they conducted user testing.

Sylaiou et al (2004) evaluated an augmented reality museum project using heuristic guidelines and cognitive walkthroughs. Twenty-nine users and ten experts were asked to complete an 8-point Likert scale test on usefulness and enjoyability. No statistical calculations were mentioned. Abawi et al. (2004) conducted user testing while Ogleby and Quadros (2004) mentions exit polls, but there was no mention of statistical testing, the number of participants polled, or any other numerical details for either paper.

In short, there appears to be a distinct lack of either user testing in virtual heritage environments with statistical calculation of the data. The iCHIM proceedings include papers on usability testing, but they avoid mention of the statistical methods used. Of the papers that discuss evaluation, they do not directly address the user-centered issue of cultural learning; they evaluate navigation and aesthetic issues.

Of the four above areas, research under the auspices of the International Society for Presence Research (ISPR) seems to have applied the most thorough and comprehensive evaluation methods. However, statistical methods were typically used to evaluate Likert-based questionnaires, the focus was on subjective response to a sense of shared presence or co-presence, and the actual content either was designed directly for the sake of the experiment, or did not directly address the notion of learning about other cultures. A paper presented at Presence 2002 (Riva et al. 2002), outlined a notion of Cultural Presence, but no evaluation method was discussed.

While HCI is a field that is focused on evaluation, it too has its own internal problems. For example, Hartson et al. (2003) have evaluated usability methods as a meta-comparison of usability studies, measuring these methods against the criteria of thoroughness, validity, and reliability. They selected 18 comparison studies and found a surprising number were incomplete or unclear. They concluded "At this point in the HCI field, it appears to be nearly impossible to do an appropriate meta-comparison of usability studies."

Bowman et al. (2005, pp. 360–367) argued that extrapolating guidelines from the 2D world of HCI heuristics to virtual environments may also obscure the distinctive characteristics of 3D virtual environments. They wrote (2005, pp. 363–365):

> 3D UIs are still often a 'solution looking for a problem.' Because of this, the target user population or interaction technique to be evaluated may not be known or well-understood... Presence is another example of a measure often required in VE evaluations that has no analogue in traditional UI evaluation.

Gabbard et al. (1999, pp. 7–9) have also written of the problems that bedevil the evaluation of virtual environments. They have written that it is difficult to discern the target audience, find an actual problem that the virtual environment is trying to solve, or separate expert knowledge from novice knowledge. In the evaluation of the virtual environment they also commented that it is difficult to decide on using within-subjects testing (which means the subjects need to experience many different conditions) or use between-subjects testing (which requires a great deal more subjects to sit the tests). The novelty of virtual environments to most users further exacerbates the problem.

It may be possible to counter the novelty factor of virtual environments by evaluating an experienced group, such as those who have played computer games for some years. Krauss et al. (2001) measured presence in a computer game using a modified version of the Witmer and Singer (1998) questionnaire on 170 participants who were asked to remember a computer game they played Singer. This resulted in 163 complete data sets of answers to questions that measured audio and haptic curse, control, ability to use the control mechanisms, and carry over behavior generated from gameplay that continued even when the participant stopped playing the game.

Respondents selected a button for each answer (based on a 7-point Likert scale), and these answers were calculated using Cronbach's alpha. The writers said the sample size should have been even larger, but they also forgot to mention if all respondents played the same computer game, using the same hardware. The paper notes that participants were recruited online to answer notions of presence in 'first person shooters.' If so, it is hard to understand how individual responses could be combined as the genre covers many different games that can be played across different platforms.

Curtis and Lawson (2002) conducted an interesting study on computer-based adventure games as problem-solving environments, and used *t*-tests and then Partial Least Squares (PLS) to evaluate schema and strategy development of 40 participants who were asked to find at least six objects in 5 minutes. The number of locations reached and objects collected were recorded, as were the extent to which they used maps and the number of moves that they made. The participants were also trained to speak aloud while solving the tasks.

However, their results (Curtis and Lawson 2002, p. 53) "suggested a strong negative path between schema and performance." Curtis and Lawson suggest cognitive overloading or high variability in decision-making adversely affected the results but there may also be other reasons. Possibly those who understood the game well were not highly motivated to perform well because they simply were not challenged and intrigued by the tasks set them.

Barfield and Furness (1995, pp. 482–483) have acknowledged that defining and evaluating a useful sense of virtual presence is still difficult. Their chapter is entitled "Components of the 'Virtual Environment' Experience", however statistical methods described in that chapter measure task performance rather than user experience. In addition, one of the components, Zeltzer's criterion of natural 'task-level' interaction which is apparently related to a notion of how intuitive is the environment, is also task performance based rather than user-experience based.

Parés and Parés (2005) have written that presence research does not typically evaluate the experience of the virtual environment, and their paper outlines a conceptual evaluation method to address this gap. However, they unfortunately do not provide statistical evaluation to verify their conceptual model.

Steed and McDonnell (2003) have written that the emphasis on task performance is typical in presence research. Unfortunately, their attempt in their pilot studies to marry the two commonly used Presence questionnaires (the Slater–Usoh–Steed questionnaire. and the Witmer–Singer questionnaire) in order to help answer this question, does not have a suitably large sample size ($n = 5$), and the tasks set still seem arbitrary.

One exception to arbitrary task-based evaluation is the evaluation of Social Presence, a sense of 'other' in a paper by de Greef and IJsselsteijn (2000), which uses a between subjects test and statistical evaluation using the General Linear Model to evaluate the variables of presence and satisfaction. However, for virtual heritage purposes, we are looking for immediate and direct evaluation of the effect of certain modes of interaction on a sense of Cultural Presence, and not with Social Presence as defined in that paper.

Presence conferences have discussed the relation of culture to presence, but not in terms of cultural learning as defined in this paper. For example, Hu and Bartneck (2005) evaluated the effect of cultural background on a subjectively perceived notion of presence. Twenty-four Chinese and 19 Dutch participants watched interactive movies of a fictional job interview. Each movie had two decision points for the participant to answer, which created four possible movie endings. There was also had a secondary screen of a Lego robot, or the actual Lego robot. In both conditions, screen condition and robot condition, the screen robot or actual robot spoke using speech synthesis software, and looked randomly at the main screen. In the robot-condition, the participant touched the left or right shoulder of the robot to make a decision.

After watching the movie, they were asked to answer questions on spatial presence, engagement, naturalness, and negative effects. Using paired sample t-tests and independent samples t-tests, statistically significant differences between the two groups were discovered.

However, there are serious problems with the experimental design. The claim that the movie was "culturally neutral" because there were Moroccan, Dutch, American, and Chilean actors, is puzzling. The test was in English, and the Chinese participants had been in the Netherlands (where the experimental design took place) for up to 2 years. Chinese students and teachers at a Dutch university are unlikely to reflect the cultural beliefs and viewpoints of mainstream Chinese society, especially given the sample size, if indeed there is one set of cultural beliefs that can be considered to be 'Chinese'. This example shows the dangers of using small samples for demographic testing.

There are other problems in using questionnaires. A recent paper by Roussou and Slater (2005) studied the learning of children in a virtual environment, and the effect of interactivity on that learning. Approximately 30 children were assigned to one of three conditions, a control, an interactive VR, or a passive VR, and a speak-aloud method was employed. The study had not been completed by the time of writing the paper, but it revealed a problem with questionnaires. For young children, it can be very difficult not just to observe and recall, but also reflect on why they undertook specific actions in the virtual environment.

In their attempt to standardize data collection and data analysis, Friedman et al. (2005) have listed issues with presence research and evaluation methods, which are relevant to this research. They noted that in presence research there is currently no large-scale verification of data. It is hard if not impossible to reconstruct the subjective experience of the user. It is difficult to compare methods as the content is not detailed, made available, or related directly to real life situations; and the experimental design is often not easily replicated.

They suggested that as presence is still a hotly debated term, (for an example, refer Slater (1999)), one requires many evaluation methods, along with questionnaires (which are often unreliable when used in isolation) to catch subjective responses not revealed by objective evaluation methods. Unfortunately, Friedman et al. (2005) focus on evaluation of task performance, and do not recommend and detail a preferred method of data collection and data analysis.

Insko (2003) also argued that due to the many definitions of presence, one should try to evaluate it with as many measures as possible. Insko added that a good meta-test of questionnaires is to see if they distinguish between virtual presence and real presence. He cited a study by Usoh et al. (2000) that evaluated a real office space and a virtual reconstruction of the same office space using the Witmer–Singer questionnaire and the Slater–Usoh–Steed questionnaire.

The Witmer–Singer questionnaire failed to show any differences in presence between the two groups, the Slater–Usoh–Steed questionnaire "had a higher marginal score for the real compared to the virtual world" (Insko 2003). Notwithstanding this potential conflict of interest, according to Insko a test of virtual presence should return a score lower than if it assessed presence in the corresponding real world, hence the Slater–Usoh–Steed test is more useful than the Witmer–Singer questionnaire. In other words, for Insko and the researchers he cited (Usoh et al. 2000), evaluation of virtual presence is based on an approximation towards real presence.

Interesting as this may be, the test will not necessarily be of help in assessing Cultural Presence, unless the virtual experience is supposed to tally as accurately as possible with a given and accessible real world experience of that culture. This is a problem if the real culture being simulated no longer exists in one place or at the current time, or if the cultural knowledge is fragmented or only circulated amongst experts and not the general public.

Riva et al. (2002) have written a paper on how to evaluate the quality of experience in virtual environments, which is a topic closer to the research objective of this book. They also argued that questionnaires are unreliable, and that relying on people who have never before been asked to measure their own experience or the content they learnt in a virtual environment, is risky. They also agreed that presence has many different definitions, and that presence is multi-dimensional. Their recommendations were to analyze as many components of the quality of experience as possible, to analyze the relation of virtual content to daily life, to use their Experience Fluctuation Model, and to compare to other evaluation frameworks. Yet their definition of culture was reliant on the notion of memes, an unproven theory of cultural propagation, and no data collection or data analysis was given.

In the paper 'Evaluating Soundscapes as a Means of Creating a Sense of Place', Turner et al. (2003a) evaluated the effectiveness of soundscapes to help create a sense of place, through a simple post-experience presence questionnaire. Forty people were randomly allocated to one of four conditions while listening to a soundscape (while being in a real place, being in that place and speaking aloud, being blindfolded and silent, or blindfolded and asked to speak aloud). The results were simply mean scores per test condition. In another paper from the same year, 'Re-creating the Botanics: Towards a Sense of Place in Virtual Environment', written with different co-authors, Turner et al. (2003b) evaluated a sense of place using qualitative data. They also took quantitative data, but the paper did not describe the latter, as they did not believe quantitative data was an accurate measure of a subjective sense of place.

Spagnolli et al. (2003) agreed with the inherent risk of questionnaires, they noted that asking people if they experience presence relies on the respondents having a clear and coherent notion of their own self-presence, and conventional tests assume that people can describe their sense of presence clearly and accurately. Their paper also suggested a method potentially applicable to cultural learning in virtual environments, with clear guidelines and questions to ask, but they evaluated dialogue not interaction or creation of cultural artifacts, and they did not appear to have conducted any statistical evaluation of the experimental data.

8.6   Evaluation Case Study: Palenque

As I noted in Chapter 5, the original Palenque project using Adobe Atmosphere (which is no longer sold by Adobe), was to determine which of three interaction modes contributed more to cultural understanding. These interaction modes were called action-based, guide-based, and observation-based.

Unfortunately, because the site was too large for the rendering engine, it was broken up into three parts. Each part was a slice of the overall site, using one of the three interactivity modes.

For example, in the 'Temple of Inscriptions Action-based world', people were asked to find artefacts and the accompanying webpage of information. However, unlike the 'Temple of Inscriptions Observations-based world', in the 'Temple of Inscriptions Action-based world' in order to find and read the information they had to carefully re-position themselves while moving trapdoors and sarcophagus lids. In the second 'Cross Group Guide-Based world', people were asked to find and click on the Cross Group tablets; and listen to the scripted guides. In the third 'Palace Observation-Based world' they were asked to find as many of the hidden artefacts as possible, and read the related information.

There were several affordances, proxemic music, glowing lights every 20 seconds, and buttons that would orient them to the next goal and tell them how far away they were. Hidden scripts recorded the time taken and how many tasks were completed and emailed the results to me at the end of their visit to the virtual environments. Photographs of real people available via the Lonely Planet Images database were mapped onto the face of each avatar. They were also allowed to fly since the steps were often huge, and the site was large for a 1 hour experiment. Only the activity-based mode had serious constraints; that is, manipulation skills were required to move the giant slabs that hid the secret passages.

8.6.1 Pilot Study

Before the virtual environments were finished, three domain experts (archaeologists and usability specialists) suggested refinements to the navigation and interaction. An archeology teacher who taught Mayan archaeology also provided feedback on the questions asked. I then conducted a pilot study of her first year archaeology class. The students were keen on exploring what options were available to them, especially how to change avatars and talk to each other. There were many requests on how to destroy or shoot things, which is rather disturbing given that they were archaeology students. Perhaps game–style interaction has created a game-genre at odds with cultural learning.

Her class of first-year archaeology students was evaluated against the prototype, in computer lab settings of up to 15 people. The 47 students were asked general questions on cultural knowledge acquired, and were tested on what they observed, asked to rank the worlds in terms of several 'presence-style' criteria, asked to judge which world had the fastest speed (frame-rate), and their in-world task performance was also recorded.

Because the students had a predilection for game–style interaction, for the study four imaginative environments were added (ballcourt, caiman creation myth, cave-diving, village-quest game). They lasted for only 3 minutes, but incorporated one specific task (mentioned in Chapter 5). However, each imaginative environment was only reached on completing the archaeological environment before it, this was meant to encourage the participants to explore the archaeological level. Finding information here could help them in the more imaginative game-like environments later on.

8.6.2 Evaluation

For the evaluation 24 visualization experts were invited to take part, and ten IT-experienced Lonely Planet employees also took part. In the evaluation, participants were asked to complete certain tasks within a set time limit of 9 minutes. At the end of 9 min, they were asked to perform tasks (for 3 minutes) in an imaginative environment. Then they were asked to record answers to a multiple-choice questionnaire, with 6 questions for each of the 3 environments. At the end of the experiment, they were asked to rank the worlds against each other, to answer questions on recalling generic environmental details, and to guess the relative frame rate speeds of the three archaeological environments. The overall evaluation and the results will be covered in a future issue of Virtual Reality journal, but here I would like to share the conclusions I gained from the study.

8.6.3 Evaluation Questions

Participants were evaluated via in-world task performance, post-experience cultural understanding (knowledge recall), observation of time passed, speed of rendering, ranking of world against certain Cultural Presence criteria, and environmental observation (Table 8.1). The ten Lonely Planet employees were also asked which interaction mode they preferred for virtual travel environments. The demographic data collected was of age group, gender, literary knowledge of Mesoamerican

Table 8.1 Evaluation measures and questions

Evaluation	Content	Objective
Task performance	Six information objects to find per environment	Compare to understanding
Cultural understanding (multiple choice)	Six multiple choice questions on the Temple of Inscriptions	Compare to preference, task performance and demographics
	Six multiple choice questions on the palace	
	Six multiple choice questions on the Cross Precinct	
Presence survey (rank from 1 to 7)	Which did you find the most challenging to explore, find or change things?	Compare to demographics and task performance
	Which was the most interesting to you?	Find personal preference in answers (A–D/E)
	Which seemed most interactive to you?	Rank the three archaeological and the four imaginative environments from 1 for highest (most, closest), and 7 for least close
	Which did you feel most closely represented the way Mayans saw their own world?	
	Which most effectively seemed inhabited by real people?	
	Which felt most like you were in the presence of Mayan culture?	
Environmental recall: did you notice? (multiple-choice)	Shadow?	Compare to demographics, to task performance and to understanding
	Real people?	
	How tall were Mayans compared to modern western people?	
	How many real or computer scripted people were in the site?	
	In future, which would you like such environments for?	
Subjective experience of time passing (rate 1–3)	In each environment, did time pass by quickest? (Write in descending order of apparent speed).	Compare to subjective preference and to demographics

Table 8.2 Table sequencing of environments in evaluation

Order	Environment	Objective of environment
	Warm-up	
A	Teotihuacán	In 3 minutes learn how to use software
B	Milpas (village)	In 3 minutes discover/share/navigation
	Archaeological and imaginative reconstructions of Palenque	
1	Inscriptions (action)	In 9 minutes move slabs to descend to bottom of temple
1a	Mayan Ballcourt	In 3 minutes action–play
2	Palace (observation)	In 9 minutes find artifacts and click on them
2b	Cave	In 3 minutes pick up and release artifacts
3	Cross group (guides)	In 9 minutes find and listen to guides, then enter temple
3c	Primal sea-mountain	In 3 minutes discover the world tree; reach the paddler gods

archaeology and culture, PC Internet and PC game experience, and travel knowledge of the region.

8.6.4 Schedule of Evaluation

Note that after the warm-up environment, we changed the sequence of environments for each participant to avoid a possible order effect (Table 8.2).

8.6.5 Observations

None of the groups enjoyed answering general knowledge questions, which were probably too hard. It is difficult to assess cultural learning via knowledge and recall questions. It is highly possible that people's answers to questionnaires do not truly reflect their sense of engagement. And although they ranked the archaeological worlds higher than the imaginative worlds in all the main criteria, it was difficult to coax experts and students from the two game-based imaginative worlds, the Cave-world and the Ballcourt.

Splitting the virtual environment into three environments because of technical constraints made life difficult for me, resulting in complex multifactorial statistical analysis. Choosing social world software like Adobe Atmosphere was also a mistake as only one level (the Village) required more than one participant. The most fundamental mistake though was the assumption that cultural learning is derived from observation, social discourse and activity-based learning. That may well be true but in practice we don't learn from strict division of these three interactivity modes, but from a hybrid of ways to learn.

I also found that people who completed the tasks or completed them more quickly did not necessarily understand or recall more cultural facts. Game–style interaction may be intuitive for navigation and task-performance, and reduce cognitive loading, but at the expense of understanding cultural significance.

However, some of the five evaluation methods showed promise. People's understanding of how quickly time passed and frame-rate did seem to relate to their sense of enjoyment, and so did memory recall of environmental details. Asking participants to rank the environments against Cultural Presence criteria may also be more revealing than asking them directly to rank or rate Cultural Presence (a vague and controversial term despite my best efforts!) However, participants should never be asked to rank too many environments, my survey had screenshots to remind them of what they were ranking, but there were still too many environments.

Further, and this was learnt from bitter experience, advanced techniques that slow down the environment in order to create more realistic effects may not be noticed by participants engaged in solving tasks. In this case, the use of dynamic lighting (dynamic shadows) may appear highly immersive to the world designer, but have little or no effect on the actual participant's sense of immersion.

8.7   Summary of Evaluation for Virtual Heritage

In summary, virtual heritage papers generally seem to avoid detailed descriptions of data collection and analysis of the intended and actual user-experience. Presence research does have a great deal of literature on data collection, analysis, and some discussion of statistical issues. However, these papers are typically derived from laboratory experiments set up purely to isolate components of presence through analysis of task performance, not thematic user-experience.

Where papers talk about cultural or Social Presence, or about content related learning, they may detail framework and concepts similar to this book. However, they either avoid or decry the use of quantitative data. In the case of museum-based evaluations, there is a focus on navigation and legibility issues, but even when data analysis methods are included, these papers do not typically analyze the content-related notions of Cultural Presence as experienced by the user, nor what they learn from the experience.

> More research is certainly needed on the usefulness of methods of user study and activity modeling in the context of interactivity in VR. As it seems, there have been no relevant studies that we know of that have been specifically aimed at these subjects, except for the one by Kaur et al. (1999) (van der Straaten 2000, pp. Conclusion, section 4, p. 3).

The first major problem for experimental designs in this area is obvious: to determine exactly what we are trying to improve through the testing of virtual heritage environments. In experimental design related to virtual heritage environments there are a myriad of issues. How can we evaluate the success or failure of an attempt to recreate digitally a past culture? How do we know whether the designer's goal is achieved in terms of the audience?

It is not clear what the experimental goal is. If we have a definition of culture, what are the outcomes of tailoring virtual environments to communicate a sense of Cultural Presence? Do we increase the participant's knowledge, or ability to extrapolate socially contextual principles of behavior?

If say, we wish to find out which independent variable most affords the dependent variable of Cultural Presence, we need to define this dependent variable as accurately as possible.

Secondly, as suggested earlier, it is difficult to run comparisons of virtual environments against traditional media (to ask for cross-media audience preferences), because the form of interaction and the technology is so different and in some cases alien to the test subjects (Riihiaho 2000, pp. 101–103). To argue that the content in a film and a game based on that film are comparable, is to conflate narrative with self directed interaction, ignore the atmosphere of a cinema, and equate high tech surround systems with a desktop monitor.

There is also the issue of time; people have had years to build up knowledge of film and television and even computer games. They may also take a long time to build up experience of virtual environments. We could use ethnographic methods or ask people in online communities to compare new interaction modes or new interfaces. Unfortunately, we do not know if they represent the complete spectrum of the potential audience, while their knowledge is typically very specific and accumulated through unhealthy amounts of time spent online (Yee 2004).

There is also the issue of which evaluation method to use. For cross-media comparisons, questionnaires are typically used but they can be problematic. Virtual environments are also seen as a 'cool' new technology, and the test audience may be biased towards this new technology, or, conversely, have unrealistic hopes of what is feasible in real-time and online media (due to previous experience with commercial game engines, or watching pre-rendered digital animations in science fiction films).

For virtual travel environments, one might wish to compare them with visiting the real place. One might argue that to evaluate photo-realism a comparison of the virtual place with the real place it attempts to replicate, is essential. However, the logistics of finding an audience that can compare real places to virtual places is often difficult if not impossible. More importantly, as Gillings (2002) noted, the issue is not how Virtual Reality can appear to be reality (i.e. be identical to the place that it recreates), but how Virtual Reality can add to the experience in a new and different way to reality: for why should we recreate what is already there or imitate what has already been done better (and probably also more accurately), in another medium?

Thirdly, in experimental design one typically employs a control group to determine whether a treatment (a new added cause) is more beneficial than the status quo (represented by the control group). For virtual environments, especially virtual heritage environments, such an approach is highly problematic. It can be very difficult to select and sort audiences by background knowledge and skills into equivalent groups (a control group versus a treatment group) for statistical evaluation, and expect initial learning styles, as well as understanding and experience of three-dimensional computer environments to be equivalent without a thorough demographic pre-questionnaire.

If we are evaluating whether a control group using a standard interaction mode performs or understands a culture better or worse compared to a treatment group that is using a new mode of interaction, we have to make sure that the two modes of interaction do not differ greatly in cognitive loading. We must also ensure that the second group is not getting the same information twice. For example, Kavakli et al. (2004) forgot to mention this effect in their interesting paper comparing learning history when playing a computer game to reading a text.

Fourthly, if we wish to understand how different interactive elements affect task performance, we may wish to have two or more groups, one being a control and the other or others using other modes of interactivity. However, we cannot then find out if a certain world-mode (a particular virtual environment with a particular mode of interactivity) is preferable to the same environment with a different mode of interactivity.

Fifthly, we may wish to compare different types of interactivity to a virtual heritage environment, but different contexts in the same environment may require different forms of interactivity. Different forms of learning and different traditional ways of navigating environments or manipulating artifacts may require particular forms of interaction.

For example, interaction appropriate to the cultural learning of a monk in a monastery may not apply to the learning in the farms that feed the monastery. In the former, one learns by instruction, while in the latter one may learn by trial and error, or by observation. The environment may dictate a specific type of interaction, or a specific combination of degrees or even kinds of interaction.

The specificity of certain forms of historical interaction may impede the creation of general design guidelines, and it may present problems to the evaluation of cultural learning across a large virtual heritage project. Hence, although there are many interesting and novel ways of evaluating virtual environments, there are a host of contextual issues, especially in terms of cultural learning, that bedevil testing this area. We are still left with the central problem of defining cultural learning, and ensuring this definition could produce clear and verifiable outcomes.

Even if we have clear outcomes that can be tested with small statistical samples, we must also ensure that the testing is as close as possible to real world use. Yet here in this emerging field the research literature is sparse, and comparisons with equivalent products and media are problematic. We must also attempt not to bore the test audience or cause cognitive overloading that may confound the results.

References

Abawi, D., Los Arcos, J.L., Haller, M., Hartmann, W., Huhtala, K., & Träskbäck, M. (2004). *A Mixed Reality Museum Guide: The Challenges and its Realization.* Paper presented at the VSMM2004: Proceedings of the 10th International Conference on Virtual Systems and Multimedia, Japan.

Aldrich, C. (2004). *Simulations and the future of learning: an innovative (and perhaps revolutionary) approach to e-learning.* San Francisco, CA: Jossey-Bass.

Barfield, W., & Furness III, T.A. (Eds.). (1995). *Virtual environments and advanced interface design.* New York: Oxford University Press.

Bowman, D., Koller, D., & Hodges, L. (1998). A methodology for the evaluation of travel techniques for immersive virtual environments. *Virtual Reality, 3*(2), 120–131.

Bowman, D., Wineman, J., Hodges, L., & Allison, D. (1999). The Educational Value of an Information-Rich Virtual Environment. *Presence: Teleoperators and Virtual Environments, 8*(3), 317–331.

Bowman, D.A. (2005). *3D user interfaces: theory and practice.* Boston, MA: Addison-Wesley.

Champion, E., & Dave, B. (2002, 24–27 October 2002). *Where is this place?* Paper presented at the ACADIA2002, Association For Computer Aided Design in Architecture 2002 Annual Conference, Pomona, CA.

Christiansson, P. (2001). *Capture of user requirements and structuring of collaborative VR environments.* Paper presented at the AVR II and CONVR2001 Conference. Retrieved 30 April 2010, from http://it.civil.aau.dk/it/reports/r_chalmers_vr_4_10_2001.pdf

Curtis, D.D., & Lawson, M.J. (2002). Computer Adventure Games as Problem-Solving Environments. *International Education Journal, 3*(4), 43–56.

Davies, C. (1998). Osmose: Notes on Being in Immersive Virtual Space. *Digital Creativity, 9*(2), 65–74.

de Greef, P., & IJsselsteijn, W.A. (2000). *Social Presence in the PhotoShare Tele-Application.* Paper presented at the Presence 2000 – 3rd International Workshop on Presence. Retrieved 30 April 2010, from http://www.temple.edu/ispr/prev_conferences/proceedings/98-99-2000/2000/de%20Greef%20and%20IJsselsteijn.pdf

Friedman, D., Brogni, A., Antley, A., Guger, C., & Slater, M. (2005). *Sharing and analysing data from presence experiments.* Paper presented at the 8th Annual International Workshop on Presence, London.

Gabbard, J., L., Hix, D., & Swan, J.E. (1999). User-Centered Design and Evaluation of Virtual Environments. *IEEE Computer Graphics and Applications, 19*(6), 51–59.

Gardner, H.J., & Martin, M.A. (2007). Analyzing ordinal scales in studies of virtual environments: Likert or lump it! *Presence, 16*(4), 439–446.

Gee, J.P. (2003). *What video games have to teach us about learning and literacy.* New York: Palgrave Macmillan.

Gillings, M. (2002). Virtual Archaeologies and the Hyper-Real. In P. Fisher & D. Unwin (Eds.), *Virtual Reality in Geography* (Vol. 17–32). London & New York: Taylor and Francis.

Göb, R., McCollin, C., & Ramalhoto, M. (2007). Ordinal Methodology in the Analysis of Likert Scales. *Quality and Quantity, 41*(5), 601–626.

Goldman, K.H., & Wadman, M. (2002). There's Something Happening Here, What It Is Ain't Exactly Clear [Electronic Version]. *Archimuse, Museums and the Web Conference.* Retrieved 9 March 2010, from http://www.archimuse.com/mw2002/papers/haleyGoldman/haleygoldman.html

Hartson, H.R., Andre, T.S., & Williges, R.C. (2003). Criteria for Evaluating Usability Evaluation Methods. *International Journal of Human-Computer Interaction, 15*(1), 145–181.

Hu, J., & Bartneck, C. (2005). *Culture Matters – A Study on Presence in an Interactive Movie.* Paper presented at the Presence 2005 Conference. Retrieved 30 April 2010, from http://www.temple.edu/ispr/prev_conferences/proceedings/2005/Hu%20and%20Bartneck.pdf

Insko, B. (2003). Measuring Presence: Subjective, Behavioral and Physiological Methods. In G. Riva, F. David & W. A. IJsselsteijn (Eds.), *Being there: concepts, effects and measurement of user presence in synthetic environments* (pp. 109–119). Amsterdam, The Netherlands: IOS Press.

International Society for Presence Research. (2003). Tools to Measure Presence [Electronic Version], 2010. Retrieved May 2008, from http://www.temple.edu/ispr/frame_measure.htm

Kavakli, M., Akca, A., & Thorne, J. (2004). *The role of computer games in the education of history.* Paper presented at the IE2004 Australian Workshop on Interactive Entertainment, UTS, Sydney.

Kim, J. (1999). An Empirical Study of Navigation Aids in Customer Interfaces. *Behaviour and Information Technology, 18*(3), 213–234.

Krauss, M., Scheuchenpflug, R., Piechulla, W., & Zimmer, A. (2001). Measurement of presence in virtual environments. In A. C. Zimmer & K. Lange (Eds.), *Experimentelle Psychologie im Spannungsfeld von Grundlagenforschung und Anwendung Proceedings,* Regensburg (pp. 358–362).

Lee, J.C., Dietz, P.H., Maynes-Aminzade, D., Raskar, R., & Hudson, S.E. (2004, 24–27 October). *Automatic projector calibration with embedded light sensors*. Paper presented at the 17th annual ACM symposium on User Interface Software and Technology, Santa Fe, NM, USA.

Lessiter, J., Freeman, J., Keogh, E., & Davidoff, J. (2001). A Cross-Media Presence Questionnaire: The ITC-Sense of Presence Inventory. *Presence: Teleoperators and Virtual Environments, 10*(3), 282–297.

Manninen, T. (2003). Manifestations in Multi-player Games. In G. Riva, F. Davide & W. A. IJsselsteijn (Eds.), *Being there: concepts, effects and measurement of user presence in synthetic environments* (pp. 295–304). Amsterdam, The Netherlands: IOS Press.

Meehan, M., Insko, B., Whitton, M., & Brooks Jnr., F.P. (2002). *Physiological measures of presence in stressful virtual environments*. Paper presented at the 29th Annual Conference on Computer Graphics and Interactive Techniques, San Antonio, Texas.

Mosaker, L. (2001). Visualising Historical Knowledge Using Virtual Reality Technology. *Digital Creativity, 12*(1), 15–25.

Nielsen, J. (2003, 25 August). Usability 101: Introduction to Usability, online article. *Jakob Nielsen's Alertbox*. Retrieved 12 March, 2010, from http://www.useit.com/alertbox/20030825.html

Nielsen, J. (n.d.). How to Conduct a Heuristic Evaluation. Retrieved 13 March 2010, from http://www.useit.com/papers/heuristic/heuristic_evaluation.html

Ogleby, C., & Quadros, N. (2004). *In the Company of Dinosaurs: 3D Animated Content. Development for the Eight Screen Virtual Room*. Paper presented at the VSMM2004 10th International Conference on Virtual Systems and Multimedia, Japan.

Parés, N., & Parés, R. (2005). *Towards a Model for a Virtual Reality Experience: the Virtual Subjectiveness*. Paper presented at the PRESENCE 2005 Conference: The 8th Annual International Workshop on Presence, London England.

Pletinckx, D. (2003). Mapping the future: Intelligent Heritage – The user perspective. *Information Society Technologies, Cultural Heritage section*. Retrieved 30 April 2010, from ftp://ftp.cordis.europa.eu/pub/ist/docs/digicult/pletinckx28012003.ppt

Relph, E.C. (1976). *Place and placelessness*. London: Pion.

Rettig, M. (2000). *Architecture for use: ethnography and information architecture*. Paper presented at the ASIS Summit 2000: Defining Information Architecture.

Riihiaho, S. (2000). *Experiences with Usability Evaluation Methods*. Unpublished Licentiate's thesis, Helsinki University of Technology, Helsinki.

Riva, G., Castelnuovo, G., Gaggioli, A., & Mantovani, F. (2002, October). *Towards a cultural approach to presence*. Paper presented at the PRESENCE 2002 Conference: Fifth Annual International Workshop on Presence, Porto Portugal.

Roussou, M. (2004). Learning by doing and learning through play: an exploration of interactivity in virtual environments for children. *Computers in Entertainment, 2*(1), 10.

Roussou, M., & Slater, M. (2005). *A Virtual Playground for the Study of the Role of Interactivity in Virtual Learning Environments*. Paper presented at the PRESENCE 2005 Conference: The 8th Annual International Workshop on Presence, London.

Schlögl, A., Slater, M., & Pfurtscheller, G. (2002). *Presence Research and EEG*. Paper presented at the PRESENCE 2002 Conference: 5th Annual International Workshop on Presence, Porto Portugal.

Slater, M. (1999). Measuring Presence: A Response to the Witmer and Singer Presence Questionnaire. *Presence: Teleoperators and Virtual Environments, 8*(5), 560–565.

Slater, M. (2003, 18 August). I'm only pretending – response to the core of presence by J&A Waterworth. Retrieved 12 February 2010, from http://presence.cs.ucl.ac.uk/presenceconnect/forum/viewmessage.asp?forumid=14&messageid=104

Slater, M. (2004). How Colorful Was Your Day? Why Questionnaires Cannot Assess Presence in Virtual Environments. *Presence, 13*(4), 484–493.

Slater, M. (2004). How Colourful Was Your Day? Why Questionnaires Cannot Assess Presence in Virtual Environments. *Presence: Teleoperators and Virtual Environments, 13*(4), 240–245.

Slater, M., & Garau, M. (2007). The Use of Questionnaire Data in Presence Studies: Do Not Seriously Likert. *Presence: Teleoperators and Virtual Environments, 16*(4), 447–456.

Spagnolli, A., Varotto, D., & Mantovani, G. (2003). An Ethnographic, Action-Based Approach to Human Experience in Virtual Environments. *International Journal of Human-Computer Studies, 59,* 797–822.

Steed, A., & McDonnell, J. (2003). *Experiences with Repertory Grid Analysis for Investigating Effectiveness of Virtual Environments.* Paper presented at the Presence 2003 Conference: The 6th Annual International Workshop on Presence, Aalborg, Denmark.

Sylaiou, S., Almosawi, A., Mania, K., & White, M. (2004). *Preliminary evaluation of the augmented representation of cultural objects system.* Paper presented at the VSMM2004: Proceedings of the 10th International Conference on Virtual Systems and Multimedia, Japan.

Thwaites, H. (2003). *Immersion and Audience: Some Considerations resulting from OSMOSE.* Paper presented at the VSMM2003 Conference: 9th International Conference on Virtual Systems and Multimedia-HYBRID REALITY: Art, Technology and the Human Factor, Montreal Canada.

Thwaites, H. (Ed.). (2004). *VSMM2004: Proceedings of the 10th International Conference on Virtual Systems and Multimedia* (Vol. 1). Gifu, Japan: IOS Press.

Turner, P., McGregor, I., Turner, S., & Carroll, F. (2003). *Evaluating Soundscapes as a Means of Creating a Sense of Place.* Paper presented at the 2003 International Conference on Auditory Display (ICAD 2003). Retrieved 30 April 2010, from http://www.benogo.dk/publications/ evaluating_soundscapes.pdf van House access date is 30 April 2010. URL is still valid.

Turner, S., Turner, P., Carroll, F., O'Neil, S., Benyon, D., McCall, R., et al. (2003). *Re-creating the Botanics: Towards a Sense of Place in Virtual Environments.* Paper presented at the Environmental Psychology in the UK Conference. Retrieved 30 April 2010, from http://www. benogo.dk/publications/2003.html

Usoh, M., Catena, E., Arman, S., & Slater, M. (2000). Using Presence Questionnaires in Reality. *Presence: Teleoperators and Virtual Environments, 9,* 497–503.

van der Straaten, P. (2000). *Interaction Affecting the Sense of Presence in Virtual Reality.* Unpublished Master's thesis, Delft University of Technology, Delft.

Van House, N.A., Butler, M., & Schiff, L. (1996). *Needs Assessment and Evaluation of a Digital Environmental Library: the Berkeley Experience.* Paper presented at the DL96 Conference: the First ACM International Conference on Digital Libraries. Retrieved 30 April 2010, from http://info.sims.berkeley.edu/~vanhouse/dl96.html

Witmer, B.G., & Singer, M.J. (1998). Measuring Presence in Virtual Environments: A Presence Questionnaire. *Presence: Teleoperators and Virtual Environments, 7*(3), 225–240.

Yee, N. (2004). The Psychology of MMORPGs: Emotional Investment, Motivations, Relationship Formation, and Problematic Usage. In R. Schroeder & A. Axelsson (Eds.), *Social life of avatars II.* London: Springer-Verlag.

Chapter 9
Conclusion

9.1 Cultural Understanding Through Digital Interactivity

The central question of this book was:

How can we increase awareness and understanding of other cultures using interactive digital visualizations of past civilizations?

In order to answer the above question, Chapter 1 examined the advantages of virtual travel as an experiential medium. Advantages include the reduction of air pollution, avoiding the after-effects of natural disasters or conflict zones, minimizing contamination of heritage sites and adverse influences in surrounding local economies by the sheer presence of large numbers of tourists.

There is also the potential to better transform the technical constraints of virtual reality technology, but turning these limitations into cultural constraints, not to limit the visitor but to encourage them to see the virtual site more through the eyes of the original inhabitants. Seen in this way, games are already a form of virtual travel. Just like the challenges of travel, games coerce players through a punishment and reward system, to act and behave in different ways in order to reach their goal.

Chapter 2 examined current limitations of virtual environments, including issues in usability and in usefulness. Virtual worlds were found by past critics to be lifeless and sparse. On the other hand, many theorists acting as proponents of virtual worlds seemed prone to vague statements as to what virtual worlds should contain, and what one would actually meaningfully do inside of them, and distinct from their typical activities in the real world.

Chapter 3 examined the nature of inhabitation and why inhabitation seems to be so difficult to design and to design for in the creation on virtual environments. Architects who wrote about virtual worlds were criticized (and hopefully not unfairly), for not emphasizing the importance of interaction. I questioned the success of current virtual environments, and asked whether they are capable of producing a platform that supports the experience and understanding of place-inscribed culture. This led me to a typology that defined different types of successful virtual environments and I suggested virtual environments are impeded by technological constraints, lack of evaluation techniques and results, and content-specific applications that contextually respond to user needs.

It is of course easier to criticize existing case studies than it is to design a solution. The issue of place has received widespread academic discussion, without correspondingly answers in design. Place may seem a vague and ethereal concept, and those that write about it may be tempted to use esoteric language not immediately accessible to the designers of places (real or digital). For example, certain writings may introduce the neologisms of continental philosophy to this field but it is not clear how hyperspace or cyberspace distinctions help us improve the design of virtual environments. They may help us understand how 'virtual reality' relates to society in the abstract, but that is arguably not as relevant to designers as the issues and reasons they had for designing the virtual environments in the first place.

A threefold separation of virtual places may help develop guidelines of more practical benefit to designers, especially when it reflects the end user's needs. A separation of visualization (for want of a better term), activity-based, or hermeneutic environments better suits the different audience and designer needs that was outlined in Chapter 1.

The last type of virtual environment, the hermeneutic, exists in two different senses. On the one hand, this type of virtual environment might act as a symbolically projected identity, dynamically customized by us as the visitor to reflect our social and individual values and outlook. On the other hand, a virtual environment might be hermeneutic when it affords meaningful interpretations of its shareholders (clients and subjects) to those that visit it. Unfortunately the sensation that a virtual environment is inhabited and 'modeled' by a thematic cultural outlook and identifiable social agency is not a feeling I associate with virtual environments.

This is truly ironic, considering the huge number and range of conferences that are held on cultural heritage, but I believe the primary issue has not been technological limitations, but understanding what culture is and how it can and should be learnt. We need to understand how culture is an interactive process of observation, instruction, and participation, and how to replicate this meaningfully in virtual environments.

In real life situations culture is our interface with society. We take cultural objects (that identify and make available social rituals) and we use them. As we use them we modify them and future users will take the enriched-by-use cultural objects and further modify erode and refine them. For example, a medieval house is not a pure form representing a pure idea; it is a collection of memories associations, uses and intentions based around changing ideas of inhabitation and social identification and possession. Unfortunately, sharing our cultural interactions (and not just our actions) with others via computers is still infrequent.

In order to facilitate cultural understanding, architectural reconstructions and virtual heritage environments must provide more than visualization or interactive navigation. They require some form of social learning, they must be personalizable (capable of some form of inscription), and allow some degree of culturally specific embodiment to the virtual tourist or traveler. In order to be engaging, virtual heritage needs to study how games are engaging through interaction, setting of mood, and contextual embodiment, but in such a way that the content is meaningfully understood rather than used as merely an atmospheric backdrop.

In Chapter 4 I attempted to provide my definition of culture and presence that may assist us in both enhancing virtual environments and also help us in evaluating these environments more accurately and appropriately. While the discussion in this chapter was of a more generic nature, I believe it has important ramifications for people who design virtual heritage environments.

There were two major arguments in this chapter, the first being that photo-realism in a virtual environment is not always necessary or even desirable, especially for cultural heritage. It is likely that in our attempts to advance technology and to preserve historical knowledge through digital means, we have over-emphasized the values of photo-realism at the expense of Cultural Presence. In many cases, photo-realism is a worthwhile goal. However, for depicting intangible heritage, and for participatory academic debate, it may not be the most useful means of depicting cultural knowledge. It may be difficult to reconcile interactivity with photo-realism, and the latter may imply an authoritative knowledge of the culture that the virtual environment designers do not in fact possess. Attempts at static realism may also prevent us from seeing the local cultural perspective, or perhaps even be fully aware of the archaeological and anthropological debates and issues that relate to the site in question.

The second major argument was to distinguish between the cultural and social. For although they greatly overlap, one can build a social world using artifacts that are never fully integrated into an appropriate cultural understanding. To visit a heritage site on this planet with another human being does not necessarily lead one to a better cultural understanding of that place. Yet in many academic papers on presence, I still see this conflation of the cultural with the social.

While culture is a projection of society, and the mirror by which society can see its own values, we need to separate the two, for Social Presence does not necessarily lead to Cultural Presence. If 300 children rush into cyber cafés around the world to meet each other in a virtual heritage environment, they may experience Social Presence. They may well make new friends, argue, or be bullied by others. Yet that very social engagement with others may destroy their feeling of Cultural Presence, they may ignore or trivialize the cultural information and setting of the virtual environment. Cultural Presence requires an encounter with a unified social agency that attempts to materialize its desires and values by giving these forces material expression. Landscapes, clothing, and even hardware tools, are all material reflections of a society's immediate goals and long-term ideals.

Virtual heritage is particularly vulnerable to the difficulty of both creating and defining socially and culturally appropriate interaction. While much excellent research has been undertaken in the Presence Research community on Social Presence, little has been undertaken on Cultural Presence, let alone how social interaction can help develop awareness of the cultural significance of a digitally rendered and explored heritage environment. Where Cultural Presence has been explored, it has not been directed towards the experiencing of culturally significant heritage, nor has it qualified exactly how to determine if the user experience achieved the goals of the designers.

In Chapter 5 I recounted the famous Salen and Zimmerman definition of digital games. Hopefully my point that the definition seems to be arguing for comprehensiveness rather than for profundity strikes a chord with the reader. I believe that a definition of a cultural activity should not just explain the typical elements of that activity but also try to capture why that activity captivates and entertains. For computer games certainly captivate and entertain. So by using game–style interactivity we can potentially increase the engagement of people in virtual archaeology (Anderson 2003). Embodiment (via an avatar) may also help increase the visceral part of the experience and interaction could be linked to the culturally situated mode of learning.

Game engines are often associated with cheap modeling packages and game level editors, they are accessible and engaging for students, they contain built in scripts and resources, and they are optimized for personal computers (and also for consoles), with powerful physics engines. The graphics can include a surprisingly high amount of detail; they can import from professional or free 3D modelers and show a large amount of terrain and sometimes even dynamic weather or lighting. They can also allow modification of the visual overlaid interface (the Head-Up Display or HUD), they often include avatars with triggered and re-scriptable behaviors and pathfinding, but they can also include maps that demonstrate location, orientation, or the social attitude of non-playing characters in relation to the player.

Yet games trivialize consequences; one takes silly risks and does not care about others unless respect and recognition of their social status is required by the gamer. Another problem is the violent nature of many commercial games. Due to their cognitive loading, there is also the issue of time for reflection. Awareness of other cultural perspectives may be far more achievable than understanding other cultures, for full immersion takes time and concerted understanding. A set interaction time may reduce cultural learning and engagement (if the task is too challenging) and the completion of a task may reduce meaningful acquisition of cultural knowledge.

Teaching history through simulating traditional forms of 'learning by doing' is an incredibly understudied research area and yet it is of vital importance to virtual heritage. Chapter 6 outlined a simple definition of virtual heritage, and then discussed 11 virtual heritage projects. While virtual heritage projects are increasingly featured and requested as special sessions in digital media, archaeology, and cultural heritage conference calls for papers, world heritage experts have actually suggested there are too many conferences and not enough serious work based on the central mission of virtual heritage (Addison 2006). And while even archaeologists and technical experts (Gillings 2002) have warned against an over-emphasis on technical achievements, there are still far too few attempts to build and test virtual heritage projects for the end user.

Virtual heritage is of course not merely a theoretical endeavor and domain specialists are not the intended final audience. To preserve and communicate social and cultural significance we also need to communicate it to a wider audience, and (or) create a platform in which shareholders (descendents or visitors) can maintain, improve and collaborate and through this social sharing, and thus learn more about what has been simulated.

Apart from the issue of how to theoretically determine, create and achieve both social and Cultural Presence, there is the added logistic issue of how to allow this to be conveyed through interactive media in a way amenable to how people best learn. And how to evaluate not just how they learnt, but why they learnt, and not just the effectiveness, efficiency, and user satisfaction of this learning, but also the awareness, understanding and (or) sense of newfound ownership or appreciation of cultural diversity, authenticity and significance. Ideally this would be in line with the aims of UNESCO or other heritage organizations.

There are new and exciting forms of social interaction that game engines can help support. Players could progress through sharing knowledge, tips, or tools online, or outside of the game. Player communication could be filtered so that they explore or advance only by developing in situ or collaborative communication. This would encourage ways of appreciating difference rather than relying on conventional cultural assumptions. Avatar representation, interaction, and ability could vary according to social role, social importance, or cultural significance. Tools available inside the game engines could allow players to modify and share aspects of their game experience.

Although I am by no stretch of the imagination an expert on augmented reality, Chapter 7 discussed this research area because of its growing importance to widespread virtual environments, ubiquitous computing, and especially to virtual heritage projects. I suggest that recent developments in locative media are stretching or blurring the traditional definition of augmented reality, that there has been a strong tendency to think of augmented reality as a visually-dominant experience, and some issues to do with the terms *augmented*, *reality*, and *augmented virtuality* are pointed out.

I briefly mention famous augmented reality projects, with phones or PDAs, HMDs, backpacks, and peripherals, and also point to some notable examples in virtual heritage. Although they are not strictly augmented reality, there is also a discussion of biofeedback and how it can be used as background interaction, and to blur the boundary between audience and participants.

Chapter 8 discussed evaluation for virtual heritage environments. This may seem a radical idea in a book that is part of a series on HCI, but universal usability is not always desirable. For our content domain, creating virtual heritage projects, it may in fact be a serious problem. Rather than attempt to bridge cultural divisions, there may be times when we wish to record, preserve, explore or share different cultural experiences.

For example, game designer Warren Spector has been quoted as saying "We absolutely must streamline our interfaces and make them so intuitive users forget they're even using an interface. We have to make sure users know exactly what they're supposed to do at all times and challenge them to figure out how" (Aldrich 2004, p. 175). However, perhaps in some situations the audience needs to feel alienated either from the environment or from the most effective forms of interaction, for social interaction is often culturally constrained.

In this chapter I surveyed evaluation methods that we might usefully apply to virtual heritage environments using the interactive methods and features we have learnt from studying popular computer games. In evaluating virtual heritage, we have to consider several problematic factors. The variety of audience in required learning style, computer experience and background archaeological or place knowledge may vary wildly. Most technology is platform dependent. It can be difficult to test cultural learning acquisition in situ. We may also need post world experience results but questionnaires often produce misleading statistics (participants may hurry to finish them, guess at multi-choice questions, or attempt to produce 'pleasing' answers).

In the evaluation chapter (Chapter 8) I discussed Palenque as a case study that highlighted the inherent difficulties of virtual heritage evaluation, especially the notion of Cultural Presence. Results from the Palenque evaluation show the importance of recording demographics (in this case age group and gender), the strong effect of context on the choice of interaction, the strong effect of navigation, and a significant relation between gaming experience, task performance, and understanding. It uncovered another factor for consideration by future researchers, and that is cognitive overloading (including too many interactive processes for the participant to cope with effectively while immersed within a virtual environment).

Game–style interaction used in the virtual environment appeared to be intuitive for navigation and task-performance, and reduce cognitive loading, but at the expense of understanding cultural significance. The results do suggest that gaming experience relates to task performance, and that social agency (via scripted agents) needs to be very believable in order to evoke a sense of presence. My interpretation of the findings is that while agents can act as powerful navigation cues, if they are not believable then they are ignored.

Pre-testing with not just experts but also beginners can also help reduce the possibility of designer (expert) bias – the tendency to make complex and difficult but aesthetically pleasing worlds. Participants engaged in solving tasks may not notice advanced techniques that slow down the environment in order to create effects that are more realistic. In the Palenque example, the use of dynamic lighting (dynamic shadows) may appear highly immersive to the world designer, but have little or no effect on the actual participant's sense of immersion. The author was too heavily affected by the designer affliction, adding in features that most members of the public would not notice.

Applying game–style interaction that is very genre-based can increase the usability but not the usefulness (for learning about another culture), as users can become 'trapped' inside the genre, only looking for objects that suit a fixed and limited mindset. The Palenque case study did however reveal important design issues; it highlighted the importance of recording demographic factors, the possibility of cognitive overloading, and it indicated how essential it is to match the type of interaction to the content in order to improve the participant's understanding and awareness of other cultures.

Several assumptions in academic literature were challenged by the results. For example, the more 'inhabited' or 'interactive' environments were not considered more interesting or more 'Mayan'. This suggests that Cultural Presence is not synonymous with Social Presence and that cultural learning is too hybrid in nature to be broken down into three distinct modes and tested. In addition, a descriptive theory does not necessarily make it suitable as a prescriptive and verifiable theory.

It also appears very difficult to gain a sense of cultural learning from multi-choice general knowledge questions. Many people (and students in particular) prefer to randomly explore and then just guess answers when in an evaluation situation. This suggests to me that evaluation should be as much an integrated part of the virtual learning experience as possible. Usability experts such as Don Norman (Norman 2001) seem to agree:

> Museums and video arcades exploit similar themes: meaningful activities, learning that takes place invisibly, not as the objective, but naturally, effectively. Exploiting social interaction and discussion. Participants don't think of themselves as interacting with technology, they think they are doing something interesting: discussing an interesting topic, playing basketball, riding a jet-ski, skateboarding. They exploit social interaction and cooperation. The result is high intense concentration, true learning, with people anxious to go back and do it again, paying for it out of their own money.

Performance data is difficult to obtain, perhaps partly because some participants prefer to explore, and some may wish to solve tasks (either with or without time constraints). Enough time should be allowed to complete all tasks, and preferably, the participants would only experience a warm up test world, plus at most two virtual environments to compare. Designers may want to convey atmosphere, but in a game–style task-based environment, the end-users want interactive control and low levels of latency (i.e. minimal lag).

On a more theoretical note, statistical correlations might be used to analyze multiple definitions of presence in order to produce a rough guideline as to the suitable description of a theory. The closer and further apart values may indicate successful (and unsuccessful) synonyms that together may produce a more comprehensive result than a single question for the vague and elastic concepts of cultural understanding and Cultural Presence.

9.2 Future Research

There is still a pressing need to design, modify, and test interactive genres for learning about historical and cultural information through trial and error-based procedural learning that best utilizes the unique real-time and collaborative potential of digital media. The paucity of studies on interaction suitable for historical and heritage reconstructions became evident through this research.

A possible solution is to match generic forms of interaction in entertainment design with social interaction in distinctive cultures and historic periods. A second approach is to apply game genres to suitable heritage reconstructions. We could also evaluate the usefulness of applying game genres' social identities on participants and compare the results to a non-socially constrained environment.

That is not to say that game design is a panacea. Excessive playing of computer games may lead to physical inactivity, exacerbate social alienation, or numb players to graphic acts of violence. Notwithstanding these concerns, there is great scope for evaluating game genres and gamers' profiles to understand how people learn by trial and error, whether current generations do process information differently, and whether we can gain a sense of place without ever having visited the actual locale. There are many people who cannot easily travel to either a classroom or a heritage site, or who have difficulty learning in conventional classroom settings, but that does not mean that they do not want to experience other places and other cultures.

One way of assessing cultural information transmitted is to see culture as a survival mechanism. Many 'Third person shooter' computer games gain their popularity through challenging the participant to survive in a hostile world populated by aggressive agents. While such computer games can be highly engaging, and do offer interesting methods of interaction, they typically do so to the detriment of cultural understanding, and certainly to the detriment of empathizing with the local inhabitants and their unique cultural perspectives.

Chapter 5 also briefly described the notion of individual avatars that can interact with each other while being surrounded by their own virtual worlds and unaware the world of the other avatar is completely different. This scenario would allow for understanding through sharing dialogue or interaction that makes the other's world or your externally perceived identity obvious to you. One might call this an example of hermeneutic transfer. I believe this method offers some rich and interesting research opportunities.

The other approach deserving further exploration is the idea that I also briefly mentioned in Chapter 5. Combing the role-playing and the spy game ideas, a promising option is to evaluate a multi-user virtual environment game where the task is to imitate local inhabitants' behavior and dialogue in order to move up the social ladder without being caught (by scripted agents or by other users). There could be a mix of scripted characters and other real-world users, all are trying to detect and catch out inappropriate behavior, interaction or dialogue (inappropriate in terms of space, time, or social encounter).

This scenario hopefully addresses some of the problems of Social Presence and Cultural Presence. On the one hand, multi-user environments are inherently engaging; on the other hand, we may wish to restrict users' contextual interaction and dialogue so that they learn about the local culture and not use the setting as a mere chat-room. By asking users to imitate inhabitants and avoid detection (by agents or other users), we are introducing challenging game elements while at the same time allowing them to learn contextually relevant behavior and local knowledge. A changing mix of scripted characters and real world users adds a form of mystery and engagement, and helps ensure a reasonable level of challenge persists after the initial learning period.

More than just visualization devices to showcase 3D content, we need to develop ways of using game engines that explore, challenge and foster social conventions, and help build awareness of social similarities or perhaps even differences, and that help educate people on the cultural significance of heritage sites and cultural practices. Game engines are not neutral and objective vehicles for displaying real-time interactive content, they are behavioral 'skinner' boxes, and they carry cultural genre baggage, and rely on perceptual affordances. There are many recent developments in psychology that we need to apply to social and collaborative virtual environments; for example, exploring how third person views may encourage desired social behavior (Libby et al. 2007; Slater et al. 2010) more than a first person viewpoint.

Tangible computing and devices like biofeedback could dynamically update or overlay or even erode the virtual environment with player sensations and experiences so that objects develop an 'aura' for future players. GPS could even be used to show the weathering of the actual site as caused by tourists. The virtual heritage environment could also be annotated or allow player created or experientially defined maps to be shared amongst players. Maps can also be developed and learnt to encourage appreciation of culturally thematic symbolic notation and description of social status and ritual importance.

Virtual heritage may help social and community-based ownership through allowing ownership of digital resources, presentation, or networking or hosting; through linking the heritage project to online or offline mapped or contactable community resources and providers; to updateable or tag-able information via feeds, comments, user tagging or ratings, and blogs. A community ranking system for new, authentic, high-quality, or popular content may help promulgate the project and support the content and interaction designers. Industry-related prizes and media releases for new and useful interaction and for finding content previously hidden, ignored, or misunderstood, could help fledging content producers from poorer countries access to internships or training in visualization, VR, and virtual heritage research centers.

Information on free game engines could be collated, with virtual heritage templates and scripts available for download to speed production and improve content production. More collation on free or low priced hardware could be provided to schools along with free versions of animation or modeling packages (such as SketchUp, Blender 3D, Unity, or the free version of Houdini, Softimage XSI, or game editors such as Unreal Development Kit).

It is now possible (although still challenging) to modify easily accessible game technology in order to present and involve participants in not just homogenous but also embodied, embedded and thematically authentic experiences that relate to the heritage of the local community, or, conversely, emphasis the alterity or exoticality of others either distant or extant. We need to create and foster more socially responsible forms of interaction, foster better social access and collaboration, and improve the objective evaluation of the user experience and perhaps even the user design experience (where the community becomes the owners, modifiers or developers of the virtual heritage content and its distribution and dissemination). For if the fundamental aim of virtual heritage is to communicate cultural significance, then creating advanced technology is not enough. We must also attempt to improve how people learn and understand culture through digital media.

References

Addison, A.C. (2006). *The Vanishing Virtual (keynote).* Paper presented at the New Heritage: Beyond Verisimiltude Conference on Cultural Heritage & New Media, Hong Kong.

Aldrich, C. (2004). *Simulations and the future of learning: an innovative (and perhaps revolutionary) approach to e-learning.* San Francisco, CA: Jossey-Bass.

Anderson, M. (2003). *Computer Games and Archaeological Reconstruction: The Low Cost VR, Enter the Past*. Paper presented at the CAA 2003 – Enter the Past + Workshop 8 – Archäologie und Computer Conference, Vienna, Austria.

Gillings, M. (2002). Virtual archaeologies and the hyper-real. In P. Fisher & D. Unwin (Eds.), *Virtual Reality in Geography* (Vol. 17–32). London and New York: Taylor & Francis.

Libby, L.K., Shaeffer, E.M., Eibach, R.P., & Slemmer, J.A. (2007). Picture Yourself at the Polls: Visual Perspective in Mental Imagery Affects Self-Perception and Behavior. *Psychological Science, 18*(3), 199–203.

Norman, D. (2001). *The Future of Education: Lessons Learned from Video Games and Museum Exhibits*. Commencement Address for Northwestern University. Retrieved 30 April 2010, from http://www.jnd.org/dn.mss/the_future_of_educat.html

Slater, M., Spanlang, B., Sanchez-Vives, M.V., & Blanke, O. (2010). First Person Experience of Body Transfer in Virtual Reality. *PLoS ONE, 5*(5), e10564.

Index

A

Acrossair, 164
Activity-based, 12, 45, 46, 53–55, 89, 96, 152, 190, 193, 202
The Advanced Visualisation and Interaction Environment (AVIE), 148, 149, 151
AEL. *See* Augmented Environments Lab
AI research, 86
Alterity, 14, 55, 178, 209
ARCHEOGUIDE, 172
Architecture, 6, 28–30, 32, 36, 37, 39–42, 48, 52, 55, 69, 79, 182
Artifacts, 2, 4, 6–8, 10, 12–14, 18, 28, 29, 33, 34, 38, 41–42, 44, 48, 49, 51, 54–60, 63, 64, 67, 69– 73, 75, 76, 78, 89, 90, 96, 98–100, 102–112, 118, 120, 121, 125, 126, 129, 138, 139, 141, 143, 149–151, 160, 167, 174, 177, 178, 182, 184, 190, 193, 196, 203
ARToolkit, 171, 172
Augmented Environments Lab (AEL), 166
Augmented reality
    ARCHEOGUIDE, 172
    ARToolkit, 171, 172
    In-Place Augmented Reality, 173
    The Virtual Showcase, 172
Augmented virtuality, 158–166, 168–171, 173, 174, 205
AVIE. *See* The Advanced Visualisation and Interaction Environment (AVIE)
Azuma, R., 157–159, 172

B

Binocular Dysphoria, 174
Biofeedback, 168–171, 205, 209
Bologna, 48

Bourdieu, P., 70
Bourke, P., 91, 93, 144, 145, 163, 164, 170

C

CAHRISMA, 28
Caillois, R., 40
Carnegie Museum of Natural History, 143
CASA, 28, 46
Cave Automatic Virtual Environment (CAVE), 17
    CaveUT, 91, 142, 178
Center for Design Visualization, 28
Champion, E., 11, 18, 36, 41, 45, 57, 59, 67, 83, 116, 130, 152, 168, 170, 178
Changing Places Research Group, 28
Civilization, 1, 73, 79, 88, 105, 112, 113, 116, 118, 129, 151, 201
Cognitive walkthrough, 179, 186
Coliseum, 30, 31
Collaborative virtual environments (CVEs), 7, 18, 145, 208
Correlons, 104
Crang, M., 23, 33, 34, 42, 43, 70, 105
Crida, 28
Cross-media presence survey, 180
Cultural VR Lab, 28
Culture
    cultural agency, 23, 52, 60, 69, 75–76
    cultural learning, 9, 10, 12, 28, 57, 63, 69, 71, 72, 75, 76, 84, 87, 95, 96, 111–113, 115–118, 151, 177, 178, 186, 188, 190, 191, 193, 196, 204–206
    world, 12–14, 28, 37, 43, 44, 48–50, 55, 67, 70–72, 75–79, 105, 106, 118, 124, 129, 149, 177, 186, 189, 192, 194, 201, 203–206, 208
Curved mirror, 91, 93, 94, 144, 170
CVEs. *See* Collaborative virtual environments

D

Dave, B., 45, 59, 178
Davies, C., 105, 184, 185
Dekker, A., 168
Digital Design Research Group, 135
Digital Studios-CUMIS, 28
3D joystick, 91, 169
3D software
  Houdini, 209
  SketchUp, 209
  Softimage XSI, 209
Dynamic places, 59, 90–94, 107, 121, 126, 151

E

Egenfeldt-Nielsen, S., 141
Egypt, 134, 142, 143
Emic, 74, 75, 79, 114, 179
Ename ICOMOS Charter, 130
Ethnography, 177, 182, 195
Etic, 67, 74, 75, 79, 114, 179
Evaluation, 21–24, 29, 48, 69, 78, 85, 90, 91, 96,
    102, 103, 110, 121–125, 150, 151,
    157, 160, 177–196, 201, 205, 206
Expert testing, 179–180
Extern, 48, 57, 58, 96, 104

F

Fassbender, E., 145, 146
Federation of American Scientists (FAS),
    137–139, 152
Feiner, S., 158, 160–162
Fidelity, 12, 20, 23, 63–65, 67–69
Film, 7, 9, 39, 40, 43, 53, 70, 85, 119, 120,
    131, 135, 195
Flynn, B., 149–151

G

Gadamer, H-G., 53, 68
Game
  ArcDig, 68, 114
  Civilization, 118
  Close Combat, 118
  Escape from Woomera, 140, 142
  Far Cry, 86, 142
  Global Conflicts, 139–142, 152
  Heretic II, 89–90, 113, 115
  Morrowind, 108, 109
  Myst, 112, 114, 115
  Neverwinter Nights, 100
  Oblivion, 108, 123, 140, 145–147
  Playing History, 140, 141, 152
  Space Invaders, 112

Tetris, 85, 112
Unreal Tournament, 91–93, 104, 142,
    143, 169
World of Warcraft, 3, 123
Game engine
  Adobe Atmosphere, 91, 116, 133, 190
  Blender 3D, 2, 3, 145, 209
  Blink 3D, 18, 132, 133
  Ogre 3D, 133
  Source, 104, 145, 168
  Torque, 56, 94, 134, 135
  Torque 2D, 110, 111
  Torque 3D, 94
  Unity, 2, 133, 140, 143–145, 209
  Unreal Development Kit, 209
Game feedback, 14, 17, 87, 88, 122, 124, 139,
    170, 171, 184, 191
Game genre
  First Person Shooter, 110, 113, 187
  Steal the Flag, 116
  Third Person Shooter, 208
Game ideas
  different perspectives per player, 117
  snakes and ladders, 116
Game-style interaction, 112
Gibson, W., 30
GIS, 90
Google Goggles, 164
Gunhouse, G., 132, 133

H

Hamlet on the holodeck, 10
HCI. *See* Human-computer interaction
Head mounted display (HMD), 20, 106, 157,
    158, 160, 161, 166, 167, 169,
    171–174, 205
Hermeneutic
  environments, 44–46, 51, 53–55, 58, 60,
    68, 89, 151, 202
  richness, 75–76, 89
  transfer, 208
Heuristics, 122–124, 179, 180, 186
Hight, J., 167
HMD. *See* Head mounted display
Hodder, I., 44
Human-computer interaction (HCI), 122, 124,
    185, 186, 205

I

IBM, 133, 134
iCinema, 148, 149
ICOMOS Burra Charter, 130
iDome, 144, 145

In-place augmented reality, 173
Interaction history, 10, 21, 24, 52, 53,
        79, 85, 90, 118, 119, 121, 125,
        126, 142
Interactors, 57, 58, 101
Internet, 3, 4, 10, 12, 51, 53, 85, 132, 134, 193

J
Jacobson, J., 91, 142, 143, 152, 170
Journey to the West, 100–101

K
Kalay, Y, 28, 29, 31, 45, 49, 50, 52, 59, 77, 78,
        135–137
Kant, I., 30
Kenderdine, S., 147, 148
Kerremans, P., 166
Key Centre of Design Computing, 28

L
Layar, 164, 165
Life history, 48–49, 58, 108
Likert scales, 181, 182, 185–187
Literature, 1, 10, 11, 23, 30, 37–39, 42, 43, 49,
        50, 67, 78, 83, 106, 112, 157, 184,
        194, 196, 206
Longinus, 30

M
Macquarie Lighthouse, 145–147, 151, 152
Malone, T.W, 122–124
Maps
    game, 77, 90, 105–111, 126, 134, 135, 151,
        204, 209
    inventory, 109, 111
    sketch, 106, 107
Mawson's Huts, 144–145, 152, 163–164
Mayan, 4, 13, 91, 95, 96, 98, 99, 116, 118,
        134, 171, 191–193, 206
MechWarrior, 170
Memes
    Aunger, 119
    Dawkins, 119
    memetics, 119
Memex, 45
Mesopotamia, 137–139, 152
Metaio, 164
Mexico, 4, 13, 32, 96, 134
Miletus, 48
Milgram, P., 157, 158, 166
MIRA Lab, 171

MIT Media Lab, 102
Mjalnar. *See* Spaces of Mjalnar
Morse, P., 144, 163, 164
Murray, J., 10

N
Nagel, D., 134, 135
Nielsen, J., 77, 180, 181
Norman, D., 207
34 North, 118 West, 167

P
Paladin Studios, 35, 134, 135
Palenque
    Ballcourt, 95, 99, 191, 193
    paddler gods, 98, 193
    sarcophagus, 95, 190
    Temple of Inscriptions, 95, 190, 192
    Xibalba, 91–93, 95
Personalization, 21, 23, 32, 44, 45,
        52, 56, 85, 89, 125, 130, 183
Phobias, 22, 66
Physiological Testing, 180, 185
Piranesi, 30
Place, 1, 19, 27, 63, 89, 130, 159,
        177, 201
PLACE-Hampi, 147–148, 152
Placeness, 39, 45, 94
PlayStation, 85, 130
Polo, M., 102–104
Presence
    co-presence, 69, 73–74, 179, 186
    cultural, 11, 12, 28, 49, 56, 63–80, 103,
        125, 179, 182, 185, 186, 188, 189,
        194, 203, 208
    environmental, 20, 74
    presence research, 22, 27, 44, 56, 60,
        179–182, 185–188, 194, 203
    presence studies, 22, 177, 180
    questionnaires, 27, 181, 186–190
    social, 12, 56, 63–80, 101–103, 178, 179,
        182, 188, 194, 206, 208
Procedural interaction, 84
Proxemics, 34
PublicVR, 143, 178

Q
Queenscliff, 86, 87, 142
Questionnaires, 11, 27, 146, 181–182,
        184, 186, 188, 189, 193,
        195, 205
Qumulus, 35

R

Realism
photo-realism, 3, 14, 23, 63–69, 75, 195, 203
photo-realistic, 63–66, 163
reality, 63–66, 68, 195
Relph, E.C., 29–31, 42, 45, 50, 54, 59, 178
Renaissance Project, 46, 48

S

Salen.K., 83, 84, 87, 123, 203
Santa Maria ad Cryptas, 132, 152
Second Life, 3, 166
Sensor pads, 92, 93
Shaw, J., 147, 148
Slater, M., 19, 22, 27, 49, 72, 178, 180, 181, 188, 189, 208
Slater-Usoh-Steed questionnaire, 187, 189
Social agency, 27, 28, 37, 51, 53, 54, 72, 75, 76, 85, 88, 101–102, 104, 126, 202, 203, 206
Spaces of Mjalnar, 148–150, 152
Sterelny, K., 95, 105, 106
Sublime, 30, 51
Kant, 30
Surveys, 11, 19, 23, 24, 148, 157, 171, 180–182, 184, 192, 194, 205

T

Task performance, 11, 76, 122, 180–181, 184–185, 187, 189, 191–194, 196, 206, 207
Tenochtitlan, 32
The 'Indiana Jones' dilemma, 131
The Popol Vuh, 91
Therapeutic virtual environments derived from computer games (TVEDGs), 66
Tilley, C.Y., 44, 67, 149
Trace, 12, 24, 30, 32–34, 38, 43, 49, 52, 58, 70, 76, 79, 105, 108, 185

Triggers, 22, 36, 38, 40, 50, 51, 59, 65–67, 96, 112, 120, 123, 167, 168, 184
TVEDGs. *See* Therapeutic virtual environments derived from computer games

U

Uncanny Valley, 66

V

Virtual Egyptian Temple, 142–143, 152
Virtual environment
collaborative virtual environment (CVE), 7, 18, 145, 208
multi user virtual environment (MUVE), 135, 179, 208
Virtual Forbidden City, China, 133–134, 152
Virtual heritage environment, 10, 11, 13, 19, 24, 46, 50, 52, 53, 58, 59, 63, 67, 68, 70, 72, 75, 78–80, 87, 89, 95, 115, 119, 121, 125, 126, 135, 145, 177, 180–190, 194, 195, 202, 203, 205, 209
Virtual reality (VR), 1, 2, 9, 13–14, 17–20, 23, 24, 30, 41, 42, 49, 63, 65, 66, 68, 76, 131, 132, 146, 151, 157–159, 164–165, 167, 171, 172, 177, 185, 188, 191, 194, 195, 201, 202, 209
Virtual Sambor, 135–137, 152
VRML, 32, 51, 53, 143

W

Wikitude, 164
Window-on-the-world, 166
Witmer-Singer questionnaire, 187–189

Z

Zimmerman, E., 83, 84, 87, 123, 203